THE C

B. Bartos-Höppner

THE COSSACKS

Translated by Stella Humphries

London
OXFORD UNIVERSITY PRESS
1972

Oxford University Press, Ely House, London W. 1

GLASGOW NEW YORK TORONTO MELBOURNE WELLINGTON
CAPE TOWN IBADAN NAIROBI DAR ES SALAAM LUSAKA ADDIS ABABA
DELHI BOMBAY CALCUTTA MADRAS KARACHI LAHORE DACCA
KUALA LUMPUR SINGAPORE HONG KONG TOKYO

First published 1959 under the title
Kosaken Gegen Kutschum-Khan
by K. Thienemanns Verlag, Stuttgart

First published 1962
Reprinted 1963, 1971

First published in this edition 1972

ISBN 0 19 272036 8

FOR
CHRISTOPHER
AND
BURGHARD

Printed in Holland
Zuid-Nederlandsche Drukkerij N.V.
's-Hertogenbosch

Contents

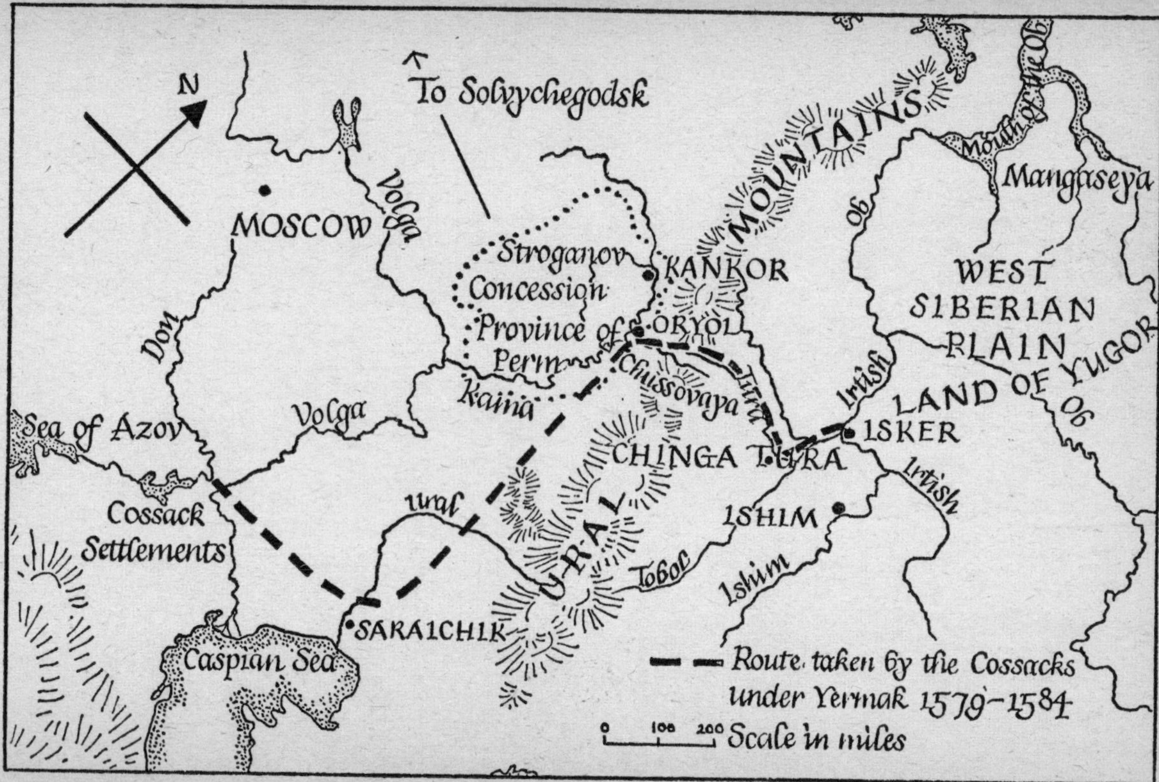
N
To Solvychegodsk
MOSCOW
Volga
Don
Stroganov Concession
Province of Perm
Kaina
Volga
Sea of Azov
Cossack Settlements
Caspian Sea
SARAICHIK
Ural
URAL MOUNTAINS
KANKOR
ORYOL
Chussovaya
Tura
CHINGA TURA
Tobol
ISHIM
Ishim
Irtish
ISKER
Irtish
Ob
Mouth of the Ob
Mangaseya
WEST SIBERIAN PLAIN
LAND OF YUGOR
Ob
Route taken by the Cossacks under Yermak 1579-1584
0 100 200 Scale in miles

1 THE STRANGER

He had ridden hard and the horse was lathered in sweat. As it fell into a weary trot, flecks of foam dripped from the bit and it snorted noisily through its nostrils.

The rider ignored its plight as he peered anxiously along the road ahead. 'The village can't be far now,' he kept telling himself. 'It must be quite close, just beyond this stretch of forest, if I'm not mistaken.'

He tugged at the reins and halted. Narrowing his eyes, he scrutinized the landscape like a man who has to be on his guard. Then he pushed his fur cap back from his forehead, took a couple of deep breaths and slid down from the saddle. He staggered a little as his feet touched the ground, but once he had stretched his powerful legs his steps regained their strength. Suddenly he dropped his arms and turned back to listen. He gave an impatient jerk at the halter as the horse's head started groping hungrily for the tender young shoots of the nearby oak trees. With an iron grip he secured the bridle and held the muzzle tight. 'The devil take you,' he hissed. 'Can't you keep still for a moment?'

Again the horseman strained his ears and listened. But all he could hear was the creaking of branches as the wind swayed the treetops.

'Good Heavens, I must be imagining things,' he muttered to himself and shook his head. 'All right then, go on. Eat your fill.' He released the horse's mouth and patted its neck. 'We had better wait until nightfall before we arrive.' The animal reached for the leaves once more and the horseman helped himself to a lump of bacon and some bread from the saddle-bag. The floor of the forest was overgrown with moss and he sat down on a hummock and chewed away hungrily at the food.

'Why did I come here?' he mused to himself. 'Why am I courting danger? But then, is there not danger wherever I go, so what does it matter? Danger! When was my life not in danger? Still, this is different. This is sticking my head straight in the hangman's noose.

'Oh, come! Don't exaggerate,' he told himself. 'It isn't as bad as that. After all, I'm not at the foot of the gallows yet. Nor will I be, either, if I keep my wits about me. But why have I taken such a risk? For one simple reason. Now that the Devil is clamouring so urgently for my soul, I had to come back for the last time. Why don't you admit it? Death and damnation! Isn't this the place you have been yearning for, all these long years? Ha! Yearning! Well, why don't you laugh? Go on! Laugh, curse you, laugh!'

But he tightened his lips instead and his fingers tugged at the beard on his chin.

It was supper-time at Vassili Metyanov's house. In the outer room were the serfs, the maids and the slaves, while the master of the house and his family sat in the inner living-room. They ate in silence, dipping their wooden spoons into the earthenware dish of thick fish soup which stood in the middle of the table, and tearing big bites from hunks of coarse bread between mouthfuls of soup.

Everyone seemed to hear the sound of the horse's hoofs at the same moment. The women looked up inquiringly, waiting for the master to give the word.

'Volodya!' he called out into the other room. 'Go and see who it is.'

'Yes, Master.'

In a short time the slave returned. 'It is a courier from Moscow. He is carrying dispatches from his most gracious Majesty. He seeks shelter for the night.'

'Show him in.'

Vassili Metyanov put down his spoon, wiped his greasy mouth with the back of his hand and dried it on his gown. Then he stood up and went to meet his guest.

The new-comer strode confidently through the ante-room towards him. As they faced each other the stranger towered above his host more than a head taller.

'You are welcome, my lord. I am happy to receive the envoy of our most gracious sovereign, the Czar of all the Russias, may Heaven preserve him.' Vassili paused reverently after these words as was the custom, and bowed his head. 'Welcome to my humble house. Everything in it is at your disposal.' He stretched out his hands towards the stranger with a cordial gesture.

'I thank you,' was the brief reply.

Vassili Metyanov led his guest to the table. 'Let me introduce my family. This is my mother, Anna Metyanova, my wife, Olga Metyanova, and this is Irina, my daughter.'

'And the lad is your son, I suppose?'

'Oh no. He is a neighbour. He is Mitya, the son of the village trapper, Nikolai Yelnikov. His father often goes hunting in the forests for several days on end, and as he has no mother Mitya comes to our house for food. His father is a fine hunter, one of the best I've ever known, and Mitya and Irina are good friends.'

Meanwhile the women and children had risen and left the table.

'Sit down, my lord,' Vassili went on. 'You must be tired after your long ride.' Then turning to the women he added, 'Bring us some ale, and bread and meat for our guest.'

'No, no, do not trouble,' said the stranger. 'I am not very hungry. Give me a spoon and a piece of bread and I will share what you are eating. And do not send the ladies away from the table, I beg you. I prefer them to remain.'

'But, my lord! I cannot allow that. I shall be most offended if you refuse the best that my house can offer. This is no way to receive a guest.'

But the stranger was already seated. Without ceremony, he pulled Vassili down by his side on the broad wooden bench which ran along two sides of the room. 'We will share a flagon of your good ale afterwards, Vassili Metyanov.'

So the spoons dipped into the soup tureen once more and the stranger's eyes darted back and forth from one member of the family to the other. Except for the master, they all sat silent with eyes downcast, but once old Anna Metyanova's spoon happened to touch that of the new-comer and involuntarily she looked up and caught his glance.

Anna's eyes grew wide and she was so startled that she spilled some soup on the table. She wiped it away hastily with her hand and no one noticed that her fingers were trembling. A moment later she stole another look at the stranger.

Vassili Metyanov was puzzled. There was something odd about this courier of the Czar's. He had not even told them his name as yet and Vassili did not know how to address him. What was more, he had never seen him at Court either. Perhaps he was on a secret mission. Of course! That must be it. That was why he was riding alone and not in his carriage. Not that that worried Vassili. On the contrary, he would only have to supply him with one fresh horse and that was much less costly than three fresh ones for a *troika.* But there was something else that worried Vassili, too. Perhaps he had seen the stranger somewhere before after all. No, he must be mistaken. Yet there was something vaguely familiar about his voice. Where had he heard that ring in it? It must have been many, many years ago. . . .

'Do you know how to look after a horse, Mitya?' asked the guest, turning to the youth when supper was done.

'Yes, my lord.'

'Then go and see if the stable-boys have attended to mine properly. It carried me faithfully to this village and it deserves good fodder.'

'Yes, my lord.'

The boy stood up immediately and left the room. Irina followed him at once.

Vassili's wife started to clear the table and as the old mother got to her feet, too, the stranger turned to her. 'Don't get up, my good woman. Stay where you are. There are younger hands than yours to fetch the beer.'

Once again they looked at each other and the glance was a longer one this time. 'You are very considerate, my lord,' said the old woman softly.

'I hope you will not think it rude of me to ask questions, but could you tell us a little how things are in Moscow?' ventured Vassili Metyanov. 'We live such quiet lives here and a visitor is a rare treat. Have you been in the service of his gracious Majesty for long?'

'No. It is quite a short time since I entered his service.'

'I should, perhaps, explain that it is a long time since I attended the Court.'

'Do you not have to pay your respects every two months, then?'

'I am excused. You see—and I hope you will not think that I am boasting when I say so—in Moscow I am considered the best falconer for miles. That is why I am allowed to spend most of my time on this estate which the Czar has been generous enough to bestow on me.'

'Is it a large holding?'

'Oh no, my lord. It is one of the smallest I know. But do not think that I am grumbling. From my point of view it could not be better. And may I ask if I have the honour of knowing your lordship's family?'

It was just at that moment that Olga Metyanova returned with the beer. She placed the flagons on the table in front of the men with something of a clatter, so that the master of the house was not sure if his guest had failed to hear his question or if he preferred to leave it unanswered.

'Do not think I am lacking in good manners, but I am very thirsty, Vassili. Let us drink,' was all that the stranger replied.

He took a few long pulls at the tankard, then pushed it away empty with a wide sweep of his arm. Vassili's wife filled it up again from the large pitcher. The stranger watched her closely. Or was he only day-dreaming? He leaned back against the wall and his eyes wandered over the grain of the wooden table. When he spoke again his voice had changed completely. 'You were asking about my family, Vassili. It is a long, long time since I was a member of any family. It will be . . .'

An oppressive silence filled the room. The stranger knew that all eyes were on him. Impulsively he leaned forward, and stretching his arms full length across the table, he looked old Anna Metyanova straight in the eyes.

'Tell me, Granny, tell me what my mother looked like,' he said softly.

Everyone seemed paralysed. They listened to the words as if they were waiting for an echo to repeat them. Then Anna Metyanova placed her skinny hands on the strong clenched fists.

'Yermak, the young master! I knew you would come back one day. I recognized you as we ate. I cannot tell you how overjoyed I am to see you again.' Tears started to her eyes. She placed her head on his hands and wept soundlessly. 'Yermak, my boy,' she whispered once more. 'Yermak, little master!'

Vassili Metyanov could not control his emotion any longer. He jumped up, gripped his guest by the shoulders and shook him affectionately. 'Are you really Yermak, Yermak whom I called my brother? Of course you are, of course. I knew it all along. There was something about you that was so familiar. . . . But how you have changed! Why, you've grown into a giant! Why did you not tell us who you were right away? Why did you not allow us to receive you with the honour due?'

'I wanted to sit among you as I always used to, to be one of the family again.'

'Olga,' said Vassili, turning to his wife, 'this is Yermak, the one who left us more years ago than I can count. Bring us food, woman, and something more to drink. Tell the serfs to slaughter a sheep! Fetch . . .'

'No, no, Vassili. Don't give anyone any trouble on my account. I must be on my way tomorrow and all I want is to stay here with you for an hour or two. Just fill up my tankard again and let us talk.'

'You don't think I am going to let you run away so soon, do you? Those dispatches from the Czar can wait another day. Now that you're home again, you shan't escape so easily.' In his joy, Vassili had not noticed that the two children had come back into the room and had been standing there listening for several minutes.

'Well, Mitya?' asked Yermak. 'How's my horse?'

'It has been turned into the best meadow. If you wish, I will stay by its side and keep watch all night.'

Yermak laughed. 'And I haven't the slightest doubt that you'd be off to your bed in five minutes. You can tell well enough that the beast is too tired to bolt. But I won't do you out of payment for your vigil. That's what you're after, I suppose.' Yermak reached in his pocket, pulled out a coin and tossed it across the table.

Mitya's eyes lit up. 'But . . . but, my lord,' he stammered. 'That's the wrong coin. It's far too much. You must have made a mistake.'

'Keep it, Mitya. How old are you, my lad?'

'They say that I'm fourteen, but I think it must be fifteen. My father makes a notch in the door frame every year when the winter starts, because I was born at the beginning of the winter.'

'And now there are fourteen notches, are there? But what makes you think there should be another one?'

'Well, some years I have to remind Father and I think that he may have forgotten one winter when I was too small to understand. See how tall I am and how strong my arms are. I could fight a bear if my father would take me with him into the forest.'

Yermak laughed again and beckoned to Mitya to come over to the table.

'If you are ready to tackle a bear, you must be able to down your ale like a man, too. Here, drink up, and then I shall tell you something. When I was a boy like you, Vassili and I shared a bed at night. And do you know what we talked about before we fell asleep? We used to brag to each other about how strong we were. And once, when we heard the wolves howling at the edge of the forest on a freezing winter night, Vassili said to me: "Would you dare to fight a wolf, Yermak?" And I replied: "Yes, of course, as long as it's not with the pack. No one stands a chance with a pack, but I'd take on a lone wolf any day of the week." "But wolves are cunning," replied Vassili. "They'll only meet you face to face when hunger gnaws at them. All the same, you are right. It wouldn't be too dangerous if you had a sharp spear." "It doesn't need much courage to face a wolf if you're armed," I retorted. "Anyone can tackle a wolf with a spear. But I would kill it with my bare hands. I would let it come closer, closer, and I would talk to it. 'Come on,' I'd say, 'show me you're not a miserable coward.' I wouldn't drop my stare for a second, I'd hold its eyes until it ran straight into my hands, and then I'd clutch its throat and I'd squeeze." '

Yermak broke off abruptly and only the reigning stillness made him aware that the others had been listening to him with breathless excitement. He knew that only Vassili could say how that night's conversation had ended, and in his mind he could still hear his friend saying, 'Hush, Yermak, hush. You must be out of your senses. No one can strangle a wolf!' And again he could hear his own voice raised. 'You can't, I know, but I could; I know how it's done. You didn't have to watch as I did, while they. . . .' 'Hush,' Vassili had said once more. 'Let's talk about something else, about the falcons and summer-time. . . .' And he had put an arm round Yermak's shoulders and he began to talk very eagerly about going hawking soon when the weather grew warmer. The complete conversation had flashed through Yermak's head like a streak of lightning.

'But do you know, Mitya, when I killed my first wolf it wasn't at all like that.' He paused again and then changed the subject. 'Still, I do believe you when you say that you are particularly strong. One can tell it by looking at you.'

'There! You see, Mitya!' said Irina eagerly. 'That's what I'm always saying. Everything turns out differently from the way we imagine it. You expect things to happen so simply but real life isn't like that. Tell him so, my lord. Mitya is such a dreamer. He wants to go away from the village and lead a life of adventure. Even Moscow won't satisfy him, and that is a long way to travel, isn't it? You must know, for you have just come from there. Mitya wants to go with his Majesty and fight the Tartars or maybe the Livonians, as there's a war against them just now, they say. Just think, my lord! He has ideas about riding by the Czar's side and carrying his banner. As if anyone below the rank of general were allowed to do that!'

'How do you know all this, Irina?'

'My father told us, my lord. He has been to Court many times and Mitya keeps pestering him to tell us all about it. That's where he gets all these silly notions which keep buzzing round his head.'

Yermak had to laugh at the girl's torrent of words.

'Don't take any notice of her.' Vassili Metyanov laid a hand on Yermak's arm. 'She means no harm. It's just the innocent chatter of a child.'

'Why should I mind, Vassili? When I hear her talking away, it reminds me of the way you used to go on, or have you forgotten?'

Irina was encouraged by Yermak's words. 'Do you know what else he wants, my lord? If he may not ride by the Czar's side, then Mitya said that he would like to . . .'

'Hold your tongue, Irina!' Mitya stamped his foot and his eyes blazed with anger.

'I only want him to talk you out of these mad ideas.'

'Oh, of course. An envoy from the Imperial Court will obviously try to stop a fellow joining the Cossacks.'

Yermak looked at the boy keenly. 'Why do you say that, Mitya? There are many Cossacks in the Czar's service, too, you know.'

'Are there?' asked the girl incredulously. 'But Father says the Czar is very angry with them because they are cut-throats and robbers and attack merchants on their travels.'

'Not all of them, Irina.'

'It's bedtime for you children,' said Vassili Metyanov, putting an end to the conversation. 'Go home now, Mitya, and you be off to bed, Irina.'

'Yes, Father. But may I just tell the gentleman that Mitya has a wolf cub at home? I could show you the way to Nikolai's hut and then you could see it for yourself. Mitya really is very brave, my lord. It isn't all bluster and boasting.'

'Perhaps we'll go and see it tomorrow, Irina.'

'Yes, my lord. Good night.'

Irina saw her friend as far as the door. 'Wait in for us tomorrow, Mitya.'

The boy did not reply. He went out into the darkness without a word.

'Mitya!' the girl called after him. 'Why don't you say good night? What's the matter?'

There was no answer.

Irina ran after him and grasped him by the arm. 'Mitya,' she pleaded.

'Leave me alone,' he said roughly and shook off her hand.

Irina persisted and trotted by his side.

'What a mean thing to do,' the words came tumbling out after a while. 'How could you tell my secrets to a stranger? A fine friend you are!'

'It's only to stop you from going away. I couldn't bear to stay here in the village if you went.'

'Do you expect me to spend the rest of life my here, skinning animals for my father and helping you to tend the cattle? No, I've different ideas. I'm leaving.'

'No, Mitya, no!'

'You'll see.'

'But not yet, Mitya, not till you're grown up.'

'I'm grown up now.'

'You're not. You're still a boy.'

'That's what you say. But I shall prove that I'm a man.'

'You can do that without going away.'

'How can I? Just tell me.'

'I . . . I . . . I don't know.'

'There you are! That's exactly what I mean!'

2 A SECRET OVERHEARD

Irina lay on her bed. The fur coverlet was drawn up high under her chin, but she could not sleep for thinking about Mitya. It was always the same. As soon as a stranger showed his face in the village the boy ached to be off and away with him. Irina could not understand it at all. Theirs was a pleasant life, when all was said and done. They could ride together over the meadows and he could go fishing in the lake with her father's serfs whenever he wished. When Nikolai, his father, took the *troika* into the town to buy provisions, Mitya could sit by his side. He was always so happy when they went gliding over the ice in winter. The *troika* went so fast, you could imagine you were flying. Soon Mitya would be old enough for his father to take him hunting, but meanwhile, there was always Grivka, his wolf cub, to keep him amused. But all these things no longer satisfied him. Mitya had made up his mind that he had to go away.

The voices of the grown-ups could be heard clearly through the thin partition which separated the sleeping quarters from the living-room next door. Irina listened. Her mother and grandmother were saying good night to the stranger. It was odd that he had wished the womenfolk to remain at the table with him. Women were usually banished when there were guests, especially such a nobleman.

Irina's eyes were wide open when her mother came and bent over her. 'What? Still awake, child? Why don't you go to sleep?'

'I can't, Mother. Mitya talks such nonsense I get quite worried about him.'

'Forget it all, Irina. He's always chattering. Try to sleep now, my dear.'

'Yes, Mother. Good night.'

The torchlight flickered over the dark wooden walls. Olga Metyanova's hair hung in a thick brown plait down her back. During the day it was always hidden by a headscarf. What a kind face Mother has, thought Irina, and such lovely glossy hair, too. I wish she didn't hide it all the time.

She edged nearer to the wall as her grandmother came in and lay down by her side.

'Are you well covered, Irina?'

'Yes, Granny.' Irina tucked her hand under her grandmother's arm as she always did. 'You're so warm to touch tonight, Granny; your skin is glowing. Why is that?'

'It's because I am so happy, my dear,' whispered her grandmother in reply.

'Happy? Has it something to do with the stranger?'

'Yes, my child.'

'But if you're so happy, why did you weep before? Was it for you? Do tell me.'

'It's no stranger, you see. It's Yermak. He has come back.'

'Yermak? But who is he?'

'Ah me. It's a long story, much too long to tell you tonight.'

'Oh, Granny, you must tell me. Please, I'm so curious. I can't wait till the morning. I can't possibly wait.'

'How you pester me! But let's wait till Mother is asleep. Then I'll tell you.'

As soon as the even breathing from the opposite corner told them that Mother was asleep, Irina crept closer to her grandmother.

'It's all right now. Do begin.'

'It's a long time ago now, more years than my old head can remember.'

'But you're not very good at counting, you know.'

'Yes, that's true. But still, it was many years ago when your father was a child like you. No, he was even younger. This estate still belonged to a nobleman then, one of the Boyars, as we call them. This was only one of the many holdings that the Czar had given him and your grandfather was the steward here. We seldom saw our master, for he spent most of his time at the Court in Moscow. But when he went hunting he would come here and he always brought his son with him, and that was Yermak. His father was kind and upright, which is more than can be said for most of the Boyars. You can judge for yourself what kind of man he was, for he always allowed Yermak to play with Vassili, your father. They were inseparable, like brothers, and whenever Yermak had to go back to Moscow he used to weep. When he grew too big to cry he stamped his foot with rage instead.

'One evening—I think it must have been in the autumn, for the roads were so muddy and rutted that carts and carriages kept getting stuck—one evening, as I say, we heard a coachman cursing and cracking his whip. When we went to the door, there was his lordship and he looked very dirty after his drive through the mire.

His wife was with him and she was so weak that she had to be carried into the house, and Yermak was there, too, staring at us with shining feverish eyes. He stretched out his hands to Vassili and said, "Let me share your bed tonight." Before long we learnt that the family were fleeing. The favour my lord had enjoyed at Court had come to an end. I don't know why it was, but these things happen, and faster than one day following the next. They intended to stay on the estate only this one night to rest and to change horses. Next day they would go on to a safer place, they thought, but the Czar's soldiers were too quick for them.'

Grandmother fell silent and after a while Irina asked her, 'What did the soldiers do?'

'I'll tell you another time, when you are older. Otherwise you may have nightmares. But we managed to save Yermak by pretending that he was Vassili's brother. When the soldiers had done, they burnt the house down, but your grandfather had it rebuilt when he entered the Czar's service as a falconer and he was given this same estate. And from that day on we had two sons and were glad of it.

If Yermak was so pleased, though, I never knew. During the day he seemed as gay and as carefree as Vassili, but when evening came he would often creep into a corner and just sit there staring into space. Or he would come across to me, and if he felt sure that no one else was listening he would ask me the same question he put to me tonight to reveal who he was. "Tell me, Granny," he would say, "what did my mother look like?" So you see, Irina, that was how I knew he missed her all the time and I have never seen sadder eyes in all my life than his when he spoke to me about her.

'As Yermak grew older, he came to resemble his father more and more, and sometimes when I was alone with your grandfather I would say to him, "If the Czar caught a glimpse of him, he would recognize him at once." And often we were afraid, not only for his life, but for our own as well.

'Then came a time when he used to go riding off by himself for the whole day and we never knew where he went. When strangers came to the village he was fascinated and would not budge from their side. Finally the day came when he told your grandfather he could not stay with us. He did not know where he was going nor if he would ever come back, but he could not remain here where everything reminded him of what had happened to his parents. It so happened that a travelling merchant had arrived in the village. He was bartering salt for furs, and he agreed to take Yermak with him. What had happened to him we never knew until today. And now, just fancy! He is actually in the Czar's service. How swiftly fortunes can change. But I must not keep you awake any longer, Irina. Or are you asleep already?'

Anna Metyanova leaned over the girl.

'Of course I wasn't! How could I sleep when the story was so exciting?'

'Oh, by the way, my dear, if anyone should question you about our visitor, just say that he was one of the Czar's couriers. Not another word, do you hear?'

'Why is that?'

'Do as you are told, my child, and don't be inquisitive. It is none of our business.'

Irina turned away with her face to the wooden partition. She kept thinking of all her grandmother had told her and she wished that Mitya had heard it, too. How he would have opened his eyes, and his ears, too!

Suddenly she heard her father's voice raised in excitement.

'Yermak!' she heard him utter, and it was a cry which mingled fear, horror and alarm. 'Are you trying to make a fool of me? That would be a sorry joke.'

'It's no joke, by Heaven. Or if you prefer it, by the Devil. I am Yermak Timofeyev and that is the truth.'

'You have taken that name to conceal your identity, then?'

'Now that you put it like that, Vassili, you bring home to me even more clearly the terrible wrong that this monster you call "our most gracious Majesty" has done to me. I have nothing left, nothing, not even my rightful name. The son of a Boyar is now a Cossack, a man whose parentage no one knows nor may inquire about.'

'But, Yermak, was there no other way than this one, the way of a . . .'

'A cut-throat and robber. You can be blunt, you know. I shall not be offended; on the contrary. But I am surprised that you of all people, Vassili, should ask me that, you who know my childhood as no one else does. For me the only path was the one of revenge. I was no general, I could not lead an army into the field against the Czar. But I took vengeance in my own way and I think I have often kept him awake at night!' The words sounded as if they might have been meant as a joke, but no laughter followed.

They were too bitter for that.

For a time there was silence. Then came Vassili's voice again, hesitant and reserved.

'Yermak, I must tell you something. It will come as a shock to you, but all the same I think you ought to know. The Czar . . . has put a price on your head. I heard it last time I was in Moscow.'

'I know.'

'You know?'

'I have just come from Moscow, don't forget. I may not be an Imperial courier, but I am determined to act the part. I chose that as cover so that nothing should happen to you and to your household. No one apart from you must know who I am. In particular, spare your mother the knowledge. I should like her to die still thinking that I am an honest man.'

'But how could you risk going to Moscow?'

'Why ever not? What could be more natural for a courier of the Czar's? Do I look so different from the genuine envoys? And here, see. Would you like to inspect his Majesty's correspondence?'

Irina could hear the sound of parchment crackling. 'Look, is not this the royal seal? Is there anything wrong with it?'

'But how did you get these dispatches and this uniform?'

'His Majesty has many messengers on the road and we do not let a single one escape unscathed if he falls into our hands.'

'Ah me. Why has everything had to happen like this? If they catch you . . .'

'Then the gallows are waiting. But I am not afraid. I have faced death too often already.'

'But it might have been so different, Yermak!'

'Listen, Vassili. Every man has his path mapped out for him by Destiny and he must follow it whether he will or no. Yours is straight and even. Mine has led me into the lowest depths. I struggled against it long enough, but I had to give in eventually. It was up to me to make the best of it, even of a fate like mine. I do not want you to think that all these years have been spent in callous slaughter and plunder. I have lived through hard times, too, you know. Life in the steppes is not so easy. It demands the last ounce of strength from us all. I have known more than enough of hunger and thirst and privations you can barely even imagine. Often for weeks on end I have had no other bed than the bare earth and a ragged cloak to cover me, and that not only in summer-time.

'But there is another side, the one which you call robbery and we call taking booty. Every Cossack has to carry out his part if the attack is to succeed, and we share the plunder fairly between us. Together we suffer want and together we enjoy prosperity. We are not squeamish—you can take your oath on that!—and we have many dark deeds on our conscience. But what are they compared with those which the Czar's band of assassins—I cannot call them anything else—have on theirs? I am not thinking only of my own family. They were but one of the many he has wiped out. But remember Novgorod. Sixty thousand souls, butchered to death in the most brutal fashion ingenuity could devise. We Cossacks have fugitives from that city with us now. And why did the Czar kill those innocent citizens? I don't know and nor do you. Probably he does not know himself. Ivan the Terrible, Ivan the Dread they call him. He is a madman, I tell you. Only a madman could behave like that. And he sentences me to death because I have done away with a handful of grasping merchants. Ah, Vassili, how ridiculous it seems.'

There was a break. Then Irina heard Yermak continue once more.

'You must not think that those years as an ordinary rank-and-file Cossack were the most difficult for me. Now that I have accepted responsibility, it gets harder. We live in communities of a hundred men, and my particular hundred elected me as its captain a few years ago. Then, more recently, five brotherhoods combined to vote for a Chieftain and I was chosen. And if Fate is kind to me, I think I shall remain their elected leader.'

'It was a big risk, Yermak.'

'Are you still harping on my visit to Moscow?'

'Mm.'

'I have but one life to lose. . . .'

'All the same, Yermak, another person would have thought twice about it. Why did you come?'

'I lived in Moscow as a child—I spent many years with you here not far from Moscow. . . .' Yermak was speaking disjointedly, almost incoherently. 'Granny is getting old. . . . You have a family. The years have been long and they have taught me that vengeance is not enough to fill a man's heart. There is a place, too, for affection, for homesickness. And since the executioner in Moscow is already knotting the rope for me, I thought it would not matter if I allowed my feelings to come into their own for once. Don't look so alarmed, Vassili,' he finished lightly. 'The hangman will easily find someone else to fit his noose.'

'But what is to happen now, Yermak? Do you intend to

tramp the countryside year in, year out, like a common vagabond?'

'We don't do so much tramping these days,' laughed Yermak and Irina could hear him bang his tankard down on the table. 'We ride, man, we ride. I shall go back to my Cossacks, and then . . . Ah Vassili, why should I worry about the future? My Cossacks are waiting for me and every man jack of them is a fellow I know I can count on.'

Irina was breathing fast. Her face felt hot. She could not hear any more: the men had lowered their voices. Her thoughts began to run round in circles, and suddenly she knew that without wishing to do so, she had overheard an appalling secret. Now she shared it with the men. And no one must know who the stranger really was; otherwise it could be dangerous for them all. For the name of the Cossack Chieftain, Yermak Timofeyev, was known and feared throughout the land.

But how could she keep it to herself? Couldn't she tell her grandmother at least?

No. Yermak had pledged even her father to secrecy.

But if she didn't tell someone, she would burst!

Irina pushed the cover away from her throat. Her hair was sticking to her forehead. There was only one person she could confide in, and that was Mitya. If only it were morning! How could she sleep with all these thoughts running round her head?

She heard the scrape of boots next door as her father and Yermak left the living-room. They're going to bed, she thought.

Soon the whole house was still.

How long until morning? Irina tossed and turned on her side. 'Sleep,' she told herself. 'Go to sleep now.'

On his pallet in the outer room the slave Volodya sat up suddenly, still heavy with sleep. He opened his black slanting eyes and peered into the darkness. I must have been dreaming, he thought; it's nothing. His head slumped back to rest.

But it had sounded as if the door had creaked.

Volodya reassured himself once more and then lay down again with a yawn. I must have been mistaken, he thought.

Irina shivered as she stood outside in her bare feet. She bent down and quickly put on her soft leather boots and tied her girdle tighter so that her gown hugged her body more warmly.

She ran to the meadow where the horses were. The dew hung

silvery in the short grass. She did not need to go far. In the grey twilight of the new day, two dark shadows loomed up before her. They stirred as Irina approached and she prodded one of them in the side with the toe of her boot.

'Hey there, Blackbird! Get up. We shall not be going far. Come on, my beauty, I'm in a hurry. We must fly like the wind.'

The horse shook itself and snorted as Irina quickly grasped its shaggy mane. With one light spring she was on its back and she dug her heels into its side.

'Come on, let's gallop. Faster, Blackbird, faster.'

Irina did not notice the keen wind which had sprung up from the east in the sickly light of daybreak. Nor did she listen to the dawn chorus as the birds began to welcome the morning. She heard neither the rushing of the stream nearby nor the dull thud of her horse's hoofs. She had only one idea in her head, to speak to Mitya.

The little cabin that belonged to Nikolai Yelnikov stood close by the forest. It was old and shabby and the woodwork had been patched up clumsily in many places.

Irina jumped down from the horse. She ran to the door and hammered on it with both her fists.

'Mitya, Mitya, wake up! Can't you hear me? It's Irina. I have to tell you something.'

'What do you want?' came a dull voice from within.

'I have something terribly important to say to you.'

'Oh, I know your "terribly important". Leave me alone.'

'But it can't wait, Mitya.'

'What is it?' Mitya opened the door a crack. His forbidding face showed that he had not yet forgotten his anger of the previous evening.

'Let me come inside. It will take me a little while to say it all. Or why do you think that I came so early? Surely that proves how urgent it is!'

She squeezed her way past him through the doorway. An angry growling from the corner greeted her immediately. Two green sparks flashed towards her.

'Down, Grivka, and don't move, do you hear?' ordered Mitya. The growling stopped, but the eyes still glowed.

'Well? What's wrong?' he asked crossly and sat down on the wide settle which ran round the big stove. 'I can hardly wait to hear,' he added sarcastically.

'Do you know who the stranger is, the man who arrived yesterday?'

'One of the Czar's couriers, of course. Is that all?'

'But he's someone else, too. Can you guess?'

'A friend of your father's, I suppose.'

'There's more to it than that.'

'Why, what do you mean?'

'He's . . .' Irina stopped. She was so excited she could hardly get the words out. 'He is . . . Mitya, promise me that you'll never tell a soul, not till your dying day, not even your father. Swear it by the holy Mother of God.'

She tugged a slender chain from the neck of her dress and held out the tiny wooden icon which hung from it.

Mitya placed one finger on the image. 'I swear. Now tell me who he is.'

'He's Yermak Timofeyev.'

'What are you saying? He can't be!' For a moment it took his breath away. 'Yermak Timofeyev, the Cossack Chieftain, the one whom the Czar has condemned to death?'

'Yes, Mitya. And that is why no one must know. We would all be killed if anyone found out that we had sheltered him.'

'But how do you know?'

'Wait a moment. I'll begin at the beginning . . . .'

It was getting light outside by the time Irina had finished, but neither of them noticed it. Mitya sat by her side, his feet drawn up and his fists were clenched in the hollow of his knees.

He did not say a word until the girl came to the end of the tale. Irina waited. She tried to read his face in the darkness, to see what impression the news had made on him.

'Well? Why don't you say anything?'

'What can I say? I'm so overwhelmed I can't quite believe it's true.'

'But it is.'

'Yes, I suppose it is.'

Again they were silent. A thin grey light came seeping through the cracks in the shutters. Irina slid down from the bench and pushed open one of the flaps. A cool breeze blew into the room.

'Do you think he will let you bring him here to see Grivka?'

'I don't know, but I don't see why he shouldn't if I remind him.'

'I want to talk to him.'

'Oh, you can do that at our house.'

'It wouldn't be the same—not what I have to say to him.'

'Why? What have you to tell him?' Irina stuck her head out of the window.

'I want to tell him. . . . No. I mean I'm going to ask him if he'll take me away with him.'

Irina spun round. 'No, Mitya, you shan't do that.' She stepped back quickly to the stove. 'Don't start that again. You're not going away. I want you to stay here.'

'Have you forgotten what I told you last night?'

'No, I haven't forgotten, but I don't want you to leave. You belong to the village. You're going to be a trapper like your father, and you can't leave him on his own, you know. He's getting old now. You can't——' Irina stumbled over the words, trying desperately to save the day. Then an idea came to her and she was so relieved that her incoherence vanished. 'And what is more,' she added coolly, 'if you say a word to Yermak you will be breaking your solemn oath.'

'Be quiet!' Mitya knew that Irina was right. The other reasons did not mean anything, but the last one was binding and a wild rage seized him. 'Why was I so stupid! Fancy giving you a promise like that. Oh, why was I such a fool! Now I must forgo the opportunity of a lifetime, a chance which will never come back again as long as I live. For once a man comes to the village whom I would follow to the ends of the earth and I cannot go because of my idiocy.'

'How do you know he would take you even if you asked him?'

'He'd take me all right; you can be sure of that.'

'But the Czar wants to hang him.'

'He'll have to catch him first. Didn't you say yourself that he laughed at the Czar?'

'Yes, but do you really want to go with a man like that?'

'More than anything in the world. Think of the life the Cossacks lead, a life I've always dreamed of. Can't you understand, Irina? Night after night I dream about strange cities with tall houses and high towers. I think of merchants speaking different tongues and of great ships sailing along mighty rivers. I can see the steppes before me and the tents of the Tartars, their golden chains and jewels, bright silks and carpets, and I am wearing a sword. I can see myself sitting round the camp-fire in the evenings with the other men. Someone strums a tune and we all hum softly to the melody. We roast a sheep on a spit. . . .'

'If you have one! Yermak said there were hard times, too, and he was often hungry.'

'All right, leave the sheep out! What does it matter as long as I am here, one of a band of brothers? Irina, release me from my promise!'

'So that you will go away and leave us? I shouldn't dream of it.'

'Irina, I always thought you understood me when I told you of my secret longings. But now I see that I was talking to the wind.' He turned away from her and got to his feet. He took a hunk of raw meat from a pot in the outer room and flung it to Grivka in the corner. The young wolf fell on it greedily. Mitya watched it, ignoring Irina even when she came up close behind him. Grivka snarled at her angrily, snapped at the meat and carried it away into the darkest corner.

Irina groped for some way of healing the breach.

'If Grivka weren't a wolf, I should feel sorry for him.'

'Why? He's well looked after here.'

'But he's a prisoner.'

'And what about me?' he retorted.

Irina stared at the lad. Those four bitter words had shocked her into realizing how deep was his unhappiness, and although she still could not quite understand her friend, she wanted to help him. Yet to do so was to lose him, perhaps for ever. Once he had gone, he might never come back. Even if he wished to return, who knew if it would be possible?

'I don't see how you can go away with Yermak,' she parried. 'You don't possess a horse of your own for one thing.'

Mitya turned on her savagely. 'That was all it wanted, giving yourself airs just because your father is falconer to the Czar! If you are going to lord it over me, you can run home, do you hear?'

'I don't have to run, I can ride. Blackbird is waiting for me outside. But if you want to go with Yermak, you will have to saddle Grivka.' And Irina slammed the door behind her so that the rickety hovel shook.

Mitya stood motionless for a moment. Then as if he would never allow Irina to come in again, he flung himself at the door and stood there panting, his back pressed hard against it.

3 A MEETING BY THE SWAMP

The whole morning Mitya sat there racking his brains to think of a way of keeping his promise and yet speaking to Yermak. But it was hopeless. He felt bound hand and foot. Still he clenched his fists, determined to find a way by hook or by crook. I'm going to ask him, somehow, he told himself. Yermak Timofeyev, the famous Cossack Chieftain whom even the Czar could not catch, was here in this wretched little village of theirs and all Mitya need do was to go to him and say . . . .

The hours went by and more than once Mitya thought about his father. If only he could ask his advice. But Nikolai Yelnikov was often away for long periods. He put up in an old shack in the forest, a bothy built of stone and peat, and he only came back when his pouch was crammed full with sable and squirrel pelts. His father was a good huntsman, but what was his life compared with that of a Cossack?

It was Grivka growling in the outer room that made Mitya give a sudden start. He held his breath so that he could listen better. Then he got up from the stove and glided to the door. He pressed his face close to it and peeped through the narrow cracks between the boards.

Two riders were coming down the path. One of them was Irina's father, but Mitya hardly saw him. He had eyes only for the other man, Vassili's companion. Then he stepped back a little from the door.

'Hey there, Mitya! Are you at home?'

As he answered a furious spitting noise came from the corner.

'Yes, I am. What is it?' Mitya flung open the door.

'Irina was too busy to come. She had to help the women in the kitchen. But I promised her that we would look in and inspect your wolf. Come on, lad, where is it?'

'Was that the only reason you came?'

'No, we were going to have a look at the falcon traps I set yesterday in any case.'

Mitya disappeared inside the house and came out a minute or two latter, dragging Grivka behind him.

'Here he is, my lord,' he said, and led him up to Yermak.

'He's a handsome beast. How old is he, Mitya?'

'The next full moon will be his fifth, my lord.'

'He looks to me as if he is not pure wolf, but has a strain of dog in him, too. His body is more compact than a wolf's would be.'

'You have good eyes, my lord, to see it so quickly.' Mitya looked at Yermak with admiration. 'You are quite right. My father had a bitch who was very strong, but savage and unpredictable. Last year she ran away, and as she did not come back for several months we thought she must be dead. But one day Father saw her in the forest again. She kept well away from him and he could not coax her to come nearer. He crept closer inch by inch and then he realized that she was not alone. There was a wolf with her. Another person might not have noticed the wolf, but my father spotted it. He thought that the two animals must have mated, and if so, the bitch would never come back. But she did return once, for we found her tracks one winter's day and this little chap was wriggling about in the snow.' Mitya paused and stroked the cub's pelt. 'Father said she brought us her whelp as a peace offering, so that we should not be angry with her any more, and I agree with him. Don't you, my lord?'

Yermak gave the boy a sympathetic nod. 'What will happen to him now? Here, Grivka, don't sulk away.'

He pulled the cub to him by his scruff. The wolf snapped at his hand and bared his teeth in anger. But Yermak laughed and held out his fist. As the animal's mouth sprang open, Yermak thrust his fist in quickly. 'There you are! Now bite it—if you can!'

'I don't know what we will do with him. Perhaps he will run away one day as his mother did. Or he may grow up into a good hunting dog if Father trains him. Who can tell, my lord?'

'But suppose his sire's blood stirs in him and he attacks you?'

'Attacks me!' echoed Mitya and his voice grew excited. 'Then we shall have to fight it out between us. I always keep a knife in my belt. But it would be a pity to kill him.'

'You are very fond of him, aren't you?'

'Yes, my lord. He is a good friend and he understands every word I say to him. He does not pay much attention to my father, but he always obeys me.'

'Your father would have done better to crush the brute's skull when it was whimpering here on the doorstep,' interrupted Vassili Metyanov. 'I said as much from the very beginning. But Nikolai will not be told. I don't see how a friend like this can ever be tamed.

'I know what you think, sir, but I still hope you are wrong.'

Yermak played a while with Grivka, who responded slowly and became less mistrustful. Then Vassili reminded him that it was time to go.

The men mounted and Yermak had already said good-bye, when Vassili turned his head as they were riding off and called to Mitya, 'Irina says to tell you it wasn't the wind you were talking to!' Then he laughed across to Yermak. 'These children! The devil only knows the secrets they have together.'

The sky was covered with thick clouds, heaving and churning like rising dough. The rough wind roared with angry gusts over the land which lay shrouded in black night. Mitya groped through the darkness. Although he did his best to tread softly, his footsteps seemed to echo aloud through the silence of the night. Or was it just his imagination? As he passed a log cabin, the dogs started barking. He jumped in alarm. Now he could see the Metyanovs' house in front of him. He swerved to one side and hurried by. The next cottage belonged to Vassili's head serf, who supervised the harvesting and the allocation of land for the crops. It couldn't be far now. If only it weren't so dark! He could barely make out the three old birch trees and beyond them the thicket which would give him his bearings. Mitya strained his eyes as he drew nearer, peering into the dark. There on the right something was stirring. Mitya stood still and his heart pounded for joy. Yes, Irina had kept her word.

Mitya gave a leap towards the thicket. The thick mire squelched beneath his feet. Then he had firm ground beneath them once more and he was standing near a horse.

'The chestnut,' he whispered happily. 'So you're really here, waiting for me.' He stroked the horse's neck and his hand groped along its back. Yes, it was saddled and the saddle-bags were full, too. The dear girl, thought Mitya, and grasped the reins. Carefully he guided the horse to the path and took care to keep it in the grass verge to deaden the sound of its hoofs.

'The blessing of the Mother of God on you, Irina, sweetheart,' he breathed and looked back into the darkness. 'I shall come back, I promise you, not once but a hundred times.'

Once more Irina was lying sleepless in bed by her grandmother's side. I wonder if he's gone or if he's just going? Has he found the horse yet? No one would notice it had gone, she decided firmly. Suppose they did, though? Then the stable-boy would be in for a beating. That was all. But tomorrow, when day dawned, the little hovel near the forest, the last hut in the village and the smallest and humblest, would be standing empty, quite empty. No. Grivka would still be there, and one evening Mitya's father would come back. That would be the hardest part, having to tell Nikolai that Mitya had gone away and for a long, long time.

Why did I make it possible for him? Why did I help him? I didn't want to and yet I did it . . . Yes, but how can you look on and watch such unhappiness? He had tried to quell his longing, but he could never quite conceal it. No, you can't stand by when your best friend has no joy in life. And now she was alone. There was no one in the village who meant as much to her as Mitya.

Without noticing it, the tears began to brim into Irina's eyes, but as soon as she was aware of them she shook them back. No, no. He would come back. He had promised and he never broke his word. She must look forward to the day of his return.

And as she imagined that day her tears flowed once more. She tried to smother a sob, but suddenly there was her grandmother bending over her.

'What is it, child! Why are you weeping?'

'I . . . I . . .' sobbed Irina. 'I had a frightful dream.'

'What did you dream, my love?'

'I . . . I can't remember, Granny.'

'There now, dearie, I'll tell you a story. That will give you something pleasant to think about until you fall asleep.'

Next morning, as soon as Yermak had left, Irina went to Nikolai's hut. In her right hand she had a wooden pail in which was food for Grivka. She walked swiftly until she saw the house not far ahead.

Her last faint hope disappeared. There was no smoke curling from the chimney. The hut must be empty.

All at once Irina felt too frightened to open the door, for there was no Mitya there to order the wolf into the corner. But no sound came from Grivka, no growling nor the infuriated spitting which made her shudder even more. Cautiously she approached the door.

'Grivka, good dog,' she called in a friendly voice, although there was terror in all her limbs. 'I've brought you your breakfast. You'll enjoy it, Grivka.'

Irina opened the door a crack, but there was still no sound. She pushed farther and placed the pail in the darkness. The light was too dim to make out the cub. She stood still and craned her neck. Then she saw close to the ground two green eyes gleaming and they were staring straight at her.

But the dog did not move.

Suppose he jumps at me? I must talk to him, she told herself.

'Come on, Grivka, eat it all up,' she said. But it was only a husky whisper. 'I'll see you tomorrow.'

She retreated a couple of steps, but all the time she kept her eyes fixed on the two green lights. Then she closed the door.

I shall come back tomorrow and every day until Mitya's father returns. But then I shall beg him to let Grivka go, to turn him loose in the forest.

Yermak had been riding for several hours. He would not allow his horse to settle down into an easy trot. He kept whipping it on, burning to increase the distance between himself and Moscow as fast as possible.

'We've a long way to go, my lad. You can rest tonight. Come on, now. Show me what you're made of.'

By noon the animal was exhausted, and Yermak recognized that if he did not allow it to rest a little it would collapse under him. He did not know how far it was to the next relay where he could change horses, so he guided it into a grove of willow trees which bordered the edge of the swamp he had been skirting now for many miles.

Yermak jumped down and tried to find a place to rest. The horse stood still for a moment, its flanks trembling. Then it started to browse on the delicate young leaves of the trees. Yermak took a loaf of bread from his saddle-bag, but his thoughts were still with Vassili Metyanov and his family. Now that he had seen them all again he had to turn his mind to the future. It had been easy enough to say to them, 'Why should I worry?' The facts were staring him in the face, and they did not look quite so simple any longer.

As Yermak chewed his bread, he saw that the horse was quenching its thirst, gulping down great draughts of water from one of the muddy pools. His own thirst began to torment him and he started prowling about to see if he could find any clean water. There was marsh all round and he kept stepping into the quagmire. As he pulled his foot out each time his boot left a deep hole and a reeking black liquid oozed in slowly. He gave up the search and went back the way he had come.

Suddenly he pricked his ears and listened. He had heard the whinny of an approaching horse. Was he being pursued, after all? Hastily he concealed himself among the bushes. His horse, too, was well hidden. He thought of stepping farther into the marsh, but then he remembered that he was wearing the Czar's uniform and there was no need to hide. Another snort followed and then came the gallop of hoofs. He peered between the twigs. Yes, there was a rider coming. Yermak waited to see if the man was alone or if there were others behind him.

No, there was only one person. Calmly Yermak freed his feet from the slime and went back to the road. He decided to ignore whoever it was approaching. It was only when the rider was almost abreast that Yermak glanced up and at the same moment he heard himself addressed.

'At last, my lord. At last I've found you.'

'Mitya! What are you doing here?'

'I left the village last night and rode on ahead. I knew that you would take this road.'

'Who told you?'

'Irina. I hoped that if we met far enough away from the village you would not be able to send me back home. I have a favour to ask you. Please take me with you.'

'You want to come with me? How can you expect such a thing? I am on a secret mission from his most gracious Majesty. I cannot take anyone with me.'

'Oh, my lord, even if you strike me dead on the spot I have to say it. I know who you are.'

Yermak gave the boy a look of such fury that Mitya thought he was going to attack him, but he did not flinch, even when Yermak's hand flew to his belt.

'I am not afraid, Yermak Timofeyev, otherwise I would never have come in the first place. And you will not kill me, I know, for in your heart you are still the son of a nobleman and a gentleman. I know why you turned Cossack and I am sure that you can always use a fellow like me.'

Yermak's hand dropped from his dagger and a hearty laugh escaped from his broad chest.

'A fellow like you!' he chortled and clapped Mitya on the shoulder so hard that he jumped. 'Fellows like you, eh? Ha, ha, ha! Yes, when they're old enough, but not when they're still playing with their toys.'

Mitya's face flushed to the roots of his hair. 'My lord!' he protested hotly and gritted his teeth together. Suddenly he whipped the knife from his girdle.

'Come on then, let's fight. You'll soon see if I play with toys!'

Yermak ignored the dagger. He looked Mitya up and down and down and up.

'Put that away,' he barked shortly. 'Why do you want to come with me? What do you imagine a Cossack's life is like? Do you think it's so simple just to come with me? I am travelling as the Czar's courier and they ride alone. Who can say where my path will take me once I am back in camp with the Cossacks? And waiting for me wherever I go there is always . . .' And here Yermak drew a hand across his own throat. 'Or do you think the hangman will take pity on me because you are with me? By the way, how did you find out who I am?'

'It was from Irina, my lord. That night when you were talking to Vassili Metyanov she could not sleep and she overheard it all. And because she knew how I longed to get away, and we have always been good friends . . . At first she tried to stop me, as she always did when strangers came to the village. But then she gave me the horse and said that if I must go, then better with you than with anyone else—because you and her father are brothers, so to speak. I will do everything you tell me. I am very strong and I am not frightened of anything. I mean that.'

'You will have to prove that.'

'Then you will take me, my lord?'

'I have not said so.'

Yermak fell silent and inspected the boy once more.

I wonder if it is a good omen that this lad is running after me, he thought to himself, a sign that life still has something to offer me, that the end is not yet in sight, the dishonourable death of an outlaw. I wonder if the Almighty has sent me this boy, who might have been my own son!

With his thumbs tucked in the broad leather belt, he paced up and down. Then he stopped in front of Mitya.

'Don't you ever want to go back to Irina, to your father and to Grivka?'

'Oh yes, my lord. When I am a man like you and when I have fought and people can say of me, "Look! there is Dmitri Nikolayev, who did not want to doze away his life in the village like us, and who had the pluck to go out into the big, strange world." That's when I should like to go back home.'

Yermak looked straight at the fresh, frank face with the clear shining eyes.

'Very well, then. Come with me, my lad,' he said at last. 'But I am telling you once more that it will not be easy to remain an honest man. Think it over carefully. You can still go back.'

'I shall go with you, my lord.'

'Come on, then. We must be on our way.'

4 BY ROAD AND RIVER

The days went by and one was so like the other that Mitya did not know how long they had been on the road. Nor could he say for certain how often they had changed horses along the way. Not one of his mounts was as dear to him as the chestnut Irina had given him and it had been a hard moment saying good-bye to it. He knew he would never see it again and it was this parting which made him realize for the first time how far-reaching his decision had been. But he did not reveal this to Yermak. He felt too ashamed of his feelings.

Days lengthened into weeks. They rode from daybreak until the gathering dusk. Yermak seemed not to know what tiredness was, and Mitya often had to clench his teeth to stop himself falling from the saddle out of sheer exhaustion. He was not used to riding for hours on end and his limbs were sometimes seized with cramp. It was all he could do to straighten his knees as he slithered from the horse's back and he could barely stagger when his feet touched the ground. At the coaching inns he stretched himself out on the floor and slept like a corpse. There were times when he had not even the strength to finish the bowl of broth which the innkeeper's wife set before him. His clothing was frequently soaked through after the rain, but he ignored it. He simply dropped to the ground and slept as he was. More than once Yermak had lifted the lad in his arms and laid him on the stove so that his clothes could dry out.

One evening, however, Yermak had some news for him. 'Well, my boy. We've done with riding for the present. There are no more relay posts after this, so we must take to the river.' And he bartered their horses for a strong raft.

Storm, sun and rain were their companions on the voyage. Day and night, the rapid current bore them farther and farther along. With his legs sprawled out in front of him and his back leaning against one of the wooden saddles they had kept, Mitya sat there for hours watching the landscape. He looked out over the broad stretch of fast-flowing water, sparkling like silver in the sunlight, and over the flat river banks. From a sitting position, reeds and stunted bushes hid the view, but if he stood up there was nothing to block the sight of the green and yellow plains which stretched unbroken as far as the horizon. Above them curved the glassy dome of the grey-blue sky, enclosing everything. There was hardly a rise in the ground anywhere for the eye to fix as a landmark. Desolate, mysterious, the vast expanses on either side of the river kept their silent secrets.

'These are the steppes, Mitya,' said Yermak.

'And what is the name of this river?'

'This is the Don.'

Mitya's eyes soon began to smart if he stared for long, so he would scoop up a handful of cold water from the river and dash it over his eyes and face. Then he would close his eyes and listen to the murmur of the waters and it brought his memories crowding back. All the dreams of his boyhood came to life again, but nearer, clearer, more pressing and more vivid. But he could hear something else in the lapping of the river, too. There was yearning in it, a longing for his father and Irina and Grivka. Mitya did not try to suppress it, and it only served to strengthen still more his urge to visit far-away places. Deep down inside him he felt that this passion for adventure and his homesickness were but different aspects of one and the same emotion.

Yermak was never tired. He stood there for hours, steering the raft all the time.

'Can't I take a turn for you, my lord?' asked Mitya, feeling uncomfortable at his own idleness.

Yermak shook his head. 'I shouldn't feel safe. In any case, you'll need all your strength presently.'

So Mitya lounged away the whole day, sometimes lying on his front and sometimes on his back. He and Yermak ate the same food and their teeth ground away at the dry barley cakes and the toasted oatmeal which formed their staple diet. In the morning when Mitya awoke he watched the ducks and geese rise from the reeds into the grey-green sky. He saw falcons and sea-eagles swooping on their prey, and they reminded him for a moment of Vassili Metyanov. When the noonday sun burnt down and he stripped off his shirt, there was nothing to do but stretch out his legs and doze. Often he awoke with a shock, for the rocking of the raft had ceased. Then he would see that they were moored safely among the reeds and that Yermak was lying by his side, sleeping soundly.

It was like that one day. Mitya woke up and the thought came to him that he really ought to relieve Yermak just this once. He picked up the long pole and tried to steer the raft out into the open water. But before he could get under way Yermak was wide awake, too. He jumped to his feet, whipped the pole from Mitya's hands and gripped him by the shoulder.

'Now listen, boy,' he said, and Mitya knew at once that he had done wrong. 'I am in charge of this raft, do you hear? There are only the two of us present and I am the one who gives the orders. Your job is to obey them. That is the law among us Cossacks and you will do well to remember it, once and for all.'

Mitya was crushed. 'Yes, my lord,' was all he could say, and he did not dare to return the look in Yermak's piercing eyes.

'And stop calling me "my lord". I am Yermak, to you and to everyone else.'

There were numerous ferry stations dotted up and down the river and from them led various routes into the interior. They never passed these stations during daylight, for not only did Yermak know every one of them but it appeared that the ferrymen knew him, too. Mitya could tell it was so by the way Yermak spoke about them. 'Now this is a worthwhile ferry,' he would say. 'They handle a lot of merchandise. But they know how to wield a sword here, too.' At another one Yermak told Mitya, 'We had a rich haul at this one not long ago, a whole consignment of goods from Greece. Do you know where that is?'

'No.'

'Never mind, it isn't important. What you have to learn is how to discriminate between these silks and brocades we capture, to decide which are worth having and which you might as well heave overboard—unless, of course, you are clever enough to hoodwink the merchants and convince them that something is valuable when it is really trash.'

Boats passed them now and then and Mitya noticed at once with what assurance Yermak made his decisions. Sometimes he would hide the raft among the rushes. At other times he would punt past calmly, although his uniform and his weapons had to be safely concealed under various bundles, needless to say. He would wave a friendly greeting to the ship, for all the world as if he were a simple peasant steering along unhurriedly to get to the next ferry post. But he had a tale to tell Mitya about every vessel he preferred not to face.

'He must have done some terrible deeds if he has to avoid recognition so often,' thought Mitya, and the urge to become a bold adventurer like Yermak Timofeyev often intoxicated him, as it grew more and more intense. The farther downstream they sailed, the higher grew the reeds by the bank, until they were more than six feet tall and to Mitya they looked like a forest. All he could see now was the strip of sky overhead and the river widening all the time, the reeds hemmed them in so completely. Mitya learned how to catch fish which he lured to the side of the raft with crumbs of bread when the waters were still.

Yermak had spoken little throughout the long journey, but now he began to talk more readily and more frequently. He told Mitya about the Cossacks in his own 'hundred' and how to behave when they arrived. But more often he asked Mitya about the village and his life at home.

'Why didn't your father take you hunting with him?' he wanted to know one day.

'I think he was afraid I might be too rash,' answered Mitya. 'You see, there were only the three of us, Father, Mother and I, and four years ago a huge brown bear killed my mother as she was gathering berries in the forest. That day I vowed I would flay the bear and afterwards Father would never allow me to go with him. He knew that I meant what I said.'

'Why didn't your father kill it?'

'Ah, he's a very cunning bear. He seldom lets himself be seen. He only comes sneaking out when he is absolutely sure of himself. When bears are old, you know, they can be very clever. But I'll get him yet, you can be sure of that.'

Sometimes when they were floating along in the darkness Yermak used to sing softly to himself. They were songs which Mitya did not know and they sounded strange and beautiful. 'They must be Cossack songs and soon I shall be singing them, too,' he thought. 'They belong to this broad river beyond whose banks I cannot see, and to hot days and cold nights when you have to buckle your belt tightly round your fur jerkin so that you can sleep, at least.'

One late evening Mitya was sitting there, his legs drawn up to his body, trying to get some sleep. Yermak had told him earlier that they would soon be landing and it seemed to the boy that his chief was listening more attentively than ever to the noises of the night.

Deeper and deeper grew the darkness. Yermak steered the raft in to the right bank and he kept it so close inshore that they kept brushing the reeds. It was difficult to make any progress at all. Big frogs leapt into the air and dived into the water, splashing and croaking.

'I suppose we'll spend the night here in the reeds,' thought Mitya, and stretched out his legs. He heard a screech-owl cry once, and then again. Mitya laid his head on his arm and closed his eyes. The owl called again, once, twice, three times. Then Mitya heard only the frogs.

With a sudden start he jerked himself awake, for now it was Yermak who was imitating the owl's call. First twice and then, after a moment's pause, three times. Mitya shivered. He did not know what it meant.

For a few minutes all was silent. Then came the call again from the rushes.

'Wake up, Mitya. We have arrived. One of the brothers has come to meet us.' Yermark punted the raft with quick movements right into the reeds and the stems all round them broke with a dull crackling. Then Mitya saw the silhouette of horses on the bank, and when he looked more closely he could make out a rider with them.

A cautious voice floated across. 'Yermak Timofeyev?'

And an equally restrained one answered with a similar question, 'Ivan Koltso?'

'At last!' replied the man from the bank. 'At last! I was beginning to think I was waiting in vain.'

The next moment the raft tipped as Yermak gave a mighty leap to the bank. Mitya could hear only a blur of voices as the two men greeted each other and then the stranger's voice came over more clearly. 'So you have dodged the Devil once again? That is good. We should have mourned you sadly, brother, if you had been caught.'

'I can't quite see it, but I believe you all the same. Hey, Mitya!' Yermak turned back. 'Throw the tackle ashore and then come across yourself.'

'Are you not alone?'

'No. Can't you hear? I have found a new recruit, someone who wouldn't leave me alone until I said he might join us.'

'Are you out of your mind, Yermak? How can you bring a stranger into our midst just now? How do you know that he isn't a spy?'

'That is *my* worry. I have my reasons.'

At that moment Mitya sprang on to the bank and stood near Yermak.

'Great heavens!' cried Koltso, bending down to stare at Mitya's face. 'Is this the scourge of the Tartars? What will this babe in arms do in camp? Who will rock him to sleep at night?'

'What's that?' shouted Mitya in fury, but Yermak stepped in quickly.

'Leave him alone, Ivan. He will soon get used to our ways. He was so anxious to come. I shall take full responsibility, of course.'

'But you know what rough lives we lead and any day now all hell may be let loose. And yet you bring us this infant with the milk still wet on his lips.'

'Don't interfere in my affairs,' said Yermak sharply and Ivan Koltso held his tongue.

'Shall we start right away or do you want to stretch your legs first?'

'No, we'll saddle the horses and be off immediately.'

'And what about the lad? I brought only one horse with me.'

'Mitya can ride behind me. You take his saddle.'

But Ivan Koltso could not refrain from teasing still. 'Now don't fret, son. Uncle Ivan will soon get a nice little horsie for you to ride, too.'

Yermak put a reassuring hand on Mitya's arm. 'Don't pay any attention to him. He means you no harm.'

They had been riding for quite some time, forcing a way through the thick undergrowth, before Ivan Koltso spoke again. He turned to Yermak and said, 'Have you any more surprises up your sleeve for us?'

'I'll tell you presently. First of all I want to know how things stand with you.'

'All is well. You know how our spirits rise when summer's on the way. Everyone has their hands full.'

'Any losses in men?'

'Only two, both from my hundred. We had a set-to with a strong caravan and they defended themselves damned well, the curs. There were more of them than we had expected, into the bargain. Not that it helped them much in the end, as you can well believe. Now you tell me.'

'We must call a council meeting.'

'Why?'

'Because our most gracious sovereign is raising an army in Moscow to send into the field against us.'

'What's that you say? A whole army? That's too much of a compliment for a miserable bunch of Cossacks, don't you think?'

'I agree entirely. Murashkin is to lead it and you and I are wanted in Moscow—dead or alive!'

'Oho!' said Ivan Koltso and gave a loud belch. Then he cleared his throat. 'I must have eaten too much mutton today. Tell me, though, does the Czar mean it or does he think the rumour is sufficient to scatter us in panic?'

'This time it's serious and what is more there will be no quarter. The Czar demands a thorough job and Murashkin is the man to do it.'

'The hound, the wretched . . .'

'Cursing won't help us.'

'Are you admitting defeat before the enemy has even struck? What's wrong with you, Yermak? I've never heard you talk like this before.'

'Nonsense! Who's admitting defeat? I am just facing facts and trying to think of a solution. I am not yet sure what is the best thing to do. That is why I shall call the council. '

'The swine! Just when summer is coming and the traffic on the Volga keeps us amused, when a fellow can actually fill both his belly and his pockets for once! And this dog of a Murashkin has to come along and spoil everything. Why can't he choose some other time!'

'Well, let us hope he doesn't ruin your sense of humour, Ivan.'

Mitya, who had been clinging to Yermak's sword belt, was listening to the conversation, all ears. 'That's a fine thing, I must say,' he thought to himself. 'So I may not have a chance of seeing anything of the world after all! Who is this Murashkin, anyway? One of the Czar's generals, obviously. Not that it matters. One day he will arrive and force us to do battle, and who knows what will happen then? I may be killed and I shall have seen nothing, nothing!'

'Don't you think it would be best if we withdrew into the steppes, Yermak?' Ivan Koltso went on. 'They'd be hard put to find us there.'

'Think a minute, Ivan. There are several thousand of us. How can we vanish into the steppes, perhaps for years on end? And how will we live? By raiding the scattered Tartar settlements, perhaps?'

They rode on in silence.

Ivan Koltso was again the first one to speak. 'You are right. There are too many of us, if we stick together . . .'

'Do you mean that we alone . . .?'

Koltso's silence was confirmation enough for Yermak.

'That would be one way out, I know. But it would mean leaving the others in the lurch, Ivan.'

'But it means life or death on the gallows to us. Not all of them are on the black list like us two.'

'Murashkin won't stop to ask people their names, you know. As far as he is concerned we are all tarred with the same brush and he will fight the whole Cossack brotherhood.'

'All the same, if it were up to me, I should not call a council meeting. I would send a message to the others to say what has happened and then set off, the sooner the better.'

'No, Ivan. We must hear what the council has to say.'

5 THE YOUNGEST COSSACK

On the third day after their meeting with Captain Ivan Koltso they reached the Cossack village where Yermak Timofeyev lived. It stood by the Volga at the point where it flows closest to the Don. The three travellers had halted at several other settlements *en route* and Yermak had had messengers sent to neighbouring districts to summon the representatives of the other colonies for a meeting at the next full moon.

A horse had been found for Mitya at their first halt and now he rode between the two men. He peered forward eagerly as they drew near to their destination. He could see the densely packed encampment, which consisted of tents and wooden cabins built on stilts, all huddling together at the foot of a low hill in front of a fringe of forest. At the top of the hill was a tall wooden turret, and from it, on either side, ran a palisade of planed tree trunks, which enclosed watch-tower and village into a rough square.

Mitya was trying to make out which was the entrance to the stockade when he heard a buzz of noise coming from the village. As they approached, the sounds grew in volume, until he could make out that they were shouting 'Yermak Timofeyev' over and over again. A few moments later a crowd of men came pouring out to meet them. Some were bareheaded, others wore the Cossack fur hat, some were dressed in tunics, others in short jerkins. They had dashed out just as they were as soon as they heard the call from the sentinels in the watch-tower. There was a sea of strange faces, smooth and wrinkled, brick red and brown. Arms waved, hands reached out to them wherever they went and above all rang the joyous cry, 'Yermak Timofeyev, it's good to have you back. God bless you, Yermak Timofeyev!'

'Greetings, brothers!' called Yermak, jumping down from his horse. The men surrounded him, kissing his cheeks and shaking his hand, still repeating: 'It's good to have you back!' They pulled him along with them into the village, talking all the time. As Yermak answered their question his eyes took in everything: the state of the houses and the tents and the strength of the stockade.

Mitya and Ivan Koltso kept their distance. 'Well, laddie?' asked Ivan, turning to the boy. 'Do you think that you're going to like it here?'

'Why shouldn't I?' answered Mitya. 'Only I was wondering if I shall have time to get used to it all before we have to leave.'

'So you heard what Yermak and I were discussing, then?'

'Yes, sir.'

'And what is your opinion? Which way do you think we should choose, eh?'

'It isn't easy to decide. You both agreed that the south is ruled out because the Nogai Khan is lying in wait to have his revenge for the looting of Saraichik. We can't go east into the steppes or we may starve. Murashkin will be coming from the north-west, so that leaves only the north.'

'Well argued, my boy! But how shall we live in the north?'

'I don't know.'

'We shall have to find out, then.'

Mitya's head felt heavy. He was not used to the crude rye spirits they had drunk at supper and he felt most peculiar. It was his first night in the Cossack village and in spite of the alcohol he could not fall asleep. He lay on a wooden settle in Yermak's cabin, which was the one nearest to the watch-tower. Until them Yermak had lived alone, but now he shared his quarters with Mitya.

There was no sign of Yermak, but the boy waited, listening to the noises that penetrated from the outside. The Cossacks were still celebrating Yermark's return and their endless songs pierced the darkness. Mitya had supposed that Yermak was still with them, but not long before he thought that he had heard footsteps outside the hut and he half wondered if Yermak might not be sitting on the steps below the front door. He felt wholly insecure when Yermak was not near. Everything was so strange and unsettling. During the past few weeks he had learnt that the Cossacks had to be prepared for attacks at any hour, and especially at night. There were Tartars living across the river, on the opposite bank of the Volga.

Again Mitya listened as more footsteps approached, but there were two men this time. He could hear them talking.

'What made the Captain bring us that young whipper-snapper?' babbled a thick voice. 'Why should we play at nurse to please him, that's what I want to know?' And the speaker hiccupped loudly.

'It doesn't worry me. Let him bring whom he likes,' answered the other. 'It's Yermak's business, not ours.'

'Oh yes, it is. We all have a say here.'

'But anyone can become a Cossack if he's a Christian and knows how to fight.'

'You don't think that babe in swaddling-clothes is any use at fighting, do you?' And a wave of hiccups overwhelmed him.

'He'll have to fight if he stays with us, or he'll soon be sprouting cherub's wings.'

'That's right!' There was a bleating laugh, which penetrated as far as the house.

Suddenly the footsteps stopped short and Mitya could hear the less truculent Cossack whispering: 'Quiet! It's the Captain.'

Mitya looked out of the window without making a sound. He saw the men ducking swiftly, dodging beneath the piles on which the house stood.

'Don't meddle in affairs which you do not understand and are no concern of yours anyway,' came a stern voice. 'And you can save your wit for a better object, Ilya. It's high time the two of you were in your beds.'

Yermak's tall figure had risen out of the darkness by the side of the two men, so he must have been sitting on the steps, after all. Mitya was grateful to Yermak for speaking up for him. In spite of the malice of Ilya and his friend, the lad's loneliness seemed less hard to bear and his self-confidence returned. He leaned out of the window and spat. Then with a sigh of relief he slipped back to his bed.

Shortly afterwards Yermak entered the room. He had to stoop as he came through the doorway. Mitya saw him throw his belt and his long greatcoat on to a stool and then he sat down on the broad bench and tugged at his riding-boots.

'Can I help you?' asked Mitya shyly.

Yermak's head turned abruptly. 'Aren't you asleep yet?'

'I was waiting for you.'

'Mm,' growled Yermak. 'So that you could take off my boots for me? I can do that by myself, thank you.' The first boot sailed through the air and the second followed a few moments later. 'I have decided you must take the oath tomorrow.'

Mitya sat up with a start. 'Oh, thank you, Yermak. I . . .'

'That will do,' said Yermak, and stretched himself out on the bench opposite Mitya. 'You still haven't told me why you were waiting up for me.'

'It was because you are so worried about the future.'

'What of that? Why should it stop you from sleeping?'

'Well, I know I can't really help you or give you good advice, but sometimes things don't seem quite so bad when you're not quite alone.'

Yermak did not reply at once. He lay there in the stillness, listening not only to Mitya's words but to the tone of his voice as well. Then he answered curtly, 'It's best to be alone.' It sounded harsh and the darkness did nothing to soften it.

'For years I have known nothing else,' added Yermak, and this time there was a hint of kindness, rebuilding the frail bridge between them.

'I know,' came the boy's voice, muffled.

'How?'

'You are so different from the others. None of them became Cossacks for reasons like yours.'

'Silence!' Again Mitya could hear the hardness of a man who will not tolerate any opposition.

Then once more came a gentle word as compensation for the blow. 'Go to sleep now, Mitya.'

There were two rows of Cossacks and they stood facing each other. At the far end were Yermak and Ivan Koltso, the most senior in rank of those present. At the other end was Mitya. His face was pale with excitement and he was still wearing the dark tunic in which he had left home.

He knew that all eyes were turned on him and that many of those present did not trouble to conceal their contempt. Mitya was as tall as most of the men present, although he was barely fifteen, but his build was still slight and his face was that of a child, in which one could read every passing emotion. What damned him most, however, was that there was no sign of a beard on his chin.

At last Yermak thought it was time to put an end to the staring.

'Brothers,' he began, 'while I was away I met a youth who wants to join our community. None of us were asked why we wanted to become Cossacks and similarly we shall refrain from probing his motives. But whoever joins us must accept our laws and he must be a Christian prepared to fight for his faith. He must obey his captain, in whose election he has a voice every year. He must be ready to take up arms as he is ordered and to share his booty with his comrades. In return he shall be given a horse, his weapons and his share of our food and drink. Now that you have heard all this, I put the question to you. Are you, Dmitri Nikolayev Yelnikov, prepared to enter our community and to keep faith with us?'

'I am.'

'Then swear it by God.'

Mitya raised his right hand. 'I swear it by God.'

Then he passed between the rows and received from Yermak's hand a dagger, a sabre and a tall bearskin cap. Next he was led into the guardroom and the Cossacks thronged round him as he was handed a pair of riding-boots, a long greatcoat, a tunic, shirt and belt. When he had dressed, Yermak went with him to the field where the horses were grazing.

'You are in luck,' said Yermak. 'At the moment we have more horses than we need. You can pick one for yourself.'

This was unexpected and Mitya hesitated. 'They are all such fine ones,' he acknowledged, and his eyes went from one to the other.

A black mare came galloping up to the two men and whinnied loudly. Mitya was about to say, 'I should like that one', when he saw Yermak stretch out his hand and snap his fingers coaxingly. 'Here, Swallow, come here!' he beckoned.

'Is that your own horse?' asked Mitya.

'Yes, isn't she a beauty? I have never known her equal either for speed or stamina.'

It looked as if the black mare's approach had been a signal to the others, for they all came trotting up behind her.

'What about the sorrel over there? Does it belong to anyone special?'

'No, I don't think so.'

'Very well then, I'll have that one.'

'Good,' said Yermak. 'But don't think that you can just mount and ride it. We haven't had it long. It was captured out in the steppes. We call it a *tarpan*. Do you know what that is?'

'It's a wild horse, isn't it?' he said cautiously, not sure if he should admit that he knew the word.

'Yes. How did you know?'

'Volodya told me. He is Vassili Metyanov's slave, you see, and he is a Tartar from Kazan. When the Czar defeated the Prince of Kazan many of his people were taken prisoner and sent to Moscow. There they were sold as slaves and Vassili happened to buy Volodya. It was he who told me that there are hordes of wild horses living in the steppes and that they roam in packs, led by the strongest stallion. Volodya said that they are hard to capture, but if you succeed in breaking one in, then you have a real treasure, a horse with swift hoofs and a small appetite, and that is very important in the vast dry plains. And once you have tamed and ridden it, he said, you'll never want any other horse. Once upon a time there were creatures in the steppes who were half man and half horse——' Mitya broke off suddenly. 'I am not sure if that is true,' he apologized, 'but Volodya told me . . .'

'Volodya is no fool, I should say.'

'You are quite right. Have you heard of these creatures, too?'

'Yes, there are many legends about them. The Scythians who lived here centuries ago are said to have been descended from such centaurs, as they are called, and I often think there may be a grain of truth in the story, for this has always been a land of men and their horses. There are no merchants or farmers, only horsemen like us Cossacks and the Tartars before us.'

The next few days flew by. Mitya hardly knew if it was day or night. He used to go down to the Volga with the others to empty the fish traps and to set new ones. Often he helped to prepare the food in the cookhouse, and whenever he had time he ran out to the fields where the horses were grazing and spent the time with the sorrel. When he returned, more often than not he was limping and dragging his feet like an old woman.

The horse he had selected was a tough nut to crack, there were no two ways about it. It was hard work just getting hold of it. And even when Mitya had caught it he had first to mount it and then to keep his seat. He was used to riding at the Metyanovs' farm, but he had never even seen such a savage unpredictable brute as this, let alone tried to ride one. Mitya could never guess whether it was going to buck or to rear and so he went flying over its head or its crupper more times than he could count. And each time he was thrown the horse ran away and he had the trouble of catching it again.

One evening Mitya was tossing on his wooden bed, groaning with all his aches and pains.

'The sorrel isn't coming on too well, is it?' remarked Yermak.

'It's all right.'

'Wouldn't you like another horse instead?'

'Certainly not.'

Yermak looked at the boy. 'I like your spirit, lad. You don't sulk about a few bruises, and this way at least you should be a first rate horseman by the time you've finished.'

A few days later Yermak spoke to him again.

'I was watching you today, Mitya. I like the way you're handling your horse, but I hope you don't beat it, do you?'

'No, of course not. How can it ever trust me if I beat it?'

'That's the way, Mitya.'

The next day Mitya was detailed for his first sentry duty. He was not looking forward to it, for he had not yet started to make friends with any of the others and he could see that they did not take him seriously because he was so young. Although breaking in the sorrel was both arduous and discouraging, he would have much preferred tackling the horse again rather than face the guard-room.

Seven Cossacks shared the watch with him. He barely knew their names, but it was not long before he realized that one of them was the aggressive Ilya who had spoken against Mitya on his first night and who had had to swallow Yermak's reprimand. He stared offensively at Mitya, but he did not dare to provoke trouble as long as Yermak was in the offing.

Mitya glanced at the others warily. Two of them were old men with grey beards, and their faces and hands were brown and tanned like hide. One of them had an empty eye socket. The next in age appeared to be Ilya. He was lean and sinewy and he had black hair and eyes which reminded Mitya of Volodya's. He wondered if Ilya was of Tartar origin.

The four remaining Cossacks were quite young. One of them had an angry red scar on his forehead. They sprawled on the benches, smoking and gossiping while Mitya listened.

As soon as Yermak had gone they started speaking more freely.

'I'd like to know what's wrong with the old man these days. He's running round in circles like a wolf when the hunters are closing in. I have a feeling there's something brewing.'

'A feeling! Only the young pay any attention to their feelings!' interrupted one of the old men impatiently. 'I rely on my eyes and my ears.'

'And what do they tell you?'

'That there's something in the wind when Yermak goes about looking so preoccupied. He wouldn't have called the council meeting for nothing, either.'

'But what's it all about?'

'You lads are so impatient! What are the possibilities? I know Yermak pretty well and I'm sure he's planning an expedition.'

'Do you think it will be like that time we attacked Saraichik?'

'I don't pretend to know, but it must be something on the grand scale.'

Mitya pretended he was absorbed in looking out of the window. If only they knew, he thought to himself.

Without warning, someone prodded him in the side. 'Hey, baby! Don't you know what's going on? After all, you share his quarters.'

It was Ilya's voice. Mitya knew it without turning.

'You don't think he confides his plans to me, do you? I'm the youngest here and I haven't shown my mettle yet.'

The others, who had waited with interest for Mitya's answer, were silent but favourably impressed. No one had really expected him to supply them with secret information, but even less had they expected him to admit his youth and inexperience. He had taken the wind out of Ilya's sails.

But Ilya was not put out, especially as everyone had heard the boy's spirited answer. 'Your mettle, oho!' he said. 'You can show us that here and now. Come on, let's see the colour of your sword.' Ilya had drawn his own sabre as he spoke and he took up his guard, waiting for Mitya. His eyes were flashing.

As the first flush of excitement faded, Mitya felt his body growing icy cold. A wave of hatred surged through him. He whipped his sword from its sheath and braced his feet. 'Come on, then!' he panted.

The one-eyed Cossack leapt up from the bench.

'Are you mad, Ilya? You know perfectly well that Yermak has forbidden duelling. The boy hasn't hurt you in any way. Yermak would have you beaten to a pulp if he found out what had happened.'

'I don't take orders from you, Igor Alexeyev,' retorted Ilya. 'Mind your own business.'

'If you don't shut that great mouth of yours you'll feel the edge of *my* blade,' was the firm answer. 'Put up your sword, Mitya. This is no way to prove your courage. You'll have occasion enough presently. Don't forget we are on duty now. Come on, fellows, look sharp! Two men to the top of the tower and the rest of you down to the posts by the river.'

6 A SHIP ON THE VOLGA

Mitya and one of the young Cossacks were posted to the farthest look-out station upstream. Mitya was pleased, for this young man was the only one of those present with whom he felt he wanted to share a watch.

Silently they strode along the river bank. Mitya stumped behind the other man and he gazed at the broad back, the corn-coloured hair which showed beneath the tall cap, the big prominent ears and the thick neck as if he had never seen such a human being before.

When they reached the lightly wooded country the other turned and spoke to him.

'You behaved very well just now. Ilya is a thorn in the flesh and none of us like him. He always tries to keep some of the loot for himself, although everyone else hands it in so that it can be shared out fairly. If Yermak caught him doing it, he'd stretch his neck till he was the tallest man in the village, but Ilya is as cunning as a fox.'

'What has he against me?'

'Why, nothing. He tries to provoke every new-comer and I don't think he'll leave you in peace until you have fought it out.'

'I'm glad you told me. I have a lot to learn, I know, but I'm not afraid of him.'

'He could tell that.'

They walked on in silence until the Cossack said almost casually, 'My name is Boris.'

After a good half-hour of steady marching they reached the lonely sentry post. Two Cossacks were sitting on a fallen tree trunk which had collapsed across the sedge. They were waiting to be relieved.

'Here you are at last!' they called. 'You've taken your time about it. Aha, so the new lad's come, has he? Good luck to you, my boy. I hope you capture a few Tartars.'

'So do I!' replied Mitya gaily and watched the pair stretching their cramped legs before returning to the village the way that he and Boris had come.

The tree trunk was not exactly comfortable, but it was broad and high so that they could swing their legs as they sat there. The reeds were tall enough to conceal them from sight, but not too thick to prevent them from watching the Volga and the opposite bank.

'Take off your cap,' said Boris. 'It sticks up above the rushes and that's not very healthy if you happen to move your head.'

Again there was silence. 'Do you know what we usually do?' said Boris presently. 'One of us sits here and keeps guard, and the other lies down in the moss and has forty winks. Of course,' he added hesitantly, 'he has forbidden it, but sometimes he expects too much of us.'

'Do you mean Yermak?'

'Yes. By the way, how did you bump into him exactly?'

Mitya looked at Boris indignantly. 'Why do you say I bumped into him? I chased after him and begged and prayed him to let me come with him.'

'You were on the run, of course?'

'I don't know what you mean. I wanted to leave home and go with him more than anything else in the world.'

'But why did you want to get away?'

'What a question! Because I wanted to. Because it was so dreary at home.'

Boris tried to smother a laugh. 'You don't think anyone here will believe that story, do you? We're not so stupid, you know. But never mind. You don't have to tell us why you are running away if you don't want to.'

'But truly, I don't understand what you are driving at. I'm not running away from justice or anything like that. Surely you don't have to commit a crime before you join the Cossacks!'

'It isn't absolutely essential,' answered Boris dryly, 'but there are quite a lot of us who found things getting rather hot elsewhere.'

'Are you one of them?'

'No. My story is nothing unique. My family were peasants, Mitya, and the only reason why they exist, as far as I can see, is for the tax collector to bleed them white. We were expected to pay more in taxes than our fields could possibly produce. We tilled the soil all day and at night we sat down to empty plates. And still the revenue man came and squeezed, when there was nothing left to squeeze. One day my father was so exasperated that he started a quarrel with the most extortionate collector. He did not kill the man; he only knocked his teeth out, but still we had to flee for our lives. And where else could we go but to the Cossacks? My father did not escape unscathed, though. That was how he lost his eye. You saw him on duty tonight, didn't you?'

'But if you have done no wrong either, why cannot you believe that I came of my own free will, and not because I had committed a crime?'

'But you are so young.'

'I came with Yermak because I always wanted to see foreign lands; because I wanted to do great deeds, something so splendid that it takes your breath away just to think of it.' Mitya's eyes lit up. He spoke as if he had forgotten that it was Boris by his side, and as though Irina was there instead.

Boris watched him out of the corner of his eye. 'I do believe you, Mitya, and I'll tell you something else. I like you. Can't we be friends?'

Boris was not sure at first if Mitya had really heard him, he took so long to reply. 'Friends? Maybe. Would it mean much to you?'

'Yes, it would and I'll tell you why. Because I think you're a decent fellow and you feel the same way about things as I do—in here I mean,' and he struck his chest a trifle self-consciously. 'There aren't many here like you.' Then as if he were speaking to himself, he added, 'Yermak as well. You make a good pair. Do you know what we all thought at first? That you were his son. Don't laugh. None of us know anything about him and there is a sort of resemblance, you know. Not so much in appearance but in your manner and bearing. And then you're sharing his quarters, and Yermak has never done that before. He has always insisted on being on his own.'

'No, no. You are quite mistaken. My father is a trapper and he lives in a village near Kaluga, not far from Moscow. I had never even set eyes on Yermak until a few weeks ago when he came to visit Vassili Metyanov in our village.'

'Do you know much about him?'

'Only the things you know yourselves.'

'Who is Vassili Metyanov?'

'One of the Czar's falconers.'

'A falconer of the Czar's? And he dared to go and see him?' Boris opened his mouth in surprise. Then he chuckled to himself. 'That's just like him! He's a real dare-devil!'

'Do you like him?'

Boris shook his head slowly. 'I don't know. When we're making a raid and he is leading a cavalry charge, then there's no one like him. I mean that. There's no one who can hold a candle to him for courage and leadership. He always thinks one step ahead of everyone else and he's always right. But he's damned strict here in camp and it's heaven help you if you break one of the laws.'

'What kind of laws?'

'Well, for instance, that no women are allowed. Many of the brothers are married and in other villages they may live with their wives, but not here. Then again he only allows us spirits on special occasions and not much beer either.' Boris looked at Mitya. 'Can you hold your liquor?'

'Not like the fellows here. But I'm not fond of drinking, so that doesn't matter.'

'Yermak is like that as well, so there is something else the two of you have in common. Do you prefer beer or spirits?'

'Beer.'

'But you are used to liquor, aren't you?'

'Oh yes.' That was a lie, but Mitya could not admit that he was so inexperienced.

'You'll learn how to drink here, my lad, in spite of Yermak's restrictions. It's a grand feeling when your head gets so light and your legs so heavy. I always want to sing when I'm drunk and singing makes you thirstier than ever.' Boris laughed. 'And then afterwards your head feels heavy, too, and you go crashing to the ground like this tree we're sitting on. But you'll find out for yourself presently, Mitya.'

'Perhaps. But now tell me what it's like when you make a raid.'

'A raid? But you don't expect to . . . Quiet a moment. I thought I heard something.'

They listened. Mitya, who was sitting in front of Boris, slid cautiously along the tree trunk and into the reeds to get a clear view of the river. In great excitement he turned his head and hissed: 'There's a ship coming!'

'Is it a big one?' asked Boris and slipped along to join Mitya.

'No.'

'That's a pity. Still, we had better report it.' Boris had caught sight of it, too. 'It's a Russian one, not a Tartar; I can tell by the shape. Will you run back to the village or shall I go?'

'Oughtn't we both to go?'

'For a little craft like that? No. You go if you like and tell Yermak.'

Mitya pushed Boris aside and began to run. It was a good fifteen minutes before the watch-tower came into sight and he was almost there when he collided with Yermak.

'What's wrong?'

'It's a ship coming along the Volga, Yermak. Boris says it isn't a very big one and it's a Russian vessel.'

The Cossacks came dashing out of the barracks.

'To the boats!' shouted Yermak and they all hurried down to the water's edge.

'Stay near me,' he ordered Mitya, as everyone ran to his appointed place.

The Cossack skiffs were arranged so that they could easily encircle the ship when it came near enough, and they let it come very close indeed.

Everyone knew what he had to do. With powerful strokes they rowed out into the stream so that there was no escape. The little ship approached steadily and the men waited for Yermak's word of command. He crouched there like a stone, keeping his eyes on the oncoming prize. Nothing stirred aboard and the vessel seemed to be drifting with the current. Were the crew lurking below in fear, or were they lying in wait? Yermak wanted to be sure and he did not give the word yet. They moved in closer until the Cossacks could almost have touched the ship with their hands. Then Yermak sprang to his feet and swung the grappling-hook. That was the signal.

At the same moment, more than thirty iron hooks swung out towards the ship and fastened in its timbers.

'Make her fast!' shouted Yermak across the water and the men in his own boat and the one opposite raised their hatchets ready to throw. With one bound he leapt over the side on deck.

But all was still on board the mysterious vessel. It seemed to be deserted, drifting with the current, abandoned. Yermak scanned the masts and the bridge. There was no one anywhere. He motioned to three of the men to follow him to the little cabin on deck. Cautiously he opened the door and then he stopped dead. A man was sitting at a table with a map spread out before him. He had no weapons in his hands and he looked up calmly as Yermak entered.

'I have come here as a friend, Cossack,' he said, and when he saw Yermak's hand on the hilt of his sword, he added, 'You do not need that.'

Yermak was taking no chances. He drew nearer, his sword pointed towards the stranger.

'You can see that I am unarmed,' said the latter. 'Why do you want to shed blood, the blood of a friend?'

'What are you doing in these waters?' asked Yermak, planting himself in front of the man.

'I am looking for your leader. Perhaps you can help me.'

'Who in particular? Speak up. Do I have to squeeze the information out of you, word by word?'

'I am looking for Yermak Timofeyev. Do you know him?'

Yermak narrowed his eyes. 'First I must know why you want him.'

'This ship contains gifts for him if he is ready to enter the service of the House of Stroganov together with his men. Now do you know where I can find Yermak Timofeyev?'

'How can you prove that your intentions are honest? The presents don't count. We shall help ourselves to them with or without your leave.'

The man behind the table stood up. He was small and well set, but his supple movements did not go with his grey beard, which was that of an old man.

'If you wish to see it, here is the Stroganov seal on this parchment. It shows that I am their envoy.' Yermak broke the seal and unrolled the scroll. Then he read in an undertone:

'Feodor Masupov has been sent at our command to seek out the Cossack Chieftain, Yermak Timofeyev, and to negotiate with him the terms on which he and his Cossacks will come to the Province of Great Perm to defend our territory. Maxim and Nikita Stroganov.'

'So you can read,' murmured Masupov, obviously surprised.

Yermak flung him an icy stare from his hard light grey eyes. 'Hadn't you heard?' he said coldly.

'Forgive me, but I can hear something else. Your comrades are looting the ship.'

A great tumult was going on below. The ship swayed under heavy kicks and blows of the axe as the Cossacks set about breaking up the vessel.

In a couple of strides, Yermak was in their midst. 'Stop!' he ordered. 'Go back to the boats. We are taking the ship in tow.'

The men followed reluctantly. They had only just started and now they were told to stop. Yermak could tell that they were likely to make trouble. 'The ship is ours anyway. Why are you waiting? Must you destroy for the sake of destruction? Back to the boats, I tell you.'

It was Yermak himself who made the slipknots and cast the cables aboard. As the sand grated under the keel, he turned to the man. 'Is there anyone with you?'

'A crew of three.'

'Call them out and then follow them into that boat.'

The three sailors were frightened as they crawled out from below decks. They protested feebly when Yermak tied their hands behind their backs, but he ignored them. He jumped after them into the boat and they were rowed ashore. Before they were allowed to land, Yermak had them searched while he looked on suspiciously.

'Nothing!' shouted Mitya, and the other searchers reported the same.

'Unbind their hands, then.'

It was not far to the village, and as they walked along Masupov turned to Yermak. 'Are you taking me to Yermak Timofeyev, Cossack?'

Yermak strode on calmly, betraying no emotion.

'He is by your side,' he answered quietly.

7 THE COUNCIL DECIDES

The flickering tallow candle in Yermak's house burned all through that night. Mitya and Boris, whose guard duty ended only with the first light of day, kept watching it from the tower. Yermak had taken the stranger, Feodor Masupov, into his house with him.

'I wonder if the man has brought him good news,' mused Mitya to himself. 'It must be important, otherwise they would not have been talking for hours on end.'

In the room below slept the three sailors from the ship. Or rather they were lying down, for Mitya kept hearing voices as they talked anxiously to each other.

The ship's cargo was already being shared out among the Cossacks. There were valuable furs among them: sables, fox and squirrel, and provisions, too. There were cakes of salt, dried and smoked fish, bread, ship's biscuit, and flour. Mitya was happy, and for the first time he felt that he belonged to the community.

It must have been about midnight when he heard Yermak coming up the steps to the tower. He looked at him eagerly, but Yermak only inquired if everything was in order. He went to the look-out and gazed at the far bank of the Volga without speaking.

'I'm surprised that those slit-eyed devils have left us alone so long,' he said more to himself than to Mitya and Boris.

'I expect they had enough last time when we gave them such a trouncing,' replied Boris, full of self-importance.

'Were you there, too?' teased Yermak.

'Have you forgotten? I rescued one of the six who had been so badly hurt that they could not walk.'

'Of course I remember, Boris. There's a future waiting for you, my boy.'

'I'm sorry I wasn't there, too,' said Mitya.

Yermak gave him a look, but he did not comment. It was only as he was leaving that he said almost casually, 'I expect you had a good time breaking up the ship tonight with the others.'

The tone in which he spoke made Mitya feel uncertain. 'But that was all right, wasn't it, Yermak? After all, I am a Cossack now.'

'It isn't always easy to decide what is right and what is wrong.'

And with that, he left Mitya standing there and went tramping down the stairway.

Mitya stayed behind, puzzled. All through the night he kept thinking of Yermak's words.

As the pallid dawn of a new day crept over the Volga, the last one before the full moon, Ivan Koltso returned to the village. He had been sent to invite the Cossack leaders from other communities to attend the council meeting.

'Have you come alone?' asked Yermak, as Ivan entered his house.

'It will not be full moon until tomorrow,' was the evasive reply. 'But the prospects look poor. Hardly anyone is convinced that the danger is real.'

'But did you not tell them . . .'

'I told them everything, but they insist that it's all our own fault. If we had not had this brush with the Nogai Khan, they say, our choice would not be so limited. So having got ourselves into this mess, we shall have to find a way out on our own.'

'But that's only one aspect. Surely they must realize that.'

'Wait until tomorrow,' advised Koltso quietly.

The council chamber was filled to the last place. At the far end of the big room at a crudely made table sat the Captains from the various hundreds. The rest of the room was filled with Yermak's Cossacks. They were all dressed in their best clothes. In place of the dark ankle-length greatcoat they wore dazzling white knee-length tunics embroidered at the throat and the hem with red, green or blue borders. Wide black trousers of heavy serge were tucked into the best boots the wearer possessed. Tall dark caps towered on their heads.

The Captains wore the same clothes, but the borders on their tunics were stitched with gold. Near each of them stood the insignia of his office as captain, a sweeping plume of horsehair nailed to the end of a long pole. On the table before them lay the mace and the great seal.

Seven Captains were the most that Ivan Koltso had been able to summon, but apart from himself, three of them were village Captains who accepted Yermak's chieftaincy in any case. The other four were from neighbouring communities, but it was doubtful if they had come in a spirit of sympathy. Their faces were hostile and hard.

When Yermak rose to his feet, a breathless silence descended. There was no shuffling of boots, no whispering or muttering. The tension which had gripped them all since Yermak's return had reached its climax. Then Yermak addressed them.

'Brothers, I thank you all for answering my request and coming here to this assembly today. I thought it was necessary to call a council meeting, because we have to come to a decision about our future.

'I was in Moscow recently, and I discovered that we are out of favour with the Czar. He blames us for harassing the Tartars and says that these attacks have provoked renewed hostility with the Khanates which border our country. Fair enough, you might say. You know for yourselves what we have done. But I do not think for a moment that that is the only grievance the Czar has against us. I think he is much more incensed that we refused to give him any assistance in his campaign against Livonia. My brothers! We are free Cossacks and even the Czar cannot force us to take part in a war which is no concern of ours. We made our joint decision in assembly on that occasion and today we shall do the same.

'Only this time a far more important decision lies before us. The Czar has ordered Murashkin to raise an army against us. Are we to stay here and fight it out or shall we pack up and leave so that he finds the bird has flown? I must make one thing clear, brothers. Murashkin is definitely on his way. Do not deceive yourselves. This is not a mere rumour. He has armed to the teeth and he has orders to annihilate the Don and the Volga Cossacks and to bring their Captains to Moscow, dead or alive.'

Yermak paused for breath. He felt that he was not choosing his words well today; he could sense the opposition which was building up against him. Nor was he mistaken. An elderly Captain with a long white beard took advantage of the pause to reply from the far end of the table.

'I do not doubt that you have spoken the truth as far as it goes, Yermak, but all the same, there is something you have left out. Only you and Ivan Koltso are wanted dead or alive! Had you forgotten that?'

'No, I had not forgotten, Sergei. But answer me frankly. Suppose Murashkin captures you instead of me? Do you think he is going to stop and ask questions? After all, it isn't the first time that the Czar has mounted a campaign against us. But this time he wants to destroy us completely.'

'But the Czar recognized our Cossack settlements here on the Don and on the Volga several years ago! He wants us to consolidate our holdings to protect the Russian frontiers against the Tartars. We were to be a community within his realm on which he could rely as on his own troops.'

'I am not disputing that, Sergei, although if it's a question of having a scrap with the Tartars, we would do that of our own accord, for there's always some booty over for us. All the same, we have held ourselves free to carry on as we thought fit; that is, we went on living according to our own laws. You from the Don sailed with your ships down to the Sea of Azov and you took into prize anything worth the taking. You plucked the Crimean Tartars and all the merchants in the towns by the Don who had anything to loot. We who live by the Volga have done the same and our watchword has been "Moscow and the Czar are far away". We guard the frontiers after our own fashion. But you must never forget, Sergei, that our Cossack communities sprang up originally as a bid for freedom. The Czar's recognition is something we value, but our freedom is worth far more to us. Murashkin is coming to bring us to heel.'

'And I answer "Let him come!" We are ready to take him on. A man from the north does not know the countryside as we do. We have grown up here. Let him come, that's all.'

Two of the Captains near him murmured their agreement. 'Well spoken. Sergei is quite right.'

Mitya, who, as the youngest member, was sitting on the back row, could see the emotion in Yermak's face as he caught a glimpse of it between two tall caps. He knew how preoccupied Yermak had been with the fate of his people during the last few weeks and for several nights he had not even slept, but wandered round the village all through the night. And now these four in front were trying to belittle the danger, to make Yermak appear as a pessimist.

Yermak clenched his fists and leaning hard on the table-top he stood up stiffly. He'll start shouting now, thought Mitya, expecting to feel the walls trembling. But he was wrong. When Yermak turned to the three Captains at Sergei's side, his voice was mild, indeed, almost gentle.

'You think Sergei is right, do you? As you please, but I must contradict you. He is wrong.'

'What proof have you, Yermak?' challenged the old man.

Mitya saw the frown as the heavy eyebrows made a firm line above the nose, and how the veins in the forehead stood out.

'Do you think I risked my neck to go to Moscow just now because my feet were itching? Do you think I spent sixteen days there, with danger breathing down my neck every hour of the day, out of sheer bravado? Do you think I returned and called an assembly simply to scare you all? And finally, do you think that the Czar is raising an army just to capture two miserable sinners, Ivan Koltso and your humble servant? The whole fate of the Cossacks on the Don and the Volga is at stake, of you and your brothers as well as me and mine. I could swear an oath that I am speaking the truth, but I shall not do so. You will have proof of my words soon enough when Murashkin is here. But as far as I and my own men are concerned, we shall not let it come to that!'

This time a murmur of applause from the rank and file interrupted Yermak's speech. He looked at hem sternly, but relief was visible in his face.

'May we know what you have in mind, Yermak, even if we cannot share your views and your plans?' asked old Sergei.

'Of course, that is why I have called you together. Or rather to be more accurate, my intention was that we should put our heads together and decide what was to be done. I have been thinking and thinking for weeks and I could not find the right solution. But yesterday I discovered the answer. It is the only way out and I shall follow it through!'

The Cossacks stared unable to guess what would follow.

'We must leave the Volga. We have a long path before us. It will lead us first south-east and then due north to the foot of a high range of mountains and it will end in the town of Oryol in the House of the Stroganovs. Yesterday a messenger arrived here by boat with a commission for me. The Stroganov cousins offer the Cossacks and their leaders honourable service in the province of Great Perm which belongs to them. We are to protect the land against the heathen Tartars, to man the fortresses and keep the peace, for the territory is so sparsely populated that every man is needed for work and they cannot spare them for military duties. In any case they have had no training. The House of Stroganov will give us all we need in the way of food, drink and clothing, and we can keep a share of our booty in addition. So I propose that we accept, brothers. I have thought it over very carefully all night and I am glad that I do not need to step before you empty-handed. Now decide.'

The atmosphere in the council chamber was tense and only gradually did it slacken. The men turned to their neighbours and talked softly in little groups. Then from the corner in which the visiting Captains were seated came a loud question.

'We have heard of the Stroganovs of course, and we know that they are a very rich and powerful merchant house. But we know, too, that a great part of their power derives from the grace of the Czar. Are they not too near to him for your safety, Yermak?'

'Your misgivings are very pertinent. I had them, too, of course.

You are quite right when you say that part of the Stroganov might derives from the Czar, but only a small proportion. The greater part of it is firmly established on their own wealth. It is a long way from Perm to Moscow and I think that every mile is twice as long when the Stroganovs do the measuring.'

'You may be right in all you say, Yermak,' said one of the Captains near Sergei. 'But that doesn't alter facts. As far as I am concerned, the Stroganov concession is too far away for me. Here we know what is ours, here we belong. Is the power and wealth of these gentlemen really so great that they can keep their promises?'

'Brothers,' said Yermak, 'let us set aside one of our rules, the one that forbids a stranger to address the assembly. The situation in which we find ourselves justifies it. Let the messenger from the House of Stroganov speak to you himself.'

'That is a good idea,' shouted Ivan Koltso, who had been sitting opposite Sergei. 'Let's take a vote. I am in favour.'

The Cossacks hesitated. But once Nikita Pan and Matvei Meshcherak, two of Yermak's Captains like Koltso, had decided in favour, more voices were added and they called out their names in agreement. The result was a majority in favour of hearing the envoy and Mitya was sent to fetch him.

Feodor Masupov entered. His back was straight and his steps were firm. The Cossacks on the front bench moved up to make room for him, but he remained standing. Mitya saw how Yermak's opponents shook their heads disapprovingly. Yermak gave them no time to start muttering, but immediately explained to Masupov why he had been called there. The sturdy Masupov threw back his head, folded his hands in front of his chest with dignity and began.

'So you doubt the power of the House of Stroganov, do you? I hope that at least you have no doubt about its honourable intentions . . .'

'No speeches now,' interrupted Yermak. 'In this gathering of ours, anyone is free to have whatever doubts he like and to express his opinion as he pleases. You are here to tell us something about the House of Stroganov, nothing more.'

It was plain from the visitor's face that these words displeased him greatly. But he remembered his mission and swallowed his anger. He thought for a few moments and by the time he began again an expectant silence had gripped the whole assembly.

'Captains and Cossacks, you use salt in your food here in the south of Russia, but you never ask where it comes from. All along the Don and the Volga, wherever men live, there is salt on the table. In Moscow the women cook with salt and so they do in Ryazin, in Tver and in Kazan. Everywhere people need salt and no one asks how it gets here. It is cheap and everyone can afford it. But many years ago things were different. Then it had to be brought to Novgorod by the German Hansa ships and there it was exchanged for the goods on sale in the market, for furs and tar, for honey and wax. And for every pound of salt we had to pay dear, for barter is business and whoever does business wants to make a profit.

'And where does the salt come from today? Today there is only one source in the whole of Russia. The House of Stroganov not only markets the salt but it extracts and refines it. Try to imagine this land in the north. It is so vast it is hardly credible. It is inexhaustibly rich in mineral deposits and in fur-bearing animals which live in the forests. The natives are Voguls and Ostyaks, small slant-eyed men who live by hunting. Imagine the broad rivers, the ships sailing along them, the barges and the ferries, and at every ferry there are relays of horses waiting to carry goods far into the country. Imagine the towns and villages with churches, monasteries and fortresses and all that has been built up by the industry and the sagacity of one single family, the Stroganovs.

'But although this land is richly blessed, it is short of one thing. It is short of men who will guard it for Russia, for side by side with wealth dwells envy, and many covet the land of Perm. That is why the Stroganov cousins have sent me with their proposal and Yermak Timofeyev has told you what it is. Whoever comes to us will earn not only the thanks of the Stroganovs. He can be certain also of the Czar's grace, for it is his Majesty who has empowered the Stroganovs to raise an armed force of their own to guard their land. And the grace of the Czar will probably be more than welcome to many of those here today, I dare say.'

Once more there was silence. Masupov's statement and the confidence with which he made it had its effect. Yermak looked at him. 'You have told us what we want to know. Go back to my house now and I shall inform you what we decide.'

When Feodor Masupov had left, Yermak spoke again.

'Brothers, now you know as much as I do. Let us close this session by voting on my proposal. If anyone is willing to come with me to the north, let him call his name aloud.'

Ivan Koltso was the first. He had utter confidence in his old friend Yermak. Then followed his fellow Captains, Nikita Pan, Matvei Meshcherak and Yakob Michailov. This meant that all Yermak's Captains stood by him. Only in Sergei's corner was there silence.

'Go with your men, Yermak,' said Sergei thoughtfully after a pause. 'For a man like you, perhaps it may be the right decision. You will not count me personally among your followers, but even if I do not agree with your decision, I promise to report faithfully to my own men all that has been said. Perhaps some of them will want to go with you and if so, I will not hold them back.'

His three fellow Captains promised the same. It was agreed that the departure should be postponed for four days and four nights. That gave everyone who wanted to go time to report to Yermak's headquarters.

With that resolution the assembly came to an end. The visitors said good-bye to Yermak as if there had been no difference of opinion, and leapt into the saddle. For a time the sounds of galloping hoofs could be heard and then the night swallowed them completely. Then Yermak went back into his house. 'The decision has been taken,' he murmured to himself. 'I wonder what will happen.'

Mitya was sitting on the steps waiting for him.

'Why aren't you in your bed yet?'

'I thought you might want to talk to Masupov alone.'

'Why should I? There is no secret about our decision. We'll be going north again, my lad, but not home.'

'No, not home. I expect it will be much farther than the distance from the village?'

'Yes, it will. Much farther,' he repeated slowly. 'Do you know how far to the north our country stretches?'

'No, Yermak.'

'Nor do I. I don't think anyone knows, not even the Czar. But something inside me tells me that even when we get to the Stroganovs our journey will not be finished.'

'But did not Feodor Masupov mention a range of great mountains in the east that can only be climbed with difficulty?'

'Many things are difficult, but it is only when you have conquered them that you can call yourself a man. Do you know, I have an idea that it will be many a long day before you return to the village.' And as he opened the door, he turned his head once more. 'Irina will have to wait a long time for you.'

The next day Feodor Masupov set out to announce that the Cossacks were coming to Great Perm.

The village was busy preparing for the great trek. Masupov had presented Yermak with a map and advised him which route to follow. The men were given their orders to demolish the settlements and shown how to load their horses. Weapons were distributed and rations shared out. There would not be much to eat, but they consoled themselves with the thought that there would be pickings on the way.

During these last few days the Cossacks who wanted to join them arrived from neighbouring colonies. The camp was full. When it grew dark and no one else was expected. Yermak counted heads. There were five hundred and forty rank and file, and their five Captains as well. Was that too many or too few? Not even Yermak knew.

At nightfall, they gathered round the camp-fires. The tents had been struck and they were to sleep under the stars. The remaining sheep were slaughtered and roasted over the open fires for the final meal by the Volga. The men took it in turns to hold the spit and their comrades watched them, lost in thought. They were on their way to a new country, that they knew, and many of them felt it in their bones that their whole way of life would be changing, too.

Even the braggarts were silent tonight. It was only when supper was over and the last of the beer was poured out that talk began to flow back and forth. Then someone began to sing, a soft melancholy tune that drifted over the whole encampment. The conversation died away in an instant. Everyone listened for a while, until another voice took up the tune. One after the other they joined in, and the simple Cossack song, melodious and soulful, soared into the night. Now they were all singing together, yet each man sang for himself alone, a farewell to the south, to the home they were leaving, perhaps for ever . . .

Towards morning, a thin persistent drizzle started and woke the camp earlier than they had intended. So Yermak ordered the men to load the boats and rafts and to ferry them over to the opposite bank. One group of Cossacks stripped off their clothes and rounded up the horses. With much shouting and cracking of whips they herded them into the water. When they reached the far side, the shaggy beasts were quickly seized and saddled, and there they stood waiting, dripping and miserable.

Soon the whole expedition was ready to start. They rode side by side in close formation into the grey morning rain. They thought that their goal was the Province of Perm, but they had, in fact, set out to conquer an empire.

8 WATERWHEELS

They rode and rode and rode.

First they made for the south-east. Then they swung round and headed due north. Yermak kept them as far as he could from any village. If it were humanly possible, he wanted to leave the south without drawing attention to the fact, for he could not afford to weaken his forces in any way and time was precious, too. The Nogai Khan was burning for revenge, so Yermak avoided every contact with the Tartar settlements in order to prevent armed skirmishes. To conserve his own strength, he gave strict commands that the tents of the Tartar nomads must not be molested and Persian and Turkish caravans making for Russia were spared, too for the same reason.

Soon the steppeland engulfed the emigrants.

On and on they went, always northwards now. On and on trotted the little horses until they were utterly weary, and on and on rode the Cossacks in their own fashion with legs drawn high, until they, too, were exhausted and cramped. A brief respite at night, a meagre fire on which to cook a little broth and then on, on, on.

The Cossacks did not endure it all without protest. They had imagined they would see some action at least to break the dead monotony. But Yermak consulted no one. 'Forward!' he ordered and, grumbling still, they climbed into the saddle once more. They rode through man-high clumps of thistles, over baked earth cracked with drought, through parched brown heather and sparse, rustling grass. The sun burnt down from the sky and sucked the moisture from their bodies. A storm raged from the east for several days, covering men and beasts with fine sand, which stuck to their eyelids. It gritted between their teeth, and infiltrated beneath their shirts. Oatmeal, biscuit and bread, everything was mixed with sand. They thought they would choke as the dark clouds of sand swept over them.

And still they went on, ever northwards. Often they were so short of sleep that they almost fell from the saddle. They had to leave it to the horses to find a few blades of dry grass for themselves, for the men were too tired to look for fodder. They did not care when the heavens opened and the rain poured down in torrents. Sodden and mud-stained, they climbed back into the saddle. To the north! To the north!

Once they had crossed the steppes, Yermak allowed them a few days' rest. In order to replenish their rations, they hunted wild boar. They built rafts and went fishing in the lakes and according to ancient custom, they exercised their so-called 'rights' over the herds grazing in the neighbourhood. Their joy in living returned and then Yermak gave his orders once more. 'Onward!'

They rode through forests so dense that no sun found its way through the leaves. They crossed broad green grasslands. Their way led through marshes where they had to file one behind the other with the utmost caution. And all the time, Yermak was determined that they should remain as inconspicuous as possible. He wanted to reach the province of Perm without the Russian army's knowledge.

One day, when they had been on the way for almost three months, they saw in the distance a village where an unusual number of high wooden waterwheels were turning slowly, looming above the deep wells they served. One after the other they came into view, and as the Cossacks drew nearer they could see that the water drawn up from the depths was being channelled into huge pans from which rose great clouds of steam. When they looked more closely they saw that fires glowed beneath the pans. Once the water was heated sufficiently, it evaporated slowly and left behind a thick deposit. These were the Stroganov salt refineries.

Yermak called a halt. His voice rang out clearly, so that all could hear. 'Brothers, the worst is behind us. We are standing on the soil of Great Perm. It will not be long before we reach our goal, the town of Oryol, where lies the House of Stroganov. You have had to restrain yourselves on this march, I know, but now discipline will be even tighter. I forbid you absolutely to enter any Russian house with intent to loot and I shall punish ruthlessly anyone who disobeys my order. Our arrival must not be heralded by terror and alarm.'

The men looked daggers when they heard these words. For weeks they had suffered want. Now they saw sturdily built Russian colonies, well-tilled fields and prosperous people decently clothed, and yet they were expected to tighten their belts to the last hole!

They grumbled bitterly to the Captains of their hundreds. 'Why must Yermak be our leader? Why can't we have someone more human? He's like a slave-driver and we are tired of all these petty restrictions he imposes.'

'Someone must take command,' was the answer. 'And don't forget that the Stroganovs' envoy came to him personally. In any case, you know very well that we have no one who could lead such an enterprise better than Yermak. Do you think we like it, any more than you do?'

So the Captains would complain, all except Ivan Koltso. He supported Yermak in everything, never swerving in his loyalty.

One more person stood by Yermak blindly. That was Mitya. He had changed a great deal on this journey. The terrible exertion had sponged the youth from his face. His cheeks were sunken, his eyes lay deep in their hollows. His hair had grown long and shaggy and his chin and upper lip were shadowed as a thin dark beard sprouted over his skin.

And something else had happened since they left the village. No one called him 'Baby' any more. Ever since—and Mitya closed his eyes and his heart began to pound. He grew hot all over as he remembered the first time they had called him 'Brother', that day when they had stopped to hunt fresh meat on their way to the north.

The beaters had raised some wild boar and were driving them towards a handful of men who were waiting ready with swords and hatchets. But by accident, they had startled an old bear as well. It must have made the acquaintance of mankind already, for it limped heavily on its right forepaw. Ilya seemed to dog Boris and Mitya, and try as they might the two young men could not shake him off. As soon as they became aware of the bear, Ilya turned to Mitya.

'Well, Baby?' he sniggered. 'What about skinning old Bruin, eh?'

Mitya stood there irresolute.

'I don't know—I think it would be wiser to clear off. It's very risky to provoke an animal like that.'

'You're frightened, Baby. That's what it is.'

'Nothing of the sort. My father is a trapper, and a good one into the bargain, but even he would not attack a bear like that. I know. They are much too dangerous when they're wounded.'

'That's a feeble excuse. You're a coward and I shall tell them all about it when we get back. You'll be the laughing-stock of the camp,' and Ilya sneered maliciously.

Boris tried to intervene. 'Leave Mitya alone. You've never killed a bear yourself, Ilya.'

But Mitya had been stung to the quick. To have Ilya tell the brothers afterwards . . . No, never. He'd show him if he was a coward or not!

They were standing in a favourable position. The bear had not yet caught their scent, but someone had disturbed its peace and it was looking for the culprit. It sat up on its hind legs, spitting angrily and twisting its small head this way and that.

'Leave it alone,' begged Boris, trying to hold Mitya back. 'I'll speak up for you and tell them the truth.'

But Mitya was deaf. 'I'm going!'

He peered at the brown shaggy mass from the side without making any sound. Boris and Ilya were behind him. The bear had still not realized its danger. Boris guessed how Mitya would attack it. He would glide as near to it as he could and then give one spring to bring down the axe on its skull.

Nearer and nearer they slunk. The bear was still spitting, but it stood up as if ready to limp off again. Its forepaw seemed to be painful, though, and Mitya stood stock still, rooted to the ground. The bear settled down on its haunches once more. That was what Mitya was waiting for.

With one bound he leapt into the little clearing and swung his axe. At that moment Ilya, who was just behind Boris, gave a great cry, 'Ooooha!'

The bear twisted round, saw Mitya, and lifted its massive paw. Mitya could not pull up in time and ran straight at the brute. There was no going back. With all his strength he struck out and brought down the axe between the narrow eyes brooding with hatred. He felt a terrible blow on his back. Then the huge beast fell on top of him and buried him.

For a moment Mitya thought that he would faint, but he struggled all the same, kicking hard against the tremendous carcass. He managed to free his head and take a deep breath. Then gathering all his strength together he told himself sternly, 'You must do it, you must, or you're finished!' He groped for his dagger, and succeeded in pulling it from his belt. His throat was tight with fear as he plunged the knife into the brown fur.

He heard someone call his name, but the voice seemed to be coming from far away.

'Mitya! Are you all right? Mitya, answer!' He could feel nothing but the searing pain down his back and the hideous pressure on his chest.

Two hands grasped his head, then his neck, and finally they gripped him under the armpits. They tugged at him and he screamed aloud, for the pain in his back was more than he could bear. He fell back on to the moss and saw Boris and Ilya dragging the bear aside.

Despite the agony in his back Mitya made an effort to sit up. He saw the crushed head of the bear and the knife sticking out of its throat; then he collapsed again. At last, at last, his legs were free.

Mitya tried to stand. His tunic was nothing but a tattered, blood-stained rag. Boris put an arm under his shoulder. 'Come along, Mitya. You'll be all right.' As if by common consent they ignored Ilya.

Walking took every ounce of Mitya's strength. He could not even speak. He was on the verge of collapse again when they met a few other Cossacks not far from the camp, and between them they carried Mitya back. The news spread like wildfire. 'Mitya has killed a bear with an axe.'

As soon as Yermak heard it he came to meet them. 'Put him down,' he ordered brusquely and then examined Mitya's back. 'We need a bottle of spirits.'

Ivan Koltso, who was standing near Yermak, slipped a hand in his trouser pocket. 'Here you are. I always carry this medicine with me. It breaks my heart to see a drop of it wasted, but the lad needs it more than I.'

Yermak unstoppered the little leather flask and poured the crude rye liquor on Mitya's wound to cleanse it. Mitya gave a shriek and then he knew no more.

When he recovered consciousness, he was bandaged with an old shirt which Yermak had torn into strips.

'You were fortunate, Mitya,' said Yermak, who was sitting by him in the tent. 'It's only a flesh wound. Your guardian angel must have been with you at that moment. Boris said that luckily for you the bear struck you with its damaged paw. It would have been much more serious otherwise.'

'Did he say anything else?' whispered Mitya, speaking with difficulty.

'No. Sleep now as much as you can. We don't want to lose any time on your account.'

When Yermak went away Boris slipped into the tent. He had been waiting for this moment.

'Shall we tell Yermak?' he asked.

Mitya shook his head.

'You're a splendid fellow, Mitya. But I'll make jolly certain that the others know what happened. Ilya's a vile dog! We shall have to wait and behave ourselves just now, but we'll get our own back.'

Mitya's mouth twisted into a thin smile.

'Good old Boris.'

They did not need to delay on Mitya's account. True, that first day on horseback was one he would never forget, but it was a little better on the following day, and after that the agony abated gradually.

One evening he was sitting by the camp fire. It was late and most of the men had already drawn their cloaks round them and settled down for the night. Yermak, who was next to him, turned to him and spoke.

'Well, Mitya, you've been through a tremendous ordeal and you've come out of it pretty well, too—in every respect.'

Mitya looked at Yermak searchingly. Then staring hard into the dying firelight he answered, 'The account isn't closed yet.'

'I realize that. Take your own time.'

9 THIRTY THOUSAND ROUBLES

Maxim Stroganov was standing by the window. He was the head of the family in the town of Oryol and his house, which was large and spacious, had been built by his father Yakob on the bank of the Kama. The courtyard before it reached down to the river, which was alive with traffic. Four big barges were tied up at the wharfs and labourers were dragging heavy sacks along and then stacking them on board.

Nothing escaped Maxim's eye. He knew every man who had anything to do with the vessels or belonged to their crews.

'That fellow's an awkward peasant,' he muttered half to himself and his eyes were fixed on one of the workmen who was carrying a sack of salt into the boat. 'He's always terrified of the water because he can't swim.' Maxim shook his head. 'I shan't be surprised if he drops the sack overboard in the end. He's as clumsy as a bear, but as strong as one, too. Otherwise I shouldn't have him working for me. Oh good. He's managed it at last.'

Maxim Stroganov turned back to the room. On a broad couch thickly upholstered with furs and cushions sat his cousin Nikita. He was on a visit, but it was a visit with a purpose.

'So you don't think he'll come?' Maxim asked his cousin.

'Would he not have been here by now?' countered Nikita.

'But even if he'd made all possible haste, he could hardly have arrived so quickly.'

'Oh, come! Masupov has been back a whole month already and he said that the Cossacks would set out four days after he left.'

'But heavens, Nikita, surely there's a difference between Masupov travelling openly and alone, and a whole army which is trying to conceal its movements. Who knows what incidents may have befallen them on the way?'

'Incidents!' croaked Nikita. 'We know what Cossack "incidents" are like!' And his reserved face seemed even more withdrawn than usual. I didn't like this business from the beginning.'

Involuntarily Maxim glanced across at his cousin. 'Are you starting that all over again?' His face with its flaming red beard and lively eyes darkened over. 'Still harping away at the same old tune! Yes, you warned us, you mentioned all the possible drawbacks, you begged us to tread with caution. But as for a better suggestion, you hadn't one!'

Nikita Stroganov, head of the family business in Kankor, listened calmly to his cousin's outburst. He helped himself to one of the biscuits which lay in a silver dish on the big table in front of him, and sipped his wine from the silver goblet which a servant had brought for him at Maxim's command.

'We both know how difficult it is to get assistance, Maxim. That was why I gave in finally and agreed that you should send Masupov to the Cossacks. But you must admit that their leader's behaviour so far merely confirms my original misgivings. I warned you that they would take our presents, promise to come and then forget it all as soon as Masupov had turned his back. Didn't I say so?'

Maxim pressed his lips together. He would have liked to contradict Nikita, but he could not think of any decisive argument.

'You have not convinced me, Nikita,' he temporized. 'Masupov's report on this Chieftain of theirs doesn't fit in with the picture you paint. And Masupov has met him personally, don't forget. Yermak Timofeyev can read and write. He grasped the implications immediately, both for him and for his men. Don't forget the gallows are waiting for him and I doubt if the majority of his rabble can expect a better fate either.

'But aren't you forgetting why he was condemned to death?'

'I know, Nikita. I know he has committed many crimes, but . . .'

'And who will guarantee that he will not treat us as he has treated so many others? That is, assuming he does come eventually and behaves himself at first. Straw should not play with fire, my dear Maxim.' Nikita's face gloated openly.

'Yes, yes. That's an old and a sensible proverb, I know, but what else are we to do? We have no body of men capable of defending this province. Do you think that just because there has been a few months' respite, the Tartars will never come back? There are always isolated bands of them popping up around Oryol. They haven't done any damage, but why are they here at all? They have come to spy out the situation. And one these days they'll be there at the door, and Heaven have mercy on us and our settlers then. I don't know how you can ignore the danger, Nikita.' Maxim had spoken dryly and factually as was his wont and his words were a challenge to his cousin.

'Of course I know the danger, my dear fellow. In fact, I came especially so that we could discuss what we should do now . . .'

A loud knocking at the door interrupted them.

'Yes?' called Maxim, turning swiftly, and both cousins waited tensely.

Feodor Masupov entered. 'Why are you disturbing us?' asked Maxim.

'I have bad news for you, sir,' said Masupov, bowing. 'Our two new villages in the foothills have been attacked by a horde of Tartars. Only one man has survived, the farms have been burnt down, and the women have fled with the children into the town here. They are completely worn out. What shall we do?'

'Give them shelter and look after them. We will decide what action to take presently.'

'Yes, sir.'

The door closed behind Masupov.

Maxim Stroganov sat down heavily on a bench. 'There you are! We must have protection, cost what it may.' And he pounded the table-top with both his fists.

'What about sending a messenger to Moscow at once with orders to explain our desperate situation to the Czar?'

'That is stupid. Have you forgotten that the Czar has refused us twice already? We can't keep running round in circles, never making progress. There is only one way. Yermak Timofeyev must come, even if I have to send another ship to fetch him.'

In the fortress towers which surrounded the town the sentries were especially vigilant that night. The Tartars had attacked villages in Great Perm and people were shocked. They knew what that meant.

Through the church windows gleamed a dim light. The priest was holding a mass for the souls of the slain and praying for the safety of the fugitives. Maxim Stroganov was among the congregation.

Darkness came late in these summer nights and the watchman could keep guard for many hours. From the southern tower one could see as far as a dense forest, and the sentinel kept his eyes glued to it. If anything was going to happen, it would certainly be from that direction.

Suddenly he started in horror. Armed riders were pouring forth from the woods.

'Sound the tocsin!' he shouted at the top of his voice. 'Alarm! Alarm! The Tartars are coming!' He stormed down the steps.

'Alarm!' rang the word through the silent town. 'The Tartars are coming!'

Men came clattering out of their houses, fumbling with swords and daggers in their excitement, rushing to the southern tower where the tocsin was ringing. Women with babies in their arms and the bigger children holding on to their skirts hurried towards the Stroganovs' house. They were seeking asylum in the stone passages where the salt was stored, as they always did when danger threatened.

Maxim Stroganov came running out of the church and made for the southern watch-tower. He dashed up the stairs to see the situation for himself.

A long procession straggled out of the forest, a train of small shaggy ponies approaching Oryol at a steady trot. Their riders sat bolt upright in the saddle and they wore dark greatcoats and tall fur caps.

Maxim Stroganov rested his arm against the wall and leaned his head on it. He gazed at the long column and he could not tear himself away. Then he turned and saw that the sentry was watching him. 'Stop that bell, you great oaf!'

And as Feodor Masupov came panting up the stairs, Maxim called out to him, 'Heaven be praised! The Cossacks are coming. Leave the gate open and have good food prepared. Yermak Timofeyev has kept his word. I shall await him in my house.' And with calm unhurried footsteps, he went down the stairs again.

An hour later Yermak Timofeyev stood before him.

'I offer you my greetings, Maxim Stroganov, and those of my Captains and all my Cossacks. We thank you for your offer and we are now at your disposal.'

Yermak did not humble himself before the man who had summoned him. Stroganov might be the master of a powerful merchant house, but Yermak was a Cossack Chieftain, a man whom thousands knew and dreaded.

Maxim Stroganov held out his hand. On his middle finger he wore a broad gold ring in which flashed an enormous blue stone.

'Welcome to Oryol. I am glad that you have arrived safely. You will be my guest as long as you remain here.'

'Your invitation is most kind and I thank you for it, but please do not be offended if I refuse. My place is with my men, but I am always at your service and will never be far away.'

Maxim Stroganov did not flutter an eyelash. Such a refusal was tantamount to an insult, but obviously one had to judge these Cossacks by different standards. In any event, Yermak Timofeyev pleased him. He had not imagined a man of such dignity and polish.

'I bow to your wishes, Yermak Timofeyev, but at least you will dine with me now, I hope. Your men will be cared for in the courtyard.'

'Thank you, Maxim Stroganov. I am honoured to be your guest.'

Maxim was amazed. Surely this was not the way the Cossacks usually spoke! Where had this man learned the language of the Court?

They sat down at table and a brisk order brought servants to them carrying dishes of roast meat and soft fresh bread which was almost white. Wine was poured into silver goblets and Maxim Stroganov begged his guest to partake.

'You have covered a tremendous distance with your men.' He continued the conversation as they ate. 'Did everything go according to your wishes?'

'I have no complaints.'

'And how have your men withstood the journey?'

'When you think of all they have endured, very well. They are hungry, of course, for we had to cut down our rations to the minimum. But a few days' rest and nourishing food and they will be their old selves again.'

'How many men have you brought?'

'Five hundred and forty men and four Captains.'

'And you are their Commander-in-chief?'

'Yes, I was elected as Chieftain last winter. I hold office for a year.'

'Why only for a year?'

'That is our law.'

'What will happen then?'

'Either I shall be re-elected or another man will take my place and I shall become a rank-and-file Cossack once more.'

'They will re-elect you; I shall see to it. Neither you nor anyone else will regret it. I am counting on your remaining in office.'

The two men exchanged frank glances.

'Thank you for your confidence in me. I have not yet proved myself worthy of it.'

'I have had to deal with strangers from my earliest childhood. I know what I am doing, Yermak Timofeyev.'

They went on with their meal in silence. Then Yermak asked:

'How long will you be able to conceal from Moscow that you have summoned my help?'

'Conceal it? From the Czar? I shall do nothing to inform him, of course, but neither shall I do anything to prevent him from finding out. But do not worry. I will guarantee your safety here. You do not know the power of the House of Stroganov. Are you tired, or would you like me to tell you our family history here and now?'

'I am not tired. Your wine has revived me and your words have given me confidence. I shall be happy to listen to whatever you have to say.'

'Good. More than a hundred years ago, during the terrible war with the Khan of Kazan, the great-grandfather of our gracious Czar, may Heaven guard him, fell into the enemy's hands. He was that unfortunate Grand Prince Vassili whom we call "the Dark", for he spent the last years of his life sightless. The Khan demanded a high ransom, much higher than the Moscow coffers could yield. They were empty, for wars cost money and Vassili had spent his whole life waging war. An appeal was made throughout the land, a call for help. The nobles and the merchants were asked, but none of them could produce the tremendous sum of thirty thousand roubles. And for every little contribution which they reluctantly squeezed out they demanded securities and pledges such as pearls and jewels, and silver and golden vessels. And still the sum was not nearly complete. Then one of my ancestors, Luka Stroganov, who traded by the banks of the Dvina, stepped in. He sold everything that could be sold. He risked his entire business and he sent the whole sum in cash to Moscow. He did not ask for securities and pledges; he gave freely without condition, and the unhappy Prince was released. Since that time our family has been linked in friendship with the rulers of Moscow. In our family house in Solvychegodsk which belongs to my Uncle Semyon, there is still preserved the charter which the Czar, may Heaven shield him, had inscribed and handed to the Stroganov family to thank them for what they did.'

Maxim Stroganov took a few sips from the silver goblet.

'I have told you this story to set your mind at rest. You can devote yourself wholeheartedly and without the slightest misgivings to the tasks which await you here.'

Before Maxim went on, he called his servants once more. They took out the empty dishes and brought in fresh ones. These contained caviare and pickled fish with subtle flavours, and more crusty white sweet-smelling bread. Once again they filled the heavy silver goblets.

'Perhaps this story does not satisfy you. Perhaps you are thinking it happened too long ago to have any weight in Moscow today. So I shall tell you more about us. We are an old trading family whose days go back to the golden age of Novgorod, that independent Free City which has cradled the most successful traders and was once the linch-pin of Russian trade. You have only to see its wonderful churches and its great counting-houses to get some idea of how prosperous and powerful Novgorod was. But the people were enterprising into the bargain. Trade with the south which delivered corn and timber, honey and tar was not enough for them. The Hanseatic merchants who came to Novgorod demanded something else for the weapons and spices they brought, something for which their appetite was insatiable. They wanted furs, more furs and yet more furs. So the fearless men of Novgorod set off on strenuous journeys and discovered that furs were obtainable from the north, but the ones from the east were even better and the supply was inexhaustible. These journeys multiplied year by year. The merchant adventurers stocked up with cheap jewellery, glass and pottery. They sailed along the rivers and came back with their furs. They did not do badly out of it either, for a single cooking-pot was worth as many sable skins as the natives could cram inside it. When trade between these unknown lands and Novgorod was becoming firmly established, one of my ancestors went out with an expedition. He had made up his mind not to return to Novgorod, but to set up a base in this unexplored territory. He built a house for himself, bartered with the natives on the banks of the Dvina and returned to his base each time as quickly as possible. Soon the word went round the Novgorod merchants. Business expanded steadily and what the father had begun, his son continued. He started a farm, and added warehouses and a village grew up round the dwelling-house. So that when storm clouds gathered over Novgorod the Stroganov family were secure.'

Maxim paused to moisten his throat. Then he rose. He went to a massive dark cupboard and fetched out a big roll of parchment.

'Are you still hungry, Yermak?' he asked, unrolling the document.

'No, thank you.'

'May I tell them to clear the table, then?'

'Yes, do.'

Again the soft summons with voice barely raised, so that Yermak felt sure the servants must be waiting just outside the door, or else they would never hear it. When one of them came in, Yermak looked at him closely. He was well dressed in a tunic of yellow silk and blue trousers and on his feet were soft shoes. Yermak was puzzled. He had never seen such leather before. Then he looked round him. The bench on which he was sitting was covered with the same skin. He stroked it interested.

Maxim Stroganov noticed his reaction.

'Don't you know what it is, Yermak?'

'No.'

'It is reindeer fur.'

'Then it must come from the far north. It is a beautiful colour and a very big size.'

'Not only that. It is wonderfully warm to wear as a tunic with the hair inside. Perhaps you will shoot a reindeer for yourself one day.'

'What do you mean? Surely you want me here in Oryol.'

'We will discuss it another time. We were just coming to the troubles in Novgorod. Let me tell you more about my family. The Grand Duke Ivan incorporated the Free City of Novgorod into his kingdom. He was the first Russian prince of Moscow to call himself Czar and he occupied the distant lands on the Dvina, too. Not that they brought him much revenue, for it's the same the world over. When the cat's away the mice will play and the Czar had more important things to do than to keep an eye on his tax collectors.

'Then Luka Stroganov, the one who had paid the ransom, offered to administer the royal possession for the Czar and he received his consent. From now on, the taxes poured in regularly to Moscow and thereby our family became even more respected at the Czar's Court. Luka's grandson was my grandfather Anika. He was seventeen when his father died and he took over part of his business. He had learnt to read and write, and he more than any of his brothers knew how to make the most of the family's far-sightedness and industry. He built his own house far away from his father's by the River Vychegda. He was not afraid of roaming through the forests nor of the loneliness. He had discovered something so important that he was prepared to face any hardship during those first few years. It was a salt lake. He was never idle for a single day. He sunk wells, and as they grew more numerous, new houses sprang up, too. Salt was much in demand in Russia, since the Czar had forbidden the German Hansa merchants to trade in Novgorod. Salt from the Crimea was very dear because of the customs duty. My grandfather's discovery solved Moscow's problem. The refineries increased by leaps and bounds, and so did the colony which Anika began to build round his own house. It became the town of Solvychegodsk.

'But salt was not the only commodity. Side by side with it was the fur trade which extended into unknown territory far to the east and the north. My grandfather discovered a great deal about it, for he went on with his exploration personally. In the salt works there were many natives who acted as interpreters, and when my father Yakob and my uncle Grigori were old enough, they were sent off exploring, too. They took household goods to sell and they came back with furs as in the old days. Their journeys did not end here in Perm, which would have been far enough in all conscience, but they crossed the Urals and penetrated east and north. And the realms they discovered seemed to know no bounds, for wherever they went they found fur-bearing animals in the forests and fish in the rivers. But the way over the high mountains into the Land of Yugor and farther still to Mangaseya always led through Perm, which at that time was still wild and uncultivated.

'Then one day my grandfather Anika set out with his son Grigori on a journey to Moscow. He asked for an audience of the Czar and laid costly gifts at his feet. He told him all he had discovered in the course of years. The Czar, who was always eager to extend his dominions and to open new trade routes for Russia, listened to it all, and when Anika asked him to bestow on him the land of Perm so that he could cultivate it and make a trade route to the east, the Czar did not need to confer very long with princes and nobles. He handed over a charter sealed with a red seal. Then Anika knew that his request had been conceded. Our gracious Czar had given the family rights exceeding those of anyone else in Russia at that time, an area of more than two million *desyatin*. They were given authority to till the soil, to build towns according to their judgement, to keep an army and to settle peasants. Furthermore, they were exempt from paying taxes for twenty years and they were to owe allegiance to no one but the Czar.

'Anika spent a whole year winning colonists for the land in Perm and then he and his sons went out there themselves. The first town he founded was Kankor, where my cousin Nikita is now head of the family. Every well brings us salt, every new farmstead wins us bread. Then iron was discovered and a foundry was set up later.

'The Czar did not stop at his original presentation. He realized that the land was in the right hands. In the year 1564 he made us a second deed of gift and the new territory covered another million and a half *desyatin*. But claiming virgin soil is a hard business. The native settlers who lived in miserable hovels by the rivers and forests had to be evicted unless they agreed to enter the service of our family. And where their huts had been, villages and towns sprang up, corn ripened in the fields and wheels turned by the side of the wells. But the natives often had their revenge, for beyond the great mountain range were their kith and kin who were much stronger than the handful of heathens we had had to shift. These pagans still threaten our safety here.

'My grandfather, who was an old man by then, made another journey to Moscow. He took more presents with him and he brought back in return another charter for a million *desyatin,* which he gave to my father and which I have inherited. They stretch as far as the Urals and the soil harbours the same wealth as in the other concessions. Our agents bring us men from the whole of Russia who wish to settle here. But the most important thing is that their security should be assured.'

'That is my business now, Maxim Stroganov, and believe me, each of my Cossacks can strike a blow for three men. Soon you will have no fears for your people. I did not realize before how vast the province is. Why, Great Perm is a whole kingdom by itself.'

'Perm? I was not thinking only of Perm. We own much more than that.'

Yermak looked up incredulously.

'You heard me aright. The land beyond the Urals belongs to us, too. We could settle it just as we did this province many years ago.' Maxim Stroganov broke off and gazed thoughtfully at the window as if he had to think carefully before going on.

Yermak watched him. Then he asked slowly, 'And why don't you?'

Maxim Stroganov returned the gaze.

'Because there is an enormous obstacle in the way. It is blocked by the Siberian Prince, Kuchum Khan, with his armies. The way to our territories in Yugor and Mangaseya passes through his dominions.'

Yermak held Maxim Stroganov's gaze without flinching.

'I see,' he said simply and an understanding smile twitched round his mouth.

10 THE PLAN TAKES SHAPE

The next few days brought much that was new, for the people of Oryol as well as for the Cossacks. The inhabitants had never seen so many armed men before, but the Cossacks were amazed, too, not only at the solidity of the town's buildings, but especially at the cannons which guarded its walls.

The men were quartered in stone barracks which had been built for an army long ago, although they had never been fully used. The few resident soldiers withdrew and left the place to the Cossacks. This militia of the Stroganovs was remarkable in its own way. It consisted of former prisoners of war bought in Moscow, the living booty from the Czar's campaigns against Livonia. These men had come from far away and spoke their own language, so that the Cossacks could hardly communicate with them at all and they had to use their hands to explain things.

One morning Mitya and Boris were washing themselves at the well, letting the water run down over their arms, for they were stripped to the waist. All at once, a hand was placed on Mitya's shoulder and someone turned him round.

'That's a frightful wound you have on your back,' said the man, who had approached them soundlessly. 'Why, it's still open.'

Mitya felt embarrassed. Would the man believe his story? His arms had grown so thin during the journey to Oryol, he did not look strong enough to have fought with a bear.

'It happened while we were on our way here . . . We were hunting wild boar and accidentally disturbed a bear, too . . . There's nothing to be done about it now . . . I killed the bear,' he added awkwardly.

The stranger nodded. 'A man who tackles a bear need not be ashamed and blush. What is your name?'

'Mitya Nikolayev.'

'Come along with me, Mitya. I want to examine this back of yours properly.'

The man drew him along by the arm. As they walked towards his house, he asked, 'Is it painful?'

'Only when I bend. Otherwise it's rather uncomfortable, but that's all.'

'How was it treated?'

'Yermak poured rye spirits over it.'

'I see. A delightful sensation, I'm sure.'

Mitya grinned. 'Wonderful!'

They reached a house that was larger and finer than the others in the street.

'I am a physician, my lad, and my name is Johannes Mohr. I expect that sounds funny to you, doesn't it?'

'Mm.'

'I am not a Russian, you see, although I let people call me Ivan, which is the same name as my own. My father was something of an adventurer, who wanted to see more of the world than the little town where he was born, far, far away in a country they call Germany. It was Anika Stroganov, the grandfather of our present master, who brought him out to the town of Solvychegodsk. And now I am a doctor as my father was, and in the service of the Stroganovs, too. I have always wanted to go back to my father's homeland, but every time I planned to leave something stopped me, and now I am too old to think of it.' He nodded at Mitya and put a hand on his fair hair. 'Now let me have a look at that wound.'

Something stirred inside Mitya. He did not feel the probing hands on his back; he could feel only the touch over his hair. Father, he thought, Father . . .

If only I could be with you now. If only you saw me as I am. If you knew about the bear—and that I've ridden right across Russia. And I've sailed on a raft, too. Oh, Father, if only you knew how hard it has been sometimes, and how I would give anything now to be able to spend just one night lying near you by the stove in our old hut. But now we are here to guard the people in Perm and it may be my turn one day . . . It was only then that Mitya came back to reality as the doctor was smearing ointment into his back and tying a bandage round the upper part of his body.

'There we are, my boy. Come back and see me in a few days' time. Don't forget now!'

'Thank you, sir. I shall come back.'

After a few days' rest and food as good as Maxim Stroganov had promised, the Cossacks were given their duties. They rode out in small patrols far away from Oryol, to keep an eye on the tiny settlements throughout the land.

This was a different country from the flat south, where they had come from, where one could survey the land for miles around. There were many rivers and swamps, but the ground was thick with standing timber, and in the clearings were the peasants' fields and log cabins which looked as if they had been wrested from the forests themselves.

The farther they rode eastwards, the more often they came across the wretched huts of the aborigines. If they showed themselves at all, these little men with their low foreheads stared at the newcomers with unveiled hostility, but they usually concealed themselves if they could. When the Cossacks rode up to a hut and peeped inside they found everything abandoned as if no one had lived there for years, yet there was still a glow to be seen among the ashes in the hearth.

'It doesn't look as if the Stroganovs' fur suppliers want to have anything to do with us,' laughed Boris to Mitya. 'And I was longing to meet them, too.'

'Oh, leave them alone. I'm not surprised that they don't want to talk to us. I suppose we are their enemies just as much as the Stroganovs.'

'Why, what do you mean?'

'Well, the Stroganovs invaded the country and took away their land. They turned them out of their homes . . .'

'But I thought that was why the Czar gave them the country.'

'Of course, but the Votyaks and the Cheremis, as the Oryol people call them, don't give a damn for the Czar. The land was theirs and they lived here in peace. So now they hate the Stroganovs and everything and everybody associated with them. Where you see fields and villages now, there were formerly forests. They were burned down ruthlessly, with everything as it stood and the people had to flee for their lives. Do you blame them for their resentment?'

'You worry too much, Mitya. I do what I'm ordered and that's that. And if one of these Votyaks doesn't behave himself when I'm about, he'll get a taste of my sabre.'

'If he comes close enough! I believe they are excellent archers.'

'Who told you?'

'The doctor who is tending my back.'

Mitya liked going to see Doctor Mohr. He often wished that he was not away from Oryol so often on patrol, and he was glad that at least he did not belong to the corps who had been sent to Kankor under Ivan Koltso to take up duty there.

The doctor had become very friendly towards Mitya. There was much to see in his surgery and he had many tales to tell the lad. One day he showed Mitya a whole handful of pearls. They were smooth, gleaming, dazzling white pearls.

'My father found them one day when he was watching the fishermen at work. They had brought the shells up in a heap together with the fish and when the shells were opened, many of them contained pearls. From that day on, shell fishing became more important than fish for food, for there was a good market in pearls.'

What interested Mitya most were the different herbs which the natives brought to the doctor. Johannes Mohr infused healing mixtures from some of them and he pounded others with pestle and mortar to mix them into salves and powders. When Mitya was with him the time seemed to fly and Mitya always had the illusion that his father was not far away.

Mitya saw little of Yermak, who was away from Oryol most of the time, although no one knew where he went. One day he patrolled with his Cossacks; another day he would ride over to Kankor with Maxim Stroganov. Once he was away for several days when his employer took him to Solvychegodsk to see Semyon Stroganov.

The great family house which belonged to Semyon was like a castle. Yermak was most impressed when he saw it. The towns on the Sea of Azov, which he knew, had great merchant houses within their walls and the ones in Moscow were equally striking. But this was a prince's palace, with its tall fortified turrets, with warehouses and servants' quarters below and over them the dwelling-apartments.

'Be prepared for a cool reception,' Maxim warned Yermak in advance. 'My Uncle Semyon is the only surviving son of my grandfather Anika. He was the youngest of the family and he has not forgotten that neither his brother Grigori nor my father shared any of the land of Perm with him. But we must see how things go. If we are to carry out our plans, we shall need his help.'

Semyon Stroganov kept his visitors waiting before he found the time to bid them welcome. He was an old man and he entered the room leaning on a stick. His face was furrowed, his grey beard was thin and very long.

'Well, well! A visitor from Perm!' he said and extended a cool hand to his nephew. He did not embrace him heartily as was the custom. Then Semyon turned to Yermak and his left eyelid drooped slightly.

'So this is what our gallant Commander-in-chief looks like, is it—the one with the gallows waiting for him? Why didn't you lead an honest life? Don't you know the commands of our church? Is there not Christian work enough for us all when we are so beset by heathen?'

'I am a Christian, sir, and so are my Cossacks. We make it a condition of acceptance into our brotherhood. But I believe that every man has his own destiny and our lives are lived as Fate decrees. Too much incense—you know the proverb, I am sure—too much incense blackens even the holy saints!'

Maxim Stroganov was horror-stricken. If anything was likely to antagonize Semyon, it was flippancy about religion.

The old man stood there, thunderstruck.

'How dare you!' he breathed. 'Don't you know where you are, sir? Never before has anyone dreamed of thinking such blasphemy in this house, let alone uttering it! My grandfather became a monk before he died and my father, too. Why, he could recite the mass like a priest. In his library were two hundred books, all of which contained the word of God. The Metropolitan of Moscow was his friend. I myself have had icons painted for our churches by the finest painters in the land . . .'

'I know that, sir. I myself have seen icons in Moscow which were commissioned by you. Please forgive me. I did not think that the thoughtless repetition of an old saying would offend you.'

'You mentioned the heathen just now, Uncle, and that was what we came to see you about,' said Maxim, quickly trying to heal the breach. 'Indeed, it is the real purpose of our visit.'

'Which heathen do you mean?'

'The Tartars and Kuchum Khan, of course,' declared Maxim Stroganov.

'I see. But why should I be concerned if they are worrying you? Perm has nothing to do with me.'

'Your old grudge, Uncle Semyon, I know. But since the Cossacks arrived we have not been disturbed. No, that is not the point.'

'Isn't it? Why are you here, then?'

'We have come about Yugor and Mangaseya which belong to the whole family, you included, Uncle Semyon. The Czar, may Heaven protect him always, gave the land to the family jointly, six years ago; so far we have not been able to make a start there. You know the obstacle as well as I. The way to our concessions leads through Kuchum Khan's kingdom.'

Semyon made a sign for the men to sit down with him.

'And you think it is time we did something about it?' His face, which had been icy before, thawed a little.

'Yes.'

'What have you in mind?'

'A field campaign.'

'And he is to lead it, is he?' Semyon's thin finger pointed to Yermak and his laugh sounded like the bleating of a sheep. 'And how do you think it can be achieved? Have you any idea of the cost of equipping an army?'

'I know that I cannot bear the cost alone. We must all contribute—you, Nikita and I.'

'You say you can't afford it.' Again came the laugh which was so like a bleat. 'Of course you can. But you prefer not to, that's all.'

'But why should I pay the whole of it? The land beyond the Urals belongs to us all. It will bring us in more than Solvychegodsk and Perm have ever produced. We have proof that it is rich in minerals: copper, iron, silver and gold—to say nothing of timber, furs and fish.'

'I know, but what use is the bird in the bush? Do you think Kuchum Khan will say, "Please, gentlemen, if you want to come here, we will leave and find somewhere else to live." He has not crossed the whole of the steppes from the south for nothing. He knew what he wanted long ago when he had Sultan Etiger murdered and then succeeded him. He wanted water, water for his herds of cattle, water for his horses. Water means life for anyone crossing the steppes. That is why he pressed on to the north. And you think that just because he is in your way he will step aside? You're a fool!'

Maxim Stroganov gritted his teeth. He was seething with anger, but he controlled himself with iron will. 'I do not expect him to step aside. I was talking in terms of an armed attack.'

'How large is the army you intend to send against him?' asked Semyon Stroganov.

'There are the Cossacks under Yermak Timofeyev, and of course we must all contribute every soldier we can spare from other duties.'

'I can spare no one,' was the brusque reply. 'You still have not said how many you can muster.'

'If we each contribute one hundred men, eight hundred and fifty in all.'

Semyon's shrill laughter rang through the room. He could hardly stop, he was so amused.

'And you intend to pit that handful against Kuchum Khan and all his vassals?'

'No, sir. *I* intend to,' declared Yermak. The laughter stopped abruptly. The contemptuous sneer was switched over to Yermak.

'Numbers are not always decisive. It is the way one uses them that counts,' Yermak continued.

For a moment all was still. Then Semyon turned to Maxim again, as if he had not heard Yermak's intervention.

'Do you really expect me to pay out good money for such a lost cause? I might as well throw it in the Vychegda.'

Maxim would not admit that he was beaten yet. He still had one card to play, and he knew it was a trump.

'Uncle Semyon,' he began again, 'there are two routes through Kuchum Khan's kingdom. One is to the north to Yugor and Mangaseya. But there is another way, eastwards, to India and China. To find a trade route in that direction is of great concern to our most gracious Czar. You know that as well as I do. Surely he had that in mind when he gave us the land beyond the Urals, indeed it must have been to the forefront. For we Stroganovs have always been forerunners, pathfinders for the Czar.'

Semyon tugged so hard at his beard that Yermak was alarmed in case it came away in his hand. Then the old man winked one eye again and darted an angry look at his nephew with the other. 'You know how to get round me, I grant you. But eight hundred and fifty soldiers against the Tartar thousands is hopeless from the start. Doesn't your reason tell you so, too, you innocent babes?'

Yermak and Maxim were both men in their prime, but to Semyon they were inexperienced boys. Nevertheless, they knew what they wanted and they went on arguing with the old man. But Semyon was adamant. He stuck to his opinion and to his refusal and he would not budge an inch. Yet Maxim got the impression that he was not quite so obstinate as he had been at the beginning.

Next day, when they were starting their journey home, the old man was standing at the door waiting for them to mount. He shook hands first with Yermak and then with his nephew.

'You will be hearing from me. Farewell.'

11 NATIVES AND WOLVES

It was autumn now. The harvest was in and there was a quiet time ahead for the farmers and peasants. They hurried to deliver the corn and cattle due every year to the Stroganovs in Oryol before the rains played havoc with the roads. The Cossacks escorted the farm-carts, for these wagons were often raided by hostile natives if they got the chance.

Traffic was at its height on the River Kama. Soon it would be a solid sheet of ice and shipping would come to a standstill. The salt transports were always used to the full during these last few weeks before winter.

The heavier the rain, the more secure from attack did the Russian settlers feel. That was so every year. In autumn and in spring military operations were impossible and the universal mud became the ally of the threatened cities against the Tartars.

Only the Cossacks were granted no respite. As soon as the first frosts set in they had to be off on their rounds again, and each time their patrols were extended farther to the east. They had to note the size of each native village and to give a report on the natives' attitude towards them.

In most cases the Votyaks were simply frightened of the foreign soldiers, but occasionally they showed their hostility openly. The men forbade them access to their huts and raised their axes threateningly if the Cossacks came too near.

The long stay in Oryol had been a dreary one and these freebooters from the Volga had taken no plunder for so long that they were spoiling for a fight. They soon found out that although the Votyaks knew how to throw an axe a fair distance, they seldom hit their target as long as the Cossacks did not wait for the blow to land. The Cossack method of attack was a decided advantage. They rushed in at a wild gallop, sword in hand, and almost invariably they got their man. The natives were always the losers if it came to a brush, and the Cossacks rode away laden with stolen furs, leaving their victims helpless with fury. The steward in charge of fur trading for Maxim Stroganov asked no questions. It was all the same to him if he was offered skins by the natives or by the Cossacks.

Winter set in and one day Yermak was doing the rounds with a three-man patrol. They had taken up quarters in a tiny Russian hamlet and there they stayed for several days.

Every morning Yermak rode out with his men to the foot of the nearby mountains. The earth lay frozen beneath a thin mantle of snow. In the north-east the sky was dark grey, the sign that more snow was on the way. Crows fluttered into the air as the riders came trotting along. The ice on the puddles broke with a sharp crack beneath the horses' hoofs.

'I'd like to know what we can possibly find in this desolation,' said Boris to Mitya and Alexei. 'These damned forests grow so thick they make me nervous.'

'I don't mind as long as we're riding,' said Alexei. 'It's when the climbing starts that I get fed up.'

'I don't know what you're both grumbling about. I like this,' retorted Mitya. 'You are from the steppes and you feel strange in the forests, but to me they seem like home. I know I'm not used to mountain country any more than you are, but it doesn't bother me in the least. A change does you good.'

'A change,' mumbled Alexei. 'A change from all this is what I need. What on earth does Yermak want around here?'

'He must be looking for something special. We follow a different path every day,' answered Mitya thoughtfully.

'Path!' protested Boris. 'That's good, I must say. Where is the path? That's what I'd like to know. We have to work our way inch by inch through the forests and then scramble up the rocks in this infernal cold, and you talk of a path.'

Mitya laughed aloud. 'Say what you like if it makes you feel any better. It won't make any difference.'

'At least if we came across a Votyak hut we could take a few furs home as a memento. This seems so pointless.'

Yermak ignored the conversation behind him. He was busy with other thoughts. Mitya's guess was right. He was looking for something, for a way of crossing the Ural Mountains, for a pass over which he could lead an army, if one fine day . . .

It was impossible for Yermak to confide in his men, for surprise was essential if Kuchum Khan were to be defeated. But every day brought the same disappointment. They could never get far enough nor high enough during daylight. The early onset of darkness forced him to return to base, for there was no lodging in the mountain which could offer him protection against the cold and the wolves.

That evening he had a talk with the village elder on whom the soldiers were billeted.

‘We are planning to build fortresses in the mountains next year to guard your homes here and I have to seek out the most suitable sites. Do you know of some mountain hut where we could spend a few nights? As it is, I have to come back to the village before nightfall and start afresh every day.’

The peasant tugged at his ear lobe.

‘That is difficult, sir. I do not know any such place, nor would any of the other Russians here in the village. We avoid the mountains, for our work is either in the fields or at the salt wells. But there are a few Votyak huts down by the forest and one old trapper lives there who often stays away for days on end, so he must know somewhere to shelter for the night. Perhaps he will guide you and your men if you take him with you.’

‘Is he reliable? That is, is he friendly towards you?’

‘We see very little of each other, but he has never shown any hostility.’

Yermak thought for a moment. ‘Very well, bring him here to me,’ he said finally.

‘Tonight, sir?’

‘Of course. Immediately.’

The elder sent his son out of the house and an hour later he returned hustling an old Votyak through the door ahead of him. The native was quaintly dressed. He wore a long garment of thick fur which started as a hood and reached down to his feet. The shaggy edge of the wolfskin hood surrounded his face so closely that only the dark deepset slanting eyes peeped out.

The man remained by the door. He threw a timid glance at Yermak and then looked down again.

‘Come closer, friend,’ ordered Yermak.

The man took one hesitant step nearer. Yermak could tell that the Votyak had understood him.

‘I have been told that you are a good hunter. I should like you to take me and my men on a hunting expedition.’

From the half-closed lids a glance of hatred met Yermak’s. Then a high-pitched croaking voice sounded from the fur hood. ‘No good hunter. Me not know where sable and fox . . .’

‘Never mind about that. You will show us where to go tomorrow and that’s that.’

‘Evil spirits in forest,’ he squeaked. ‘Bad devils in mountains—demons everywhere, there—there.’ And he lifted his hands and pointed upwards.

‘Evil spirits? Nonsense. There are no such things.’

'Afraid, lord. Much afraid.'

'Nonsense. Don't argue. You will come with us and show us where we can spend the night.'

The old Votyak turned to the door to go.

'Oh no. You are staying the night here with us. We are not going to wait for you in vain tomorrow. Come on. Up you go!'

Reluctantly, but without a further word, the old man came back. He could tell that protests were useless and so he clambered up the narrow ladder which led to the loft and the Cossacks followed him. Yermak removed the man's axe and his knife and then told him to lie down in the middle.

'Wouldn't it have been better to let him go?' asked Mitya softly. 'The other Votyaks may think that something has happened to him.'

'We must face that when it comes. If we had let him go tonight, every hut would have been deserted by the morning.'

As they left the house early next morning they saw traces of recent footsteps in the fresh snow. The village elder put a thick wooden beam across the door and he did not open so much as a shutter once they had ridden away.

The Cossacks trotted through the snowy wood and soon they began to climb the mountain-side on foot, leading their horses all the time. Yermak kept the Votyak by his side whenever the path was wide enough. Otherwise he made a sign for the native to lead the way.

The snow was not yet deep and they made good headway. Once when the Votyak tried to turn back, Yermak reiterated, 'Mountain hut.' The old hunter crawled ahead of them like an animal. They did not feel the cold, for they were climbing fast. Sometimes the Cossacks thought they could hear the barking of dogs not far away. They had never heard it on their previous expeditions and Boris, Alexei and Mitya discussed it among themselves. Yermak, however, made no comment.

Towards noon and long before they had expected it, they came across a mound of earth, roofed with slabs of stone which jutted out through a thin covering of snow. They had discovered the first hut, a typical mountain bothy.

The Votyak made a sign that he wanted to go home now, but Yermak was adamant. He pointed higher up into the mountains and repeated, 'Hut.' The old man obeyed dumbly and they set off once more.

As the day faded it grew colder. The Votyak began to hurry and before it was quite dark they found another mountain shelter. They cut dry branches from the trees and stacked them in the fireplace. The old man struck flints until the sparks caught. They melted snow for water and added rye spirits. Then they dipped their hard bread in the mixture and ate. The horses nibbled at any green twigs they could find and scraped away the snow with their hoofs to get at the moss.

'We shall keep watch in twos,' said Yermak. 'The wolves don't hunt in packs so early in the winter; there's still plenty of food about. All the same, we had better be on the safe side. I don't want to lose a horse.'

The Votyak was ordered to keep the fire going.

Boris and Alexei kept watch first. They stayed by the door and from time to time they got up to see to the horses. Then they sat down again. Mitya squatted on the ground on one side of the hearth, while the old hunter occupied the other side. Yermak lay down behind the door.

Mitya could not get to sleep. He listened into the night. Everything was still; only the snorting of the horses made him start up occasionally. He wondered if Yermak was asleep and tried to listen for his breathing. Then he gazed across at the old man, who seemed to have closed his eyes. He sat there motionless with his legs crossed, but every time Mitya thought he must be asleep he stretched out an arm and laid another branch on the fire.

Again Mitya thought he could hear a dog barking, but it sounded a different noise by night. He fell asleep, still trying to account for it.

When Yermak woke Mitya for them to take over the watch, the boy was startled. The cold struck him as he got to his feet, although the fire was still burning brightly. They changed places with the others and after a while they went on their rounds. Mitya could hear the barking much more clearly now. He shuddered. He knew what it was at last.

'They won't attack us, Mitya,' Yermak reassured him. 'We are too many for them.'

The horses did not sleep either, for they had heard the wolves as well. They scraped their hoofs restlessly and huddled close together. Sometimes Mitya thought he could see a shape gliding through the trees, but then he was annoyed with himself. But he kept a sharp watch to make sure that the fire did not go out.

It could not be long before the first grey light of day appeared, and Mitya looked forward to it impatiently. There was no mistake about it now. There were several wolves prowling round the camp.

Then all at once, as if someone had given a signal, the beasts vanished. Mitya peered anxiously across the clearing. He could not make out what had scared the wolves. If people were approaching, that might account for it, but was that likely in the midst of this wilderness? Mitya listened. Yes, there was a faint noise.

It was a soft gliding sound, muffled and cautious, and it seemed to come from behind the hut. Keeping hard up against the wall, his axe in his right hand, Mitya edged his way forward and peeped round the corner. At the far edge there was the dark figure of a man crouching. He was facing the forest and as Mitya watched he raised an arm and beckoned. Then, suddenly suspicious, he turned his head in Mitya's direction.

The first glimmer of dawn and the snow gave light enough for them to see each other, but only the fraction of a second. The thick-set figure lifted his hatchet and Mitya knew that the stranger was about to hurl it at him.

'I must throw my axe first,' it flashed through his head. 'I must hit him or he will kill me. I must be faster. He is still bending down. I must not allow him to straighten his back.'

Mitya could not take his eyes off the man. He fascinated him. 'But you killed the bear,' he told himself. 'All you must do is to bring down the axe as you did then.' But this was no bear. It was a human being.

'He may be the son of the hunter in the hut, a trapper's son just as I am. What harm have I done him that he should want to kill me?'

Then the figure rose quickly and immediately Mitya flung his axe. He knew that his aim had been true, but he did not stop to look. He turned back swiftly.

'Yermak!' he cried. 'We are being attacked. The Votyak are coming from the forest over there. One of them just gave the signal.'

The next moment Alexei and Boris were on their feet, too.

'Quick. Tie up the old man, Mitya.' He and Alexei bound his hands behind his back and drove him out of the hut before them. Yermak gave a leap on to his horse's back, drew his sword and pulled his hatchet from his belt.

'Tie his legs, too,' he cried. 'Come on Boris, after them!'

The three Votyaks were lurking so close to the wall of the hut that they almost missed them.

'You hounds!' shouted Boris. An axe flew past his head, taking his cap with it, and he struck out with his sabre. Before Mitya and

Alexei could get there, Yermak and Boris had overpowered the Votyaks.

'And now the old man will get his share, too,' cried Alexei.

'Leave him alone,' called Yermak. 'He is not to blame.'

Mitya had dismounted and bent over the fallen men. 'One of them is still alive,' he said.

'Hit him on the head with your axe,' bawled Alexei.

'No!' shouted Mitya. 'I shan't do that.'

'But what are you going to do with him?'

Mitya looked up at Yermak uncertainly.

'That is not our worry,' said Yermak and rode over to the old man. 'How many men lived in your hut?' he demanded.

There was no answer, but a look of hatred.

Alexei, who had come up behind Yermak, raised his axe. 'How many men?' asked Yermak once more.

The old man looked away, as he answered, 'The fingers of a hand.'

'Good,' said Yermak. 'That accounts for them all probably. All the same, we must still be careful. Untie him and let him attend to the wounded man.' He then turned back to the Votyak. 'You can go home.'

Boris and Alexei were incredulous. 'You're going to let that devil go free?'

'Yes. I don't want to make any more enemies in Perm than I have to. He has been punished sufficiently.'

Mitya untied his bonds.

'Go home,' repeated Yermak to the old man and pointed in the direction in which they had come yesterday. Then the Cossacks mounted and rode off. Mitya was the last. He could see how the old man crept up to the slain Votyaks, how he looked into their faces and then lifted the survivor on to his back. Then Mitya turned and kept his eyes ahead of him.

They climbed higher and higher. The trees grew more and more stunted and the rocks more numerous, so that progress was difficult. They zig-zagged forward into the growing light of day. Boris and Alexei were beginning to curse again as they had done on previous days.

Mitya did not answer them back. His thoughts were still with the little mountain hut. I have killed a man, he thought, a man. But if I had not been quicker than he, I might have been lying there instead. Yes, but it was I who did the killing.

He could see the man's eyes in front of him wherever he looked.

Perhaps it would have done if I had only wounded him, if

I hadn't aimed at his head.

But it's too late now. I can't do anything about it. Mitya did not feel the cold. His body was warm and the more his thoughts obsessed him, the hotter he grew.

I wonder if he felt any pain? What was he thinking as he died? His last thought must have been that he hated me.

Mitya did not hear Boris speaking to him. 'You were magnificent, Mitya: You killed the Votyak with a single blow. You're a real Cossack now, brother. You're one of us and no mistake!'

'They would have slit our throats like sheep if you hadn't stopped them,' acknowledged Alexei generously. 'We'll have to put you on guard every night.'

And he clapped Mitya on the shoulder.

'Oh, leave me alone.'

The others thought that he was being modest and they started praising him in even stronger terms.

'Oh, shut your mouths for heaven's sake!' Mitya roared at them.

'All right, all right.' Boris gave in with good humour. 'But we shan't forget that you saved our lives.'

Yermak had been keeping an eye on the young men behind him. When they decided on a short rest and took hunks of bread from their saddle-bags, he found himself by Mitya's side as if by accident, for the lad had drawn apart from the other two.

'Not much appetite,' observed Yermak casually.

'Of course. I'm very hungry,' protested Mitya and he took a large bite.

'I know how you feel. It was your first, wasn't it? I don't suppose you thought about that side of things when you decided to join the Cossacks!' He did not expect an answer.

But one came nevertheless.

'No,' said Mitya. 'Not that.'

That day they stumbled on a narrow path which circled the summit of the mountain and when they reached its highest point they could look down into a valley below. A broad plain with dense forests stretched away to the east.

'We've done it!' said Yermak breathlessly, leaning against a rock.

'What was the point of coming up here?' asked Alexei.

'I wanted to enjoy the view, brother. Don't you think it's worth it?'

Alexei looked at Yermak as if he doubted his reason.

'To whom does this land belong?' asked Boris. 'To the Czar in

Moscow?'

'Yes and no,' answered Yermak. 'It was once the kingdom of a Sultan named Etiger who placed himself under the protection of the Czar and offered him one thousand sableskins a year as tribute. So that made him a Russian vassal. But Kuchum Khan assassinated Sultan Etiger and occupied his throne. He would not dream of paying tribute to the Czar. He regards this as his country and he will have nothing to do with Russia. Now you tell me to whom the land belongs.'

'To be frank, I don't care. All that interests me is what are the prospects for booty? Whenever I hear about Khans and Tartars I remember our life by the Volga. I can see their rich carpets and the gleaming coloured silks and I can hear the chink of golden chains and the creak of merchants' wagons . . .'

'Stop!' Yermak laughed aloud and tugged Boris's beard as he spoke with enchanted eyes and nodding head. 'We'll have plenty of adventures here in the north, too.'

'Are you sure of that?' asked Boris, and Alexei added, 'And about time too.'

'But you'll have to wait until the winter is over.'

'And then I suppose you'll come back here and show all the Cossacks the wonderful view?' asked Boris slyly.

'I'm sure they will admire it, too! Come on. We want to be back at the hut by nightfall.'

When they arrived there, there was nothing to be seen of the dead Votyaks.

'I wonder who carted them away. The old man can't have disposed of all three bodies by himself,' said Boris.

'Perhaps the wolves gave him a hand,' suggested Alexei.

'There are houses lower down and a few women live there,' said Yermak and once more they lit a fire, melted snow, poured out spirits and devoured their evening meal.

The wolves were bolder still that night. They could smell the blood which had flowed in the morning. To hold them at bay more easily, the Cossacks took three of the horses with them into the hut. They had to huddle close together for there was hardly any room left, but they could watch the clearing in front more easily and fling burning faggots at the wolves if they threatened to come too close.

The wolves retreated and then advanced again, trying to attack the horses, but they were out of luck. The light of dawn made them feel unsure and when Yermak caught one beast with his axe, so that it lay there yelping loudly, the others disappeared.

The Cossacks set off quickly and early in the afternoon they reached the village. The elder came to meet them joyfully.

'We were deeply distressed, sir,' he said to Yermak. 'We saw how the Votyaks went up into the hills with stretchers. We thought . . .'

'We are still alive and kicking,' said Yermak. 'All we want is a hearty meal and a bed.'

12 A LETTER TO THE CZAR

That winter in Oryol saw little change. Soon, such intense cold prevailed that no one went out of doors unless he had to. Maxim Stroganov presented the Cossacks with long sheepskin greatcoats which reached down to their ankles. They inspected them at arm's length, tried them on and grinned at each other.

'They are good skins,' they said, 'and made to last for many years. They will certainly keep us warm when we go on guard.'

They sat round the fire in their stone barracks and talked about the Volga and the raids they remembered. They quarrelled when someone bragged too much, but in the evenings the *balalaikas* played and the Cossacks sang to the music.

It was in these winter days that the first murmurs were heard about the distant lands which the Stroganovs owned beyond the Urals. No one could have said who had started these tales. The Cossacks might have heard them from the people of Oryol, or perhaps Yermak himself had dropped a hint. No one knew for certain.

To the south stretched the River Taiga, so they had heard. There were thick forests crossed by broad rivers and these rivers were said to be mightier than the Volga and alive with fish. When winter took the fish by surprise, so the story went, they froze into a solid wall on the banks, so that when the ice melted in the spring you had only to bring baskets and collect them by the hundredweight. Some of the men were incredulous, but there were others who assured them it was true.

The summer was said to be a good season in Siberia, with game in plenty, wild geese and ducks, hares, deer and bears. But winter was a different matter. It was very long and severe. The land stretched far to the north, too. There were no forests there, but sparse, slender trees which grew more and more stunted the farther one went. Then came vast expanses of bleak moorland, which were known as the tundra. There was ice and snow there and it was always winter, even when it was summer in the south. Still, you could hunt polar bears in the north and their magnificent white fur fetched a high price. There were seals galore, too, and reindeer as well, in herds numbering over a thousand head. The native inhabitants, however, were bad men. *Samoyed* they were called and the word means 'cannibal'.

'What nonsense!'

'But it's the truth, the gospel truth. I swear it by the Holy Mother of God.'

'Are the Samoyed heathen?'

'Of course they are, stupid. Does a Christian eat his grandmother when she gets old and useless? Does he roast his children for supper when guests arrive at his tent?'

'Oh, be quiet! You're making my stomach turn, the way you talk.'

'But it's true.'

'All right, have it your own way. All the same if I don't get a swig of liquor pretty quick, I'll vomit.'

The paunchy wine-bottle went the rounds and then they went on talking about witch-doctors and the idols which the Samoyed obeyed and to whom they prayed.

'If only we knew what it's really like!'

'I'm telling you, if only you'd listen. When Maxim Stroganov's grandfather was still alive, the first explorers went to Mangaseya. They went by river as far as they could, but when that was impossible they dragged the boats behind them overland, although they took to the water once more whenever it was practicable. They brought back this information and if you don't believe me you can go and find out for yourself. Get the Samoyed to invite you to dinner!'

'Oh, how I'd like to see it all with my own eyes. Anything would be better than sitting around here. I'm sure we could make our fortunes in Siberia.'

'Forget it. It's no good.'

'Why ever not?'

'Because Kuchum Khan bars the way. He would never allow anyone to pass through his kingdom.'

'Don't make me laugh! Haven't you heard what happened to the Nogai Khan and his capital, Saraichik? Don't tell me the Cossacks would be put off by a handful of heathen Tartars!'

Since the recent affair in the mountains, Mitya had grown more reserved and silent. The loud voices and the rough behaviour of the brothers often tried his nerves. His mind was never still and he needed peace and quiet to work things out for himself. He could not speak to Yermak, for he doubted if the Chieftain could put himself in Mitya's place. When Yermak had caught sight of the Votyaks that day he had struck out immediately. He would never have been so squeamish when danger threatened.

Mitya spent much of his spare time with Doctor Ivan. For the most part, the boy watched him work in silence, but sometimes he would ask the name of this or that herb and what it was good for. He looked on as wounds were bandaged; he learnt gradually which salves would relieve pain and which were intended to speed up healing. More and more often he found himself anticipating the jar or pot the doctor would need and he would hand it to him before he asked for it.

'You're an observant lad,' Doctor Ivan told him.

One day Mitya started talking to him about that day in the Urals. 'I wonder what happened to the Votyak who was wounded. Do you think he lived?'

'Why not? These people are tough. You can't dispose of them so easily. It depends on the injury, of course, and how hard the man was hit.'

'Of course,' echoed Mitya. Then hesitatingly he murmured, 'I hit the first one good and hard.'

Now the words were out. The doctor looked at Mitya.

'Yes,' the lad went on, 'I killed him all right.'

'You mustn't brood over it so much. What else could you do? It was your life or his, your enemy's.'

'But why was he my enemy? I had never hurt him.'

'You had taken the old hunter with you. His friends did not know why, but they suspected the worst. You could not talk to them and explain. The axes were the only language you had in common.'

'Yes,' said Mitya. 'If only we could have spoken to each other . . .'

'I doubt if they would have believed you. Let me give you a little advice, Mitya. Don't think so much. A good Cossack doesn't do that.'

'I'm not a good Cossack, I know,' sighed Mitya. 'You lead a better life here, Doctor,' he added involuntarily. Then he changed the subject quickly as if to unsay his last words.

Yermak often visited Maxim Stroganov. By day Maxim was too busy to sit down and talk, but in the evening they spread out their huge maps and discussed their plans.

'Now, this is where you must take to the water if you want to travel fast,' said Maxim. 'You must leave the horses behind, of course.'

'I have thought it over most carefully, but I don't want to do that. My army will not be flexible enough. We will be sitting targets and the Tartars on the river banks can pick us off with their bows and arrows like a skein of geese.'

'The rivers in Siberia flow swiftly. You will be moving all the time.'

'I know, but Kuchum Khan's army is still more mobile. In any case, we must have horses. Cossacks and horses go together. You can't imagine one without the other.'

'Yermak, you know how highly I esteem your capability, otherwise you would not be sitting opposite me now. But for this campaign you must eliminate horses from all your calculations. Believe me, I know Siberia. You can only penetrate it by means of its waterways. In autumn and in spring your army would be stuck in the mud. The broad rivers are Siberia's highroads. You must use them if you want to advance. You don't know the moors and forests, the sudden violent cloudbursts that turn even firm ground into bog and marsh. I know that when it comes to fighting cavalry is best, but your biggest difficulty will be to cover the length and breadth of the land with your army. Once you have conquered it, you will find horses enough. They say that Kuchum Khan has horses by the thousand.'

'Forgive me, Maxim, but this "They say" of yours is too vague for me.'

'I have reliable reports.'

'So much the worse. They will be able to chase us to the ends of the earth. And what use will my Cossacks be then?'

'What is behind all these objections, Yermak? You have been splitting hairs all evening. Speak up, man.'

'Maxim Stroganov, I have fought with the Tartars for many years and I know that they are splendid warriors. War is their element. But they need two things, their horses and their arrows. Kuchum Khan's army is many times larger than ours. If I am to achieve anything at all against them, I shall have to use much more than cunning. I need practical assistance.'

'For instance?'

'For instance firearms, Maxim. Guns!'

'So that's it.' Maxim Stroganov's hands lay on the table before him, and he twisted the ring with the blue jewel. 'Not a bad idea, eh! They have never smelt gunpowder, so they might be shocked into surrender? Is that the idea? Mm. But how can we do it? Who will pay? Firearms cost a mint of money.'

'The money will soon be recovered when we have conquered Siberia for you.'

'I cannot bear the cost alone.'

'No, but there are your relations, They, too . . .'

'Yes, you are right. It is high time I spoke to Nikita. You must come with me, Yermak.'

The following day in the biting cold they set off by sledge for Kankor.

Nikita Stroganov received his guests with cordial hospitality. He was studiously polite to Maxim and condescendingly friendly to Yermak.

They set out before him their careful proposals to defeat Kuchum Khan, but his answer was an uncompromising 'No'. All the persuasive accounts of the great commercial benefits which the lands beyond the Urals would bring to the family were lost on him. He was not prepared to sacrifice a single man—or a single rouble for such a dubious enterprise.

The sledge in which Maxim and Yermak returned to Oryol seemed very crowded. They were so smothered with thick furs and rugs that sitting was uncomfortable, but that was little compared with the discomfiture which Nikita's 'No' had created. It filled their minds; it oppressed their spirits and the keen east wind could not blow it away.

They did not discuss it, for each knew what the other was thinking. It was only as they drove through the north gate of Oryol that Maxim Stroganov spoke with grim determination. 'I shall force him! Yes, I shall force him to contribute. He doesn't know me when I am roused!'

Before the winter was quite over a messenger arrived from Solvychegodsk. After the briefest glance at Semyon's letter, Maxim Stroganov sent a servant post-haste to the stone barracks where Yermak lived.

'The Master wants you immediately.'

Maxim Stroganov was pacing up and down the room. He looked out of the window across the courtyard, but that was only habit. The agents with whom he had been discussing business for the coming spring only fifteen minutes before had been sent packing.

When Yermak entered, tall, broad and erect as ever, Maxim Stroganov regarded him as he invariably did with approval. The sight of this intelligent capable leader of men cleared away the last doubts which sometimes worried even that hardheaded businessman, Maxim Stroganov. The moment Yermak stood there assured, confident, he knew that there was no one else who could bring his schemes to fruition.

'You are in a good mood, Maxim Stroganov.'

'Yes, I am indeed. My Uncle Semyon has sent me word.'

'I do not need to ask if it is favourable. I can see that for myself.'

Maxim Stroganov laughed.

'Sit down, Yermak. Of course, he has not given me a definite "Yes" to offset my cousin's "No". He makes a string of conditions, to protect his business interests of course. I wouldn't have expected anything else from the old skinflint. But the important thing is that he is coming in with us.' Maxim Stroganov rubbed his hands. 'Beware, Kuchum Khan, we are on our way.'

'And your cousin, Nikita?' asked Yermak.

'I have devised a plan . . .'

The next day the messenger returned to Solvychegodsk with a letter, but before an answer could reach Oryol the thaw set in, and without warning, as happens with so many things in that vast country. Any movement was impossible. The smallest rivers swelled into roaring torrents which flooded the countryside. The few roads turned into thick squelching mud with big black puddles in which the grey sky was mirrored. Then heavy gusts of wind swept over the sodden land and dried it out again.

It was spring, and winter's respite came to an end. The salt transports could sail along the Kama once more; the peasants began to sow their fields. The Cossacks took up their old patrols around Oryol and Kankor and more and more often these rounds took them up into the mountains.

By this time Semyon and Maxim had exchanged more correspondence and they had agreed to write once more to the Czar in Moscow, this time to complain to his most gracious Majesty about their cousin Nikita. They decided on the contents of the letter which Maxim would write and sign and then send to Semyon for his signature. From Solvychegodsk it would be dispatched by the fastest possible route to Moscow.

'You are banking on the Czar's support, aren't you?' said Yermak.

'I am indeed,' replied Maxim. 'I know exactly what I shall achieve and Semyon would never have consented to the letter if he were not just as sure as I am of what is at stake. The idea of winning Siberia for Russia is much too tempting for Moscow to deny us its backing. Just think, Yermak. All we ask is a letter to Nikita which will make him feel a bit hot under the collar. Can any ruler ask for a whole empire more cheaply? In any event, our family has many friends in Moscow. If the Czar asks them for their opinion, they will all advise him in our favour.'

'But your cousin is one of the family, too.'

'Ha, ha!' chortled Maxim. 'The presents we are sending come from Semyon and from me, not Nikita. And then, Yermak, one of the most important nobles in the Kremlin is on our side, and that is Boris Godunov. That time when the Czar struck his son and heir and killed him, it was Boris Godunov who tried to intervene. Indeed, he got hurt, too, for who escapes when the Czar—may Heaven guard him—flies into one of his rages? My father happened to be in Moscow at that time, and as I have told you already, he was very interested in the art of healing. It was he who attended to Boris Godunov on that occasion, and they talked a lot about Siberia. Godunov was most interested, for the land really belongs to no one. When our envoy reaches Moscow, Boris Godunov will be on our side. I'm as certain of that as I am of the "Amen" at the end of a prayer.'

Maxim Stroganov had drafted his letter with meticulous care. There was nothing in it about a campaign to conquer Siberia and equally little about Yermak and his Cossacks. But he complained bitterly that Nikita was unreliable and not ready to devote his money and his men to the defence of the land, so that they lived in constant fear of an attack by the Tartars. The enterprise of three generations was in danger of annihilation.

Just as carefully as he had worded his letter, so Maxim chose his presents. There were twenty magnificent sables, five superb black foxes and ten ermine skins for the Czar. There were ten magnificent sables, three superb black foxes and five ermine skins for Boris Godunov. Furthermore there was a gift of two hundred shining roubles for the Metropolitan Archbishop and silver for a candlestick. He would leave it to Semyon to select suitable icons, but even so, Maxim was not sure that he had been quite generous enough to attain the desired object. He decided to add further gifts for other influential friends of the family.

The preparations were complete, but as Maxim sprinkled sand over the wet ink of his signature a noise outside startled him violently. A Cossack came galloping through Oryol, standing in the stirrups. He was leaning over the horse's neck and lashing the beast mercilessly. People in the streets scattered on all sides in panic.

Maxim Stroganov saw the rider dash into the courtyard. He

jumped up from his chair and tore open the window. 'What's the matter? Is the Devil after you, man?'

'The Tartars are coming! Yermak Timofeyev sends you this message. Prince Beguli from Pelym is on the march with a whole army. You must prepare your people.'

Maxim Stroganov was already at the door.

'Masupov! Feodor Masupov!' he shouted so loudly that the servants practically fell over themselves in their haste. 'The carriage! The horses! Have them put to at once!'

Masupov came running up immediately. 'Do you really want me to go now? If the Tartars . . .'

Stroganov did not let him finish. 'You must leave at once and for that very reason. You must not lose an hour. Drive until the horses drop; travel night and day, do you hear? Do not delay in Solvychegodsk, but tell Semyon what has happened and make sure that you do not mince your words when you get to Moscow. Pack the presents quickly and God-speed!'

When Masupov had left, Maxim dispatched another messenger post-haste to Kankor. He begged for Nikita's help even if he could spare only one troop of soldiers, to hold in reserve in Oryol.

13 A JEWEL FOR A DRINK OF WATER

In a swirling cloud of sand, earth and dust, the Cossacks from Kankor came that night. As they hurtled past the walls of Oryol, the nervous inhabitants crossed themselves at the thunder of hoofs and the wild war-cries of two hundred horsemen eager for battle. At their head stormed Ivan Koltso. Ruthlessly he spurred on his horse, impatient to join up with Yermak's forces.

Yermak had set out to engage the enemy earlier in the day. His own army consisted of the main body of the Cossacks and the militia from the town. It was a clear night and Ivan Koltso soon caught up with the main force.

'At last!' Ivan called aloud as Yermak turned and came riding towards him.

'Yes, you're here at last,' said Yermak. 'I have been waiting anxiously for you, although I don't see how you could have got here before.'

'Oh, that was not what I meant,' laughed Koltso. 'I meant that at last this boring, peaceful life is over. I felt as rusty as an old sword in recent months, but now I know I am still the fighter I was. Now, Yermak, tell me what it's all about.'

They rode up to the camp-fire, where Matvei Meshcherak had just finished a bottle of spirits. He got up as they approached.

'I can't say exactly how strong the attack will be, but probably there are seven or eight hundred Tartars at a guess,' answered Yermak. 'They charged along the banks of the Chussovaya River and occupied the Russian villages. You can see their present position from the top of that hill.'

'What is the plan of action?'

'You and I will wait a little. Michailov and his men have advanced already and, as you see, Matvei is now collecting his hundred and will set off right away. They will attack on the flank and drive the enemy straight into our arms.'

'Good,' said Ivan Koltso. 'We shall embrace them so ardently . . '.

'I wish you would be serious for once,' frowned Yermak. 'You and I will make a wider detour towards the south. I want the main action to take place at the junction of the Chussovaya and the Kama.'

'That will suit me admirably, Yermak. But I think we had better be on our guard. If the scoundrels anticipate our intentions, they may break out northwards before we are in position.'

'Yes, you are right. We shall have to be very wary. Will you take the left flank, Ivan, or shall I?'

'I will, Yermak. You know I always do.'

'Very well. But I'll lend you a few of my men as a scouting party. They know the countryside better than yours from Kankor.'

'Splendid. And what about afterwards?'

'Afterwards!' repeated Yermak. 'We must wait and see if the heathen know how to fight! By the way, I have taken the precaution of giving orders to withdraw to Oryol if we are worsted. We must not allow the Tartars to get through to the city, come what may.'

'And if Fortune is with us?'

'May Heaven have mercy on their souls.'

The main Cossack force under Yermak rode through the night. A few scouts reconnoitred the way ahead, but everything was quiet. The Tartars were still some distance away.

Towards morning, Yermak saw a clearing ahead and he halted his army under cover of the forest. The horses had to be rested before they could go on. As the sun rose slowly over the treetops, they set out again and forded the river which crossed their path. Peasants came trudging towards them, trundling their pathetic belongings and the smaller children in little hand-carts, and the women hurrying alongside with terror-stricken faces. The Cossacks rode by in wild haste.

All at once the advance scouts came galloping back. 'The Tartars are here!' they cried from afar as soon as they sighted Yermak.

Yermak brought his horse to a standstill. Calmly he gave his orders. The men were to remain at the edge of the forest, concealed in the undergrowth, packed tightly into a compact fighting force. The battle-cries of the Tartars rang out from a long way away. Yermak kept his eyes on the open valley which lay before them. The enemy must emerge from the forest opposite. Their blood-curdling yells could be heard ever more clearly. Now the first horses appeared, the lances with the bright-coloured pennants, the harsh red of the pointed Tartar caps with the broad band of fur. The next moment the scene was alive with them; their ranks came closer and closer. On they rode: more, more and still more of them.

Yermak remained calm. The horses were trembling with excitement and flicking their tails.

The mass of the Tartar army filled the valley and their advance guard stormed up the hill.

Then Yermak swung his sabre. It was the signal for the attack. The Cossacks burst out of the forest like a tidal wave. The first ranks of the Tartars stopped dead in surprise, but their own men coming up behind pushed them onward. It was only a matter of minutes before the two armies clashed together in close combat. But Yermak had achieved his aim. The Tartar archers were too close in to do any damage and the Cossacks were able to use their swords in the hand-to-hand fighting at which they excelled.

'Stay close beside me!' cried Boris, easing his horse next to Mitya's. 'Don't get cut off.' Then he laughed and added, 'You are going to see something worthwhile now, brother. The moment has come.' And Boris clicked with his tongue and egged on Mitya's horse with encouraging shouts. Then he broke into a string of curses mingled with the most fearsome oaths, and swinging his sword lustily, he urged his horse on, using the hard pressure of his thighs.

Mitya was crouching in the saddle, his whole body wracked with cramp. He stared wide-eyed at the screaming welter of horses and human bodies whirling round him, and although he saw Boris next to him, he felt as if he stood alone to stem the inexorable tide bearing down on him. His hands began to shake and the strength ebbed from his bones so that he expected to fall at any moment. He could not think, he no longer knew that he was riding a horse. His eyes grew blind and he could not remember why he was there at all. Even when Boris's voice called out: 'Mitya, lie close to your horse or they'll mow you down!' he did not come to his senses. He obeyed blindly, closing his eyes for a second and would have liked to cover his ears.

It was the neighing of his horse, the spittle which splashed his face, the flowing mane which blew into his parched open mouth and made him almost vomit, that brought him to himself. It was only then that he realized how low he was crouching, how his legs were gripping the horse's flanks, that his hands were damp and the sweat was running down his back. 'I'm frightened,' thought Mitya, and once he had admitted it to himself, his mind began working normally. 'But I will not be afraid. My brothers are round me and Yermak is here. I shall fight like the rest of them.'

'I don't suppose you thought of that.' He could hear Yermak's voice in his imagination. 'No, I didn't,' he told himself, 'but now there is no excuse and I must face it.'

Mitya saw that Boris was making for a group of Tartars who had surrounded two Cossacks and he rode after him. When he was close enough, he struck. He did not close his eyes as the blood spurted under his blow. He gritted his teeth and thought, 'I will hate them as they hate me. For whoever kills a man must know how to hate, or how else could he do it?' Mitya's eyes stared boldly, full of curiosity. 'I want to know what it is like when I kill a man. I want to know what it's like when a man dies.'

Horses slithered to the ground, burying their riders beneath them. Boris's horse was hit, but Boris jumped up behind Mitya. They struck and lashed out all round them, one in front and the other behind. They stood on the horse's back, a dagger between their teeth, swinging their sabres and smiting the Tartars left and right.

Ivan Koltso's hundred now appeared on the left and behind the Tartars were Nikita Pan and Matvei Meshcherak with their troops.

The Tartars were encircled, but they refused to admit defeat. The battle lasted a long time, until at last they recognized that flight was the only way out for their beaten army.

Yermak had not been able to penetrate the bodyguard which had fought round the person of Prince Beguli. Now when he saw that the Tartars were fleeing, he was seized with rage. He collected a few of his men and set off in pursuit. The Tartars rode like the Devil and every now and then faithful followers of the leader sprang to the rescue of their prince and barred the Cossacks' way. Ivan Koltso fended off the attackers and kept Yermak's back covered, so that at last he managed to catch up with the Prince's bodyguard and once more there was bitter fighting.

The outcome was inevitable. A ring of dead bodies surrounded the Prince Beguli and still the wounded Tartars rose up again to defend their leader.

'Yield, you pagan!' cried Yermak, but the Prince, who had already lost both lance and sword, raised his hand which held a dagger. Then one Cossack lunged at the Prince's horse. As it collapsed, its rider fell and lost his knife. Yermak jumped down from the saddle and stood over him with pointed sword until he had been bound captive. Then he handed him over to Nikita Pan and galloped away in pursuit of the fleeing Tartars. They overtook only one tiny contingent whom they captured and took prisoner. In the valley the bodies of heathen and Christian lay side by side, and the groans of the dying were just as terrible to hear, no matter what their faith. Riderless horses wandered aimlessly among the corpses or dashed away in panic to the nearby forest. Wounded Cossacks rose laboriously to their feet and tottered to the edge of the woods, where their brothers had pitched camp. The prisoners were herded together and sat on the ground with heads downcast. But along the banks of the Chussovaya was the grim trail which the Tartars had left in their wake, the burnt remains of houses, slaughtered families, slain cattle and trampled fields where the new corn was thrusting forth its tender green shoots.

When evening came Yermak ascertained that the Cossacks' losses were not so high as he had feared at first. It is true that a large number were injured, but most of the casualties were the soldiers from Oryol.

Ivan Koltso, Yakob Michailov and Matvei Meshcherak were sent back to Oryol with the bulk of the army, but Yermak remained with Nikita Pan and a hundred Cossacks to guard the prisoners. They had lit camp-fires at the edge of the forest and they intended to remain until daylight. It was not wise to march through thickly wooded country in darkness with a train of prisoners.

Mitya was one of those who remained behind with Yermak. He could not sleep and he kept listening to the sounds coming from the valley. He had seen so much that day that the pictures grew blurred before his eyes. What was the life of one Votyak compared with all he had done today? The lad grew so restless that he could not lie there any longer. He got up and as if some unknown force were driving him thither he slipped back to the battlefield. He passed a heap of captured swords. In the light of a nearby fire he could see four Cossacks examining the weapons and testing their quality. 'Splendid workmanship,' he heard as he went by. 'Oh, that's nothing special. I'm taking this one. It's much finer.' 'No, give it back to me. I had that one first.' 'I say, look at this one! See how the blade is carved and the jewels in the hasp.' 'Sh! Don't let Yermak catch you.'

Mitya shook his head and hurried on. As he ran, he stubbed his foot against something round which rolled away. When he looked closer he saw it was a head. He avoided the next body. The corpses were lying thicker here and he had to step over them. Then he heard a loud moaning and drew closer. Between two dead Tartars lay a Cossack. Mitya knelt down and tried to make out his face. The man seemed not to notice Mitya. A thin stream of blood poured from his mouth without stopping. Mitya turned away.

There was another wounded man, a soldier from Oryol.

'The thirst!' he groaned. 'Water.' His eyes were closed. Mitya looked round. There was nothing nearby in which he could carry water, but he knew where the stream was, for they had watered the horses not long before. He hurried back to the camp-fire, untied one of the cauldrons, and ran to the brook. Then he hastened back to the battlefield, but he could not find the wounded man who had begged for water. He searched everywhere but it had grown darker than ever.

Another Cossack tried to hold him fast by his trouser leg as he moved away. Mitya bent down, put his hand under the sick man's head and placed the vessel to his lips.

'Brother . . .' said the man and fell back. Mitya knew that he would have liked to say more, but he was too weak.

Mitya passed one man with a Tartar arrow stuck in his breast. He turned away. He could not help him any more, but he found many wounded who wanted water and he gave them some to drink.

Near one dead Cossack lay a Tartar who held out his hands imploringly. Mitya turned aside. He wanted to help his comrades, not those who had caused their deaths. But the echo of the words in a language he did not understand rang in his ears. He struggled with his conscience. He is a Tartar when all's said and done. But he is as thirsty as a wounded Cossack. Mitya turned back and gave the Tartar a drink, too. He could tell that the dying man was still very young, no older than himself. Mitya knelt by his side and looked into his face. Suddenly he thought of his father and the notches in the door and he wondered if Nikolai had remembered to cut another one that winter.

The young Tartar raised his hand, but Mitya's thoughts were far away. When he came back to earth he heard something hard rolling in the cauldron. Then the Tartar's hand fell back and it did not move again.

Mitya went on, and among the many lying there he found Ilya with a layer of blood thickly crusted over the breast of his tunic. Mitya bent over him. Ilya did not stir, but now and then a long-drawn moan came from his mouth.

Mitya straightened his back. So someone else had done what Mitya himself had planned to do. 'Now Ilya is suffering as I would have done had the bear in the forest been swifter. That is life.' A feeling of triumph mounted in Mitya's throat. 'I am still alive and you are dying,' he gloated voicelessly, 'and I did not even need to lift a hand.'

Mitya remained squatting there. He could hear once more quite plainly the cry with which Ilya had warned the bear of Mitya's approach. But as he recalled it the cry became reality. Suppose Ilya were not mortally wounded; suppose he recovered? 'What if I carried him over to where the wounded are? This is the man who betrayed me to the bear, who loathed me from the start, who always behaved abominably to me. And he it is whom I must carry over to the brothers and save his life. No. I cannot do it.'

Mitya stood up and stepped over Ilya's body.

'He has escaped me every time so far, but this time I shall have my revenge. I shall not finish him off, but I shall leave him there as if I had not seen him.' And Mitya bent over the next Cossack. Once more he dipped his hand in the pot and cupped a palmful of water. He let it run into the man's mouth and then went on his way. Again and again he moistened the lips of the dying. Then suddenly he felt something hard at the bottom of the cauldron. He picked it up and saw that he held a precious stone in his hands. It was a smooth dark red and it gleamed dully in the darkness. Then Mitya fell a-thinking again as he had done by the side of the young Tartar. A ruby for a sip of water, he thought. Could a sip of water be worth so much?

'Should I not have given Ilya something to drink, too? After all, I gave one to a Tartar and to deny one to a Cossack . . . No. He was more treacherous than any Tartar. In any case, the water would not have saved his life.'

Then Mitya went on farther and it was a long time before he returned to the camp-fire again. The Cossacks were asleep. He sat down near Yermak, who was leaning against a tree, watching the flames with half-closed eyes and chewing a dry biscuit.

'What have you been doing? Why weren't you resting like everyone else?'

'I went down there,' said Mitya, jerking his head in the direction of the valley.

'I see.'

'Many of them were glad of a drink of water,' said Mitya.

'And you gave it to them?'

'Yes, to some of them. Do you know, Yermak, it occurred to me that many of them would live if a doctor attended to them, someone who understood how to dress their wounds.'

'But where could we get a doctor? There are so few of them. And you don't really think that a learned gentleman like a doctor would march with us into battle?'

'No,' said Mitya slowly. 'Of course not. I did not think of that. You are quite right.'

The next morning the Cossacks rounded up their prisoners and marched them off to Oryol. At the first village they came to they asked for carts and horses to be sent to fetch the wounded.

Three days later they were back in Oryol. Maxim Stroganov hurried to meet Yermak as soon as he was told that they were approaching the town.

He kissed him on both cheeks and shook him by the hand.

'Thank you, my friend. You have protected us from great danger. We are greatly indebted to you. And you have brought the Prince as a prisoner, too. That is well done. I thank you.'

'Are the Cossacks from Kankor still here?'

'You mean Ivan Koltso and his men? Yes, they are still here, and what's more they will not return there.'

'But the danger is over, Maxim Stroganov. The heathen will not attack Oryol again in a hurry.'

'All the same, I mean what I say. Come with me and I will show you why.'

As Maxim Stroganov gave orders to have the prisoners locked in the dungeons, Yermak looked around him and he saw that Doctor Ivan was standing by the carts on which the wounded lay. Near him stood Mitya, and the boy appeared to be very excited as they spoke together.

'I sent a messenger to my cousin Nikita and begged him for the help of his militia,' Maxim Stroganov went on. 'I wanted to be prepared for the worst and you know that our own soldiers went with you. But Nikita replied that if the Tartars advanced he would need his own troops to defend Kankor. I should have to make do with the Cossacks and he recommended me to put my trust in the Lord as he did himself. But this much I tell you, he will not get a single Cossack back now, not even if Kankor is burnt to the ground. Uncle Semyon raised a small but well-equipped contingent at once and sent them to Oryol. But once Ivan Koltso brought me news of your victory I sent word that they should turn back. I did not need them, at least, not for the moment.'

'Not for the moment? What does that mean?'

'That things are getting serious. I am tired of sitting here, waiting to be attacked whenever the Tartars feel inclined. The time has come for action, Yermak. Prepare your compaign against Kuchum Khan.'

'With guns, Maxim?'

'Of course with guns. How long do you need?'

'Summer is nearly here,' declared Yermak, thoughtfully, making rapid calculations in his head. 'By the time it is over, we shall have the Urals behind us.'

14 NINETY-SIX RAFTS

Work went on in feverish haste during those next few weeks and Oryol hummed like a beehive. The women sat day after day sewing uniforms for the Cossacks and those with especially gifted fingers were given the honour of embroidering the army's banners. Yermak had insisted on these banners when he made out the orders for the expedition. He wanted to impress the Czar's future subjects.

In the bakeries mounds of dough were set to rise for all the bread and biscuit required. Stacks of oats were ground into meal, which was then baked crisp and brown in the traditional manner. The Stroganov boat-builders were given precise instructions from Yermak himself, for he knew exactly what type of raft was most suitable to launch an attack on Kuchum Khan's kingdom.

Yermak appeared to be everywhere at once. He seemed to take no rest at all. One moment he was visiting the flour mills; the next he was with the gunsmiths, who were instructing the Cossacks in the use of the harquebus. These hardened warriors enjoyed their target practice immensely. So far they had relied on sabres, daggers and axes when they went into battle, but now they would use powder and shot, and they were as delighted as children at the crack of the guns and how they would startle the unsophisticated heathen.

The Cossacks were bursting with enthusiasm. They had been told just what lay ahead and what were Yermak's plans. Everyone approved the general design, but the Captains were not happy at waging a campaign without horses. They could not visualize a Cossack army on rafts. Yermak worked hard to convince them that he was right, just as Maxim Stroganov had won him over in turn. But they would not feel really happy until they were in the saddle again, on the steeds supplied by Kuchum Khan's stables.

One evening Yermak returned home to find Mitya waiting for him.

'Why have you come?' asked Yermak.

'It's about the wounded.'

'I thought they were getting on quite well. The doctor sees to them every day and I'm told you have become quite a useful assistant to him.'

Mitya flushed a little.

'I try to help,' he said diffidently, 'but that is not why I came. I have been thinking that if we are going to fight again, there will be more injured and I talked to the doctor and he thinks it is a good idea.'

'What is a good idea?'

'If we take some healing powders and ointments and bandages for the wounded with us in our kit. I know which are the most important things.'

'Do you? But who will attend to the wounded, who will use this equipment?'

'I thought I might. Believe me, Yermak, many of the injured do not need to die.'

Yermak did not reply at once. He looked at Mitya and seized him affectionately by his short beard, lifting the boy's face to his own. 'Do you want me to speak to Maxim Stroganov about it, you ointment-mixer, you pounder of pills?'

'Yes, Yermak. Tomorrow would be a good day. The doctor is going to speak to him, too.'

'What's this? A conspiracy? It looks as if the pair of you have been working hand in glove! But perhaps you are right. Perhaps it is a good idea to carry these things, as you suggest.'

During these weeks of preparation, Feodor Masupov returned to Oryol. He brought good news from Moscow. An Imperial messenger had accompanied him most of the way and then carried on to Kankor. He had a letter with him addressed to Nikita Stroganov and it carried a black seal. A black seal! Maxim knew what that meant. Money and troops from Kankor would soon be on their way.

He proved right.

The troops from Solvychegodsk arrived at the agreed time, too, and old Semyon actually accompanied them. He examined all the preparations meticulously, and in the evening he talked things over with those concerned: his nephew, Yermak and the Cossack Captains. He screwed up that left eye of his as Yermak explained his plans, and now and again he squinted at the map, and pointed his finger as Yermak referred to some place or other.

'Hm,' muttered Semyon into his beard. 'It will be a splendid thing if you succeed in defeating Kuchum Khan and conquering Siberia for Russia. Your plan is bold and it has its merits. I can see that you are a good general. But remember that you are fighting a powerful enemy. Kuchum Khan is a descendant of the great Genghis Khan and you must never forget it. The Tartars are blindly devoted to his memory, down to the last man. The very name of Genghis Khan intoxicates them even to this day. To fight for him is not only their duty. It is their glory. They feel they must win.'

'I do not forget it, Semyon Stroganov, but there is another factor which is important, too. Not all Kuchum Khan's subjects are Tartars. Even at the foot of the Urals where his kingdom starts there are Voguls and Ostyaks. They are heathen and worship pagan gods, whilst Kuchum Khan is a Mohammedan and prays to Allah. So they are not a united people. They include many vassals and I am convinced they will pay their taxes as eagerly—or as reluctantly, if you prefer it—to us as to Kuchum. We are not worse masters than the Tartars. Then there is something else, too. We are coming with thunder and lightning in our hands, something that only the gods possess. Think of the effect that will have!'

'Your guns, you mean. But they cost a fortune, you know.'

'They will enable us to win.'

The Captains looked at Yermak with pride. They had known him for many years, but they had never seen him like this. The way his mind worked; the answers he had ready! What a Cossack he was! Why, he was—how could you describe him? A giant among men, a hero!

Maxim Stroganov sat at the table with a complacent expression and in his mind's eye he could see the rafts plying along the rivers marked on the map. But they were no longer laden with Cossack provisions; they were heaped high with furs.

For the first time Semyon Stroganov looked Yermak full in the face. 'You are not only a good general, you are not only a bold man, you are a thinker, you are . . .' Suddenly his two eyes bored through Yermak's face. 'Who are you, really?'

Yermak did not blink. 'I am Yermak Timofeyev.'

There was something in his voice that took one's breath away. For a moment it was deathly still in the room. Semyon did not take his eyes off Yermak.

Then Maxim spoke. 'Are you quite satisfied now with Yermak's plans, Uncle?'

But Semyon did not reply.

'Hm,' he mumbled, and his left eye drooped once more. 'Perhaps I am mistaken . . . There was someone at the Czar's Court long ago . . . you resemble him . . . No, I must be mistaken.'

* * *

The last evening in Oryol had arrived. The rafts and skiffs were laden and stood ready to sail along the Kama. The Cossacks gathered in the church for Mass. They stood together shoulder to shoulder and watched the candles on the altar which flickered silently whenever the priest bowed. Before the altar knelt the ensigns who carried the red silk banners for the priest to bless. As the flagstaffs swayed, the embroidered portraits of the saints smoothed or crumpled with every movement. The priest swung the censer for the last time, and the Cossacks went up to the altar one by one and kissed the cross which he held out to them.

Next day began the journey into Siberia.

The Cossacks marched eagerly down to the Kama and the citizens watched the great expedition as it got under way. The rafts were tied in pairs and there were ninety-six of them, each strongly built and designed to take eight or ten Cossacks with full pack. Each 'hundred' travelled together and they towed an extra raft for their provisions. These were packed in sacks and covered with tarpaulin to keep them dry. The gunpowder and shot were protected with special care.

On the first raft with Yermak and his men was a native Ostyak who had been a servant of the Stroganovs for many years past. He was to be the interpreter. The sky above them was a pale blue, and the countryside was changing from the lush green of summer into a dull autumnal olive and grey. On the rafts which carried the Captains of the hundreds flew the shining red banners. Everyone was in good heart. At last something was happening; at last the monotonous uneventful life was over. It had had its good side admittedly. There had been no shortage of food and Maxim Stroganov had looked after them well. But now they were off on an adventure; now the life they loved, the life of action, could begin again.

'Long live Yermak, our leader! Long live Yermak!'

The shout went up spontaneously as the current carried them away.

The Cossacks ware in a mood to fight and conquer, not only for themselves and the Stroganovs but also for Russia. That would bring them more than rich plunder, for the Czar's grace would be their reward. They would no longer need to hide away as outlaws. They would be respected throughout the land.

Confident, optimistic, their morale was as high as ever when they left the Kama and followed the course of the Chussovaya. The strenuous work started now, for they had to row the rafts upstream.

Dense swampy forests covered the banks on both sides of the river, but in the clearings they saw the houses of Russian settlers who came running out to see the Cossacks, full of awe and curiosity.

'Where are you going?' they asked.

'We are off to deal the heathen such a blow that they will never trouble your villages again.'

'God's blessing on you!' cried the settlers and hastened to bring out flagons of beer, a few eggs and fresh white bread.

The Chussovaya came to an end and flowed into the Serebranya. Ever onwards sailed the rafts and the going grew harder still. The mountains came within sight and the Cossacks observed that they were being spied on. When they made a halt or set up their camp for the night they often caught a glimpse of native scouts as they slunk away, only to reappear a few miles farther on.

'You had better look out, you heathen wretches, or you'll soon taste our steel,' cried the Cossacks, shaking their fists in anger.

They were eager to try out their new weapons but Yermak forbade it absolutely. The enemy would hear gunfire soon enough, he told them. Once they were over the 'Big Rocks', the Urals, then the shots would ring out to their hearts' content.

During the day they rowed their rafts until the sweat soaked their shirts. The mosquitoes pestered them as if it were still high summer, but the nights were perceptibly cooler and they could tell that autumn had come into its own. They ignored the golden-brown leaves on the trees, but they watched the numerous squirrels as they scurried past, taking their winter fodder to secret hiding-places. 'You are wasting your time,' they called to the squirrels. 'The trappers will soon be out hunting again and your labour will be in vain. You stupid creatures, don't you know nothing ever turns out the way you expect?'

The time came when things grew more difficult still. They had reached the foot of the Ural mountains and they had to carry their rafts bodily overland to the other side. Last winter, Yermak had discovered an excellent pass where the mountains were not too high, and he had worked out in advance how best they could transport all their stores and equipment over the top.

Two camps were pitched, one at the foot of the mountains and the other just below the summit on the far side of the range. Thus with tents at both points, food and the even more precious gunpowder and weapons would be protected from the rain.

Yermak and Ivan Koltso led the first contingent with half the tents. Yermak supervised the arrangements and when he was satisfied he left Ivan in charge, and returned to the lower camp. There he divided the men into small groups and told each one exactly what stores they must carry, until the flour and salt, the oats, biscuit and buckwheat, the guns and gunpowder were all accounted for. One by one the little bands climbed to the top and then came back for more. There was a constant coming-and-going.

Night brought only a few hours' sleep and at dawn everyone resumed the laborious transport once again. Yermak organized the loading-up below and Ivan Koltso disposed of the stores above. The other Captains went back and forth, supervising and helping.

At last they had nothing left to carry but the heavy rafts. They had to be taken to pieces and the Cossacks worked and swore till the mountains echoed and the men were not far from exhaustion.

'If only we had our horses with us,' they groaned. 'There they are, idling away in Oryol, while we have to work here till we drop! A Cossack without his horse is like a ship without water, a sail without a breeze.'

Their grumbling did not help them. They had to carry on and it was only when the whole camp was safely over the other side that they were allowed a whole day and a night to rest. Then Yermak pressed on with the descent. He had to find winter quarters behind stout walls before the onset of the cold weather. He knew that no one could survive a winter in Siberia under canvas and he knew, too, that the frost there strikes suddenly and hard.

So he sought a river which would carry them eastwards and they came to the Sharavlai. A fresh camp was pitched on its banks, and as soon as the tents were erected the timbers of the rafts were carried down first and assembled again. In that way the provisions could be loaded straight on to the rafts as the men carried the sacks down from the mountains.

Before they pushed off again Yermak collected his men and spoke to them.

'My brothers, we have already covered a difficult stretch of our journey, but so far we have been on Russian soil and among Russian people. We have seen only a few tribesmen of different nationality. Our next goal is the River Tura, and there Kuchum Khan's dominions begin. From now on we must be prepared to fight. Once we take to the river, there can be no going back. We are heading east and we shall return only when we have conquered Siberia.'

'Bravo!' roared Ivan Koltso, and Yakob Michailov shouted: 'We shall win!' 'Death to Kuchum Khan!' yelled Nikita Pan, and

Matvei Meshcherak with the red face and the lumpy nose cried, 'We will smash them as we did Beguli and his army!'

'God be with us!' said Yermak, and in good heart the whole company climbed on to the rafts.

Four days later they entered the waters of the Tura. They were in the kingdom of Kuchum Khan.

15 A TOWN IN FLAMES

From the rafts, the Cossacks kept a constant watch on the shores. To their left the ground was flat, with thick forests stretching away into the distance. The right bank was rocky and rose steeply out of the water into sheer cliff.

Wretched tents were pitched on the stony verges of the river. Behind them were fields with horses grazing and a few sheep here and there. Dogs nosed in and out among the other livestock. As soon as the inhabitants of these dirty little hamlets caught sight of the rafts and the men on them, they ran away shrieking and hid themselves. Sometimes the Cossacks saw troops of horsemen who followed their movements for quite some time and then disappeared into the forests.

'I have a feeling that we shall soon be making the acquaintance of these pagans,' said Boris as he watched a bunch of riders vanishing between the trees.

'I'm not really worried about the left bank,' answered Mitya nonchalantly chewing away at a crust of bread. 'I am more concerned with the other side. We can see people coming out of the forests, but what is happening on those cliff-tops no one can guess.'

'You are quite right,' conceded Boris and henceforth he, too, kept his eyes glued to the right shore.

The river grew broader now and Yermak insisted that the rafts must be kept to the middle of the stream.

'The Chieftain thinks that there's something in the wind, too,' Boris started again. 'He has hardly slept for days.'

But nothing happened. They ate their oatmeal, they drew water from the river, they dragged nets behind them and when they hauled them in there was always a sizeable catch. 'It's good water,' said the Cossacks and laughed. The shimmering silvery bodies made their mouths water and they looked forward to the next meal. 'Baked fish with salt is much better than this eternal oatmeal.'

It was the sixth day of their voyage along the Tura and they had made good progress. The cold, golden morning was just emerging from the horizon.

Boris was already awake and he tickled Mitya under the nose with a fish bone. Mitya, who had been fast asleep, hit out clumsily as he woke up. Boris's hearty laughter soon made him wide awake.

'Breakfast for you!' shouted Boris and threw the bone in Mitya's face.

'Beast!' said Mitya and flung it into the river. Then he bent down quickly and, scooping up a good handful of water, he flung it in Boris's face. Yermak who was standing fore, turned round to see what Boris was making such a fuss about. He smiled to himself and saw that the other men were laughing and doing the same. Soon there was a cheerful battle in progress with everyone trying to splash everyone else. They're a good crew, he thought; you can do something with men like these. They were all bursting with health and energy and when he looked at the Stroganov militia who were split up among the various rafts he could not complain about them either. They fitted in well with the Cossacks and they had something to fight for. If the campaign were successful, they would be given their freedom.

'That's enough!' cried Yermak presently as the splashing got out of hand and the raft began to sway dangerously. He turned back to watch the course of the Tura.

According to his calculations they must have reached the territory held by Yepancha, a vassal prince of Kuchum Khan's. What would he do? Yermak kept the rafts one close behind the other, and the oars were ready. Ever and again Yermak's eyes scanned the steep right bank. Suddenly he seemed to detect a movement among the rocks. Yes, there they were! A long row of tall fur caps could be seen along the cliff-top.

'Alarm!' Yermak's instantaneous cry echoed loud across the water. 'The rowers to their oars! The rest to the guns!'

But before his orders could reach the last raft a shower of arrows rained down on the Cossacks.

'Steer to the left!' shouted Yermak. 'And row now for all you're worth!'

The Voguls who appeared along the rocks covered the whole length of the rafts. They seemed to possess only head and arms. With incomparable agility they spanned their bows, let fly an arrow, slipped in another one which they held ready between their teeth, shot once more and disappeared. At once a fresh row of heads popped up in their place. A hail of arrows descended from the heights. They poured into the water, stuck in the timber of the rafts, hit the provision sacks and struck among the men.

The Cossacks recovered from their surprise. Just as they had practised in Oryol, they lifted their heavy harquebuses, loaded them and fired.

The mysterious crack rent the stillness. It broke against the rocks and came echoing back. They loaded once more, lit the fuses and again the shots went thundering up to the enemy on the rocks. Here and there a native was hit and rolled right over the rocks and into the river with a splash.

'You need a bath, you dirty infidel!' shouted Ivan Koltso as the water spurted up round his raft, and he loaded for the third time. When he lifted his gun to take a sight, there was not a single target to aim at. It was the same the whole length of the flotilla. Not an arrow descended, not a head showed itself. The Cossacks looked up in amazement.

Then a great rejoicing broke out among them. The first skirmish had gone in their favour. It was a good beginning and they hoped that the heathen would report it fully to Kuchum Khan. His turn would be next.

Ivan Koltso manoeuvred his raft alongside Yermak's, which still held the lead.

'Brother,' he cried and leapt across to embrace his friend. 'Those guns were the best idea you ever had.'

'They will help us to bring victory, Ivan. What were your losses?'

'One man was killed and two are wounded.'

'What about Nikita and Matvei?'

'Nothing much. No one killed, a few injured.'

'Good. Then take Mitya with you when he has finished here.'

Mitya had thrown open the wooden box in which he had packed his bandages and healing medicaments. He came to the first Cossack who had an arrow stuck in his shoulder. Mitya's hands were trembling. He gave a cautious tug and the Cossack screamed aloud and pushed Mitya away with his good arm. Mitya made a sign to Boris to kneel on the healthy arm and keep it down.

Mitya knew that he must follow the doctor's advice. 'You must close your ears, my boy. Always remember you must often cause pain before you can help.' It was well and truly said, but when it came to putting it into practice, it was not so easy.

'Keep still, brother,' said Mitya firmly. Then he gave one strong tug and pulled out the arrow.

The man gave a moan behind clenched teeth.

'The worst is over, brother. The pain will soon grow less.' He bandaged the wound and then leapt across to Ivan Koltso's raft.

'Mitya, come here first,' came a call from the next raft.

The Cossacks beckoned to him. He sprang again on to another raft which had glided alongside. The men were crowding round a figure lying on the raft. They stood aside as Mitya approached. He looked at the wounded man and started in alarm.

'You don't think I can work miracles, do you?' he said humbly. 'I don't know much about these things, but not even Doctor Ivan himself could help this poor devil.'

'Can't you remove the arrow at least? Perhaps it would help his breathing. Or it might put him out of his pain quicker.'

'I don't know,' Mitya shrugged his shoulders. 'It can't do him any more harm, but it will cause him terrible pain if I wrench it out.' He bent over the wounded man again, but he knew he could do nothing. 'It's best to leave him alone,' he said to the Cossack who had called him over. 'He is unconscious. Let him remain so.' Mitya saw the other man was grey in the face. 'Is he your friend?' he asked, and paused for a moment.

'He is my son,' replied the other man, and knelt down by the side of the dying youth.

Ivan Koltso rowed slowly upstream and Mitya jumped from one raft to the other, carrying his wooden box with him. He needed only to bandage now, for the Cossacks had removed the arrows themselves. Then once again he bent down to a man, whose staring eyes no longer recognized him. 'The steppe is so beautiful,' he whispered, 'see how far it stretches. The sun is shining but the breeze is cool.'

Mitya stood up. He felt his gorge rising. 'I can't bear it any longer,' he thought. 'If I have to stand that all the time . . . I shall do it today, but never again.' Then a shout from the next raft brought him back to the present and he sprang across once more.

'Look at this! A neat piece of work, isn't it?' cried the men and they showed him a Cossack with an arrow straight through his outer ear.

The man had a pockmarked face, a bald head and a thick ginger beard. He stood there with his hands clasped over his bloodstained tunic grinning broadly and basking in admiration from all sides. He would not dream of pulling out the arrow and he pushed Mitya aside with his big coarse hands.

'I shall keep this ear-ring as long as it pleases me, and I don't need you to pull it out either, laddie.'

Mitya had to join in the laughter in spite of his surprise. The others all cheered and stepped aside to that Mitya could leap to the next raft, and so he went on until he was back with Ivan Koltso's hundred.

When he had finished and returned to Yermak's raft the noise grew louder along the whole flotilla.

'Huzza for Yermak! Three cheers for our Chieftain who gave us guns! As long as Yermak leads us we shall conquer.'

Yermak looked at his men.

'The guns are from the Stroganovs,' he called, and refused to take credit for them. 'And don't feel too sure of yourselves yet. You don't know where the enemy is lurking.'

But the Cossacks were too excited to listen.

'Let them come. We shall mow them down with powder and shot.'

'You'll have to go carefully with it, brothers. We have only limited supplies.'

Mitya sat down near him.

'How are the wounded men?'

'They're all right, Yermak,' he said, a little uncertainly. 'At least, as far as I can tell.'

Yermak clapped him on the shoulder. 'I know I can rely on you, Mitya.'

Then Mitya forgot all about his revulsion at the sight of the terrible wounds, for the man he admired more than anyone else had shown confidence in him. He could not speak for a moment. To hide his emotion he changed the subject quickly. 'Where's your cap, Yermak?' he asked and then blushed furiously at such a silly question.

'My cap?' laughed Yermak. 'Have I lost it?' He looked round. 'Ah, here it is behind me. I had better put it to rights.' Mitya's eyes stared in horror. There were two arrows stuck in the cap.

'They are good shots,' said Yermak placidly. The other Cossacks fell silent. They were all thinking the same thing.

'The hell-hounds shall pay for it!' came one voice.

'A plague on the villains!' cried another.

Yermak threw the arrows into the water. 'Yes, they shall pay for it,' he said coolly.

Towards evening they saw an encampment in the distance. It consisted mainly of big round tents known as *yurtas*. They were pitched close together and there were many of them. Yermak gave orders to drop anchor and he summoned his Captains to him.

'Before us lies the township of Turinsk,' he said, pointing to the right. 'This is where Prince Yepancha lives, the one who greeted us so charmingly this morning.'

'He had better look out,' said Yakob Michailov. 'We have a debt to pay.'

'Yes, we have,' nodded Yermak. 'We shall wait for darkness and then close in. Nikita, you will remain with your hundred and guard the rafts. If anyone approaches you must strike—and give no quarter.'

'Very well.'

'The rest of us will attack Turinsk from the right. We have no horses, so we shall have to wait until nightfall. Then we must move swiftly in order to reach the town before the watch can give the alarm. And we must get Yepancha dead or alive. I don't care which, but get him we must.'

The red-faced Matvei Meshcherak glanced across at Yermak. 'Would it help if I took care of the sentries?'

Yermak looked at him appraisingly. 'Yes it would, provided you can make a neat job of it.'

'Well, I'm damned!' exploded Matvei indignantly. 'Haven't you always been able to rely on me? Have I ever let you down?'

'I did not say you had. But you must remember that they are expecting us. They know perfectly well that we shall seek revenge and the guards will be keeping a sharp look-out. How many men do you need?'

Matvei thought for a moment. 'Twenty will do, but I'd prefer them all from my own hundred. I don't know the others well enough.'

'Very well, I shall be counting on you. The rest of us will be there when the moon rises over the forest. I will vouch for that. The password is "Kuchum Khan". We have one thing in our favour. Yepancha will not expect a battle before daylight. We must exploit our advantage to the full.'

When dusk fell Meshcherak and twenty of his Cossacks rowed towards the bank. Silently they disappeared among the reeds.

Matvei's raft was towed back and roped to Yermak's. Then the whole flotilla drifted farther down the Tura.

They steered close to the right bank and when they found a suitable place for landing Yermak called a halt. One raft was moored as near as possible to the shore and then the first landing party crawled through the reeds and the undergrowth to the land. The rest followed from raft to raft, using the moored one as a bridge.

Meanwhile Matvei's little band had crept close to the town of Turinsk. Matvei climbed a tree and watched the sentry patrolling down to the river in a big semicircle. Matvei could see the town itself, humming with soldiers. Stone houses seemed to occupy the centre of the town and the largest one in the middle was probably the Prince's residence.

Matvei climbed down again and gave detailed instructions to his men. Then they edged closer still. Before every single movement they felt over the ground ahead so that not a single dry twig should betray them.

As the narrow sickle of the moon rose pale over the forest, Ivan Koltso saw a figure crawling on all fours through the undergrowth. He held his breath. The figure appeared not to have seen him and it was creeping towards the very tree behind which he had concealed himself. As it came close he lifted his battleaxe. The figure rose abruptly. 'Kuchum Khan,' it whispered, and 'Kuchum Khan,' replied Ivan, letting his axe drop.

Five paces farther another furtive figure joined Yermak. They, too, exchanged the password. Yermak could tell it was Matvei by his voice.

'Have you done it?' breathed Yermak softly.

'Yes, all's well,' and in the blue-black darkness, Yermak could just make out Matvei's familiar grin.

Yermak raised his arm and beckoned. All at once the forest came to life. The Cossacks had been crouching on the ground so far but now they jumped to their feet. As they came closer to the town, they fanned out into a circle. They reached the first tents and passed them unscathed. The advance party had already reached the inner core of houses as the rearguard were setting fire to the tents and *yurtas*. And by the light of the flames, the whole Cossack army invaded the town of Turinsk. Their battle-cries mingled with howls of rage from the Voguls, who had been taken completely by surprise. They did not know which way to flee, for there were Cossacks everywhere.

The night grew lighter as the flames flared high. When the tents were well alight they fired the wooden shacks, and in and out between the burning buildings the Cossacks attacked. Yermak with his hundred made for the house of stone in the centre and Ivan Koltso defended his rearguard, for Yepancha's warriors had come into action at last. But the Prince's personal bodyguard would not yield, so Yermak gave the order to shoot. At the sound of gunfire the heathen ran screaming as fast as they could and within seconds the door was deserted.

'Surrender, Yepancha!' shouted Yermak, raising his gun.

Nothing stirred within the house, which was completely surrounded by now. Shutters splintered under the blows of the axes, burning faggots were tossed inside and clouds of thick smoke poured forth. Through them came a hail of arrows. The Cossacks pressed themselves close against the walls. The arrows stopped and a man hurled himself out of a window, only to fall straight into Russian arms. Once again shots were heard but the only sound from the house was the fire crackling.

The battle was over. The Vogul survivors surrendered. Not a single house was left standing. The men assembled in the light of the conflagration, and after conferring with his Captains, Yermak decided that they would wait for daylight on the outskirts of the town.

Next day they captured a few horses which had fled to the forest in panic during the previous night. One squad went off to loot the huts in the neighbourhood, for they too belonged to Yepancha's subjects. Meanwhile the Cossacks buried their dead and there was more than enough for Mitya to do. Indeed, Boris had to help him, there were so many casualties.

The day dawned cold and hostile. A sharp north-easter whipped up the river, but the men cast their nets and brought in a heavy catch. They were glad at the prospect of a good hot meal, but Yermak was impatient. It was high time they were settled in their winter quarters. The frost could set in any day now and they must be away from the river by then.

The prisoners crouched together in the charcoaled remains of their town. Yermak used the native interpreter from Oryol to ask questions about the Prince. The captives did not reply, but shrugged their shoulders obstinately, although none of them dared to look at Yermak.

'I must know if Yepancha was killed or not during the fighting,' Yermak insisted through the native. Again there were sultry, defiant looks. Then Yermak picked one man at random from the huddle. His brown hair hung down his back in long plaits. He was broad-shouldered like his fellow citizens, but he hardly reached to Yermak's shoulder. Beneath his fur tunic showed a coarse grey gown. This was the usual clothing of the Voguls, and the women wove the cloth from the fibres of the stinging nettle when they had harvested them in the autumn.

The man followed Yermak reluctantly and the others behind him began to shout abuse. But the Cossacks lifted their swords menacingly and then there was silence again.

Yermak motioned to the interpreter to accompany them.

'Why haven't you a beard?' was his first question and the Vogul was so taken aback that he actually looked up for a moment. Astonishment was clearly visible in his eyes.

'None of us have beards, my lord,' translated the native.

'Why not? Doesn't the hair grow on your faces when you reach manhood?'

'Yes, of course, but we pluck the hairs out. A beard would freeze in the winter when we go hunting and it would get in the way when we creep through the woods.'

'Are you a good hunter?'

'Yes.'

'Why don't you look at me when you speak?'

'I am afraid. You have been sent by the Devil.'

'The Devil? Why do you say that?'

'You carry thunder and lightning with you.'

Yermak thought for a moment. Then he bent down to the prisoner and looked hard into his eyes.

'Thunder and lightning do not come from the Devil. The gods have given me these gifts. The gods, do you understand?'

The Vogul's eyes opened wide. He forgot his terror and his defiance.

'The gods have sent you?'

'Yes. That is so, so that I shall destroy Kuchum Khan, who is a heathen. I am not concerned with you and the people of your tribes. I have come to capture Kuchum Khan.'

The Vogul threw a sideways glance at Yermak from his dark deep-set eyes.

Yermak left him time to think things over.

'What animals do you hunt? Bears?'

'Yes.'

'Are there foxes here?'

'Plenty of them.'

'Sables?'

'Very many.'

'Is Yepancha still alive?' Yermak did not look at him.

'No, my lord. He escaped from the house, but he was killed. But his son . . .' The Vogul stopped abruptly.

'Winter will soon be here. Can you feel it?'

'Yes.'

'You would like to go hunting again, wouldn't you, and the other prisoners, too?'

The man's eyes lit up for a moment. 'Yepancha's son has fled,' he said dully and then turned his face away.

'Tell the others that they will be set free when we leave. But if you should pursue us, then thunder and lightning will strike you dead, every single one of you. Now go.'

Nikita Pan and Matvei Meshcherak faced Yermak, scarlet with indignation. 'You're going to let him go? Alive? Have you gone mad?'

'Have we come here as their benefactors or as conquerors?' challenged Yakob Michailov. 'We obeyed your orders. For a whole year we kept our hands off plunder in Oryol and now we want our reward.' Even Ivan Koltso looked as if he disapproved.

Yermak gazed calmly into the fire and warmed his frozen hands. 'What do you want—their nettle shirts? Or do you prefer their fur tunics? Their lice would probably enjoy a taste of Russian blood for a change.'

'We aren't joking, Yermak. On the Volga we always received ransom if we released prisoners.'

'And who is to pay it here, the wolves or the bears?' taunted Yermak, looking from one face to the other.

Ivan Koltso made a loyal attempt to smooth things over.

'Yermak,' he said, 'we know you always have good reason for your orders and I suppose there is one now. But we can't see what it is, so don't you think you had better explain?'

'We are not living by the Volga now,' said Yermak, blowing on his hands. 'We cannot make our own laws here and live by them. We have come to conquer an empire. Our prisoners are men who fought against us at the command of their overlord, but no one will lift a finger to save them now. The Prince is dead and Kuchum Khan is much too far away. He will not pay a ransom for them. Are we to feed them with our rations, until we have nothing left? If we spare these men and do not harm them the news will soon spread all round the countryside. That will serve us well, and not only for the time we have to spend in winter quarters. It will quickly become known that we have no quarrel with the natives, that we are out to destroy Kuchum Khan, who is not one of their tribe and who remains a stranger to them because he does not worship their gods. Don't you think that our clemency will stand us in good stead in our future battles? Brothers, trust me, I beg you. I will listen to your counsel at any time and take it when it is good, but on a campaign like this only one person can be leader and you have chosen me!'

'This campaign, this campaign!' grumbled Matvei, who always was one for banging his head against a brick wall. 'For whom is this precious campaign, anyway?'

'It is for Russia, Matvei,' said Yermak sternly. 'Don't forget why we had to leave the Volga.'

'Very well,' said the others. 'It shall be as you say.'

They turned and went away, but a little while later Ivan Koltso returned. He laid a hand on Yermak's arm. 'You have many thoughts which sound strange to us, Yermak, ideas which cannot penetrate our thick skulls. But one thing you should know. You can always count on me, no matter what happens and even if they all turn against you.'

Yermak nodded.

Next morning when the Cossacks returned to the rafts, the river banks were covered with a thin sheet of ice. A bitter wind blew in strong gusts. Yermak urged on the company in a great hurry. The rafts were pushed as quickly as possible into the middle of the Tura and the men had to row hard to combat the strength of the wind.

Yermak knew what had to be done. They travelled the whole day and the cold seemed to increase from hour to hour. Even by night the rowers knew no rest. The moon was visible only in tiny snatches and racing clouds covered its cold light.

Next day they saw on the right bank the remnants of old huts and houses and a few broken tent poles sticking up in the air. Yermak made a sign and the whole fleet steered for the bank. They had reached their winter quarters, the remains of an old Tartar town, Chinga Tura.

Half the Cossacks were set to unloading the rafts, while the others went into the nearby forests. They felled trees, cut off the branches and trimmed them into suitable lengths for log cabins. What was left of the stone houses was brought into use and it was not long before missing walls were replaced by thick lengths of timber.

The first few nights they had to spend under the open sky. They covered themselves with furs and crept close together although the cold grew more and more intense. These nights gave them an inkling of the severity of a Siberian winter. When they awoke in the morning after the third night, there was a thin layer of snow on their fur coverlets. They shook it off, spat on their hands and went to work with greater zeal than ever. As they could not build houses fast enough, they pitched their tents and covered them with thick layers of brushwood. Now the Cossack tents looked more like the native *yurtas*. When an armour plating of snow and ice enclosed the brushwood, the tents were kept even warmer.

The days were mainly clear, but snow fell every night, and blizzards sometimes lasted until almost noon. But the more the men had to do the higher their spirits rose. Once they had built the houses they erected a wooden palisade round the settlement and in the midst they heaped as much firewood as they could carry. As long as daylight lasted one could hear the blows of the axe felling timber.

They thought they had plenty of fuel for the days ahead, but they soon saw how necessary it was. The days grew shorter, the temperature dropped even more and the snowstorms grew more violent. Often in the morning the tents were so covered with snow that the Cossacks inside them and the ones in the huts had to shovel a path to find each other again.

When the days were clear they went hunting. The enforced inactivity had made them inventive. They designed traps and many of them carved arrows. The wild game grew hungry in the long bitter winter and roamed far and wide, so the hunters never came back empty-handed. They brought deer and hares, foxes and sables, and the daring ones roused the bears from their winter sleep and then killed them. The empty sacks were filled with pelts and meat was a welcome change from the monotony of their daily fare.

Mitya, who was sharing a cabin with the wounded soldiers, was one of the keenest hunters. The injured men were recovering and needed less and less attention, so he had plenty of time to wander through the dense forests with the others. He often thought of his father during these weeks and many things he had heard from his lips came back to him. Yermak often hunted with him and Boris and two or three of the others, and then it was not uncommon for them to speak of home. But invariably it was Yermak who would break off the conversation, and he did it so abruptly that the others thought he must have regretted starting it.

Nevertheless, Mitya's thoughts were usually far from Chinga Tura, and when night came distance dissolved beneath the cloak of darkness. There were times when he imagined the snoring in the corner must be coming from his father Nikolai as he lay by the stove. Did he often think of his son? Was he angry with him for running away? No, not that. But he would be waiting for his return day by day and night by night. Perhaps Irina went to see him sometimes. Irina! Mitya could see her still as she let him take back his promise. There were tears in her eyes, but she had sobbed them back angrily. 'Dearest Irina,' thought Mitya and passed a hand over his face. His fingers lingered over his beard which was now thick and dark. He had had no beard at all when he went away. And then it occurred to him that Irina must be older too. Why it was almost two years since he had gone and Irina was fifteen now. She would wear a kerchief over her hair like her mother and she would not go riding any more or watch the fishing. She would have to stay indoors and help with the cooking and the sewing. It was strange. He could not imagine her so domesticated.

Mitya lay quite still. The storm shook the walls of Chinga Tura, but for Mitya they might have been the door and the shutters of his father's old hut rattling in the wind. The wolves came prowling round the wooden palisade and their long-drawn howls sounded through the tempest. But at home, too, there were wolves prowling round the village in winter. He saw Grivka's eyes before him when they flashed across the darkness into the living-room. And suddenly Mitya remembered fragments of what Irina had told him, how Yermak had spoken of the wolves that first night he had met him at Vassili Metyanov's. 'I would put my hands round its neck and I would squeeze and squeeze.' Then he had added: 'You couldn't do it, Vassili, but I could.' Mitya propped himself up on his elbow. Why did Yermak want to strangle a wolf? Why just that? It was strange to think that he alone among the Cossacks knew who Yermak really was. None of the others had any idea. But they certainly would not find out from Mitya.

These winter months showed how right Yermak had been to treat the Voguls as he did. One day a string of eight light sledges approached Chinga Tura drawn by a team of strong dogs. Each sledge had a man in it and Yermak went out to meet them. He called for the interpreter from Oryol, and he ordered the Cossacks, who had also come hurrying out, to sheathe their swords.

'You don't think they're going to attack us, do you?' he laughed, and shook his head.

As the sledges came closer the heavily swathed figures got out and walked towards the Cossacks warily.

'Ask them what they want,' said Yermak.

'They want to take an oath of allegiance,' the interpreter told him when he had spoken to the men. 'They are the elders of their clans. They have brought presents with them.'

'Tell them to come into the house,' said Yermak and strode on ahead.

The men unloaded furs from their sledges and laid them on the floor at Yermak's feet. Then they themselves knelt in submission.

'Tell them that I thank them for their gifts and that I will be their friend on certain conditions. They must swear that they will offer loyalty to no other lord, and that they will pay me tribute as the viceroy of the Czar of all the Russias who has sent me here.'

'My lord,' said the interpreter. 'They want to know who is the Czar of all the Russias.'

'Tell them that he is my sovereign and theirs. From him have I received thunder and lightning, and if they will take the oath of allegiance they must kiss my sword.'

'Yes, my lord, they will,' the interpreter informed him.

Then Yermak drew his sabre, and each man placed his right hand in it and touched the blade with his lips.

Next day the Voguls went away again.

16 THE STARS FORETELL

Winter rules Siberia for many months. When the people in Moscow are already pushing their warm caps back from their foreheads and loosening their furs, when they blink joyfully into the sun as it warms the walls of their houses and the women need fewer logs for the stoves, Siberia is still buried under ice and snow.

Yet spring was in the air, too, even in Siberia. It nestled in the branches of the tall birch trees whose dull winter brown was bursting into glossy red. The snow slid from the fir trees with a thud, and beneath the ice, whose surface was riddled with small puddles, the river sucked and gurgled all day long.

The Cossacks grew impatient. Every day they stood on the banks of the Tura, asking each other how long they had still to wait before they could continue their campaign and subdue Kuchum Khan. Yermak ordered an inspection of the rafts and set the men to work repairing those that were damaged, and so the days passed a little more quickly.

In Isker, the capital of Siberia, preparations for the Festival of Spring were in full swing. Everywhere was excitement and bustle. Many people had come from the outlying districts either as spectators or to participate, for Kuchum Khan, their overlord, had been lavish with his invitations.

The soldiers were rehearsing for the tournaments and the various competitions. Some shot arrows at distant targets, others practised riding and horse-racing. Everyone wore their best clothes, loose mantles of silk in red, green or blue tied at the hips with a girdle, and over them the warm *chalat,* a broad stole of gaily-coloured cloth. On their shaven heads were embroidered skull caps to match their silken coats.

As well as the invited guests, many merchants had come to Isker, hoping to do good business with such crowds and all in holiday mood. They spread carpets for sale in the streets, they piled bales of cloth in tempting heaps and offered honey, rice and spices to the passers-by. People were clamouring for food and drink and a bed for the night at all the inns in the city.

With the pedlars came the fortune-tellers, too. They would prophesy the future from the stars or read people's hands for a few coins, but when they were asked into a prosperous tent or especially into a house their price for such intelligence rose considerably.

A group of men entered Isker by the west gate. Among the elegant Tartars, they were conspicuous in their trailing, bedraggled furs. One of them, whom they kept in their midst, seemed very young, more a boy than a man. He limped heavily and leaned on his companions.

'Can you tell us the way to the house of Kuchum Khan?' they asked one venerable Tartar. 'We have urgent business with the descendant of Genghis Khan whom Allah has blessed with such great wisdom.'

The man pointed up the hill. 'Can you see those tall masts where the green banners of the Prophet wave in the breeze? That is the Khan's palace.'

'Thank you,' said the boy, and he went on with the others.

The Tartar watched them go. 'I wonder who these wretched strangers are who come to our town in rags,' he muttered half aloud.

An astrologer who was squatting on the ground by the wall of the house overheard him. He clapped his hands to his swarthy face, closed his black eyes and shook his head with its soiled white turban.

'My lord, they bring evil tidings. The sun will never rise again over Kuchum Khan's kingdom, even if spring is here. It is sinking deeper and deeper, into darkness and blood.'

'Silence,' ordered the Tartar. 'How dare you bring such bad news to the land!'

'The stars, my lord, the stars have told me.'

'The stars!' was the contemptuous echo. 'Allah alone is almighty. He who bestowed such wisdom on our ruler will not allow him to be destroyed.'

Meanwhile the new-comers had reached the Khan's palace. The royal bodyguard barred the way, but when the youngster told him his name and why they had come he was conducted to an ante-room by one of the sentries. He was as tall and as massive as a tree trunk and he wore a light blue tunic with flowing white trousers. He held a mighty scimitar in front of the boy as they walked. At his word a servant disappeared into the interior of the house and in a while he came back and motioned to the boy to follow him.

He was shown into a large chamber which lay in twilight. There were thick, patterned carpets everywhere, on the floor, hanging like tapestries, and draped over the wide divans which lined the walls to left and right. In the middle of the wall at the far end of the room stood a low arm-chair and in it sat the ruler of Siberia, Kuchum Khan.

It was difficult to see his face in the dim light. Even a searching gaze could make out little more than the thick white eyebrows, a sparse grey moustache on the upper lip and a pointed chin which quivered a little.

The lad bowed low and murmured a timid greeting, but the sound of his own voice frightened him so much, he thought he must be shouting.

'Come nearer, stranger,' said Kuchum Khan and beckoned.

The boy straightened his back and limped a couple of steps closer. It was only then that he noticed there was another man present. Or had he just emerged from behind the hanging carpet? This man, too, gave him a sign to come closer and as the boy hesitated he gesticulated vigorously. The boy advanced another step and then stopped again. He inquired dumbly if he should approach nearer still and the man nodded. Now the boy could have touched the Khan with his hands if he had dared to do so.

Kuchum Khan's face bent over the lad and his eyes stared blankly.

'Sit down. Tell me who you are and where you have come from.'

'My name is Ubak and I am the son of your vassal Prince Yepancha, whose town lies on the River Tura.'

'Yes,' nodded Kuchum Khan. 'He is the head of the Vogul tribe and he has sworn an oath of fealty to me. What has happened?'

'My father is dead, mighty Khan. He was killed defending your kingdom.'

'Killed? By whom?'

'By a mighty army as strong as a wild beast. It is led by a man to whom the gods have given thunder and lightning as weapons. He travelled along the Tura on rafts which sail faster than the hurricane. His men are as powerful as bears and as savage as wolves. Whatever stands in their way they tear apart. But the man who leads them has let it be known that he is going to fight you, great Kuchum Khan, and that he will destroy your kingdom, for the glory of his master whom he calls the Czar of all the Russias.'

Kuchum Khan bent down lower still. 'How do you know all this?'

'I fought against them, and when we were defeated faithful

servants of my father's lent me their clothes as a disguise so that I could escape. But my leg is shattered. I lay for many months in a lonely hut to heal it. The man who leads your enemies let all the prisoners go free. From them I learnt what I had not seen and heard for myself. My aim was to get well quickly so that I could bring you the tidings.'

'I am grateful to you, even if you bring me bad news. Stay near me, Ubak. If I need you again I shall send for you.' He clapped his hands softly and a servant appeared who led the young Prince away.

When Kuchum Khan had heard the door close gently he turned to the man at his side.

'Are you still there, Tausan?' he asked. His eyes groped in the direction he thought was the right one.

'Yes, Kuchum Khan.'

'Step nearer.' The tired lids drooped over the slanting black eyes. 'You heard what the boy said. What do you think of this challenge?'

'Not so much that your kingdom is in any mortal danger, and not so little that you can allow this army to penetrate any deeper into your dominions.'

'You think we should fight, Tausan?' Kuchum leaned back in his armchair, his head sunk on his breast. He mused with his eyes closed and he did not open them when he spoke again. 'A strange army, to come by river, and without any horses. And they have come to conquer my realm, have they?' His lips twitched in scorn. 'This is a trivial affair to a man like you, Tausan, who have been my counsellor and my General since we both reached manhood. Ride forth today and summon my vassals. They can deal with this Russian army and smite the invader who dares to threaten my kingdom.'

'Yes, Kuchum Khan, I shall do what you command . . .'

By his voice, the Khan could tell that Tausan had not finished yet. He lifted his alert narrow face and rubbed the palm of his hand impatiently against his brocade cloak which was worked in bottle-green and gold.

'What else?' he asked and knitted his brows.

'How many Tartars will you give me?'

'Tartars? None. Why else have these petty princelings sworn their oaths of allegiance to me? Now is the time to prove their loyalty.' And his words cut short any further protest from his general.

'I will do your will.'

Kuchum Khan sat leaning forward, listening. Just as Tausan reached the door, he shot another question at him. 'What did Ubak mean when he said that the enemy had weapons of thunder and lightning?'

'I do not know, Kuchum Khan. Perhaps the battle was so hot that the fire of fear danced before the boy's eyes. Who knows?'

'You do not think that there is some magic in the hands of these invaders?'

'No, I do not. May I go now?'

'Yes. And prepare for the campaign.'

Tausan's face was contorted with bitterness. His hand rested involuntarily on the hilt of his dagger, but he did not dare to draw it. The skirt of his bright coat flapped persistently against the side of his boot which was made of soft leather. 'To wage war with vassals—whilst he keeps his Tartars for himself,' he muttered between clenched teeth. Then he left the place and made for his luxurious *yurta*.

In May, Yermak decided that it was time to advance. The days were warm and fruitful and new life surged forth from the over-long sleep of winter. From the thick forests came the musty smell of spring and the ancient trees awoke from their slumbers and stretched their creaking branches. Slowly the marshes came to life and the frogs' chorus grew louder each day. Wild ducks and grey geese nested in the undergrowth by the banks of the Tura. Eagles and falcons sailed across the green-blue dome of the sky.

The gay Cossack banners fluttered on the Captains' rafts in the windy gusts of a bright May morning. The Tura had overflowed its banks and its yellow waters carried the convoy along at a tearing pace. Every now and again the men broke into their old songs, they were so full of confidence and eagerness. Kuchum Khan and his dominions obsessed them. They thought of the fame and honour they were to win and of their triumphant return to Russia, laden with treasure.

With every hour the Tura grew wider and the helmsmen had difficulty in steering the right course. Two days after they had left Chinga Tura, they reached the point where the river flowed into the Tobol. The Tobol was a dirty, grey, featureless torrent as it roared along menacingly. The Cossacks had to use their oars to follow the right direction, for the current flowed northwards.

Yermak kept the boats close in to the right bank. He had seen tents and *yurtas* in the distance. His mission was to conquer

Siberia and to perform his task thoroughly, he must make every tribe take the oath of loyalty to Russia. This was especially important here in the heart of Kuchum Khan's kingdom, not far from the capital itself.

The Cossacks saw the village, too, and they rejoiced at the sight of it. For once, there was no forest behind into which the pagans could disappear and then, with familiar cunning, shoot arrows at the invaders. Behind this settlement the green plains stretched afar into the distance, almost as endless as the steppes they knew so well, and the bank was crowded with low bushes, again like the Volga at home. The Cossacks could hardly wait to land. The oarsmen rowed so fast that their faces were scarlet with effort. The others kept their eyes on the shore which came nearer with every stroke. The first raft went crackling into the sedge. The next one bumped into it so that it rocked and swayed and the third rammed the one ahead with a dull thud.

Yermak had warned his men that once they landed there must be no hesitation. The rafts must be cleared in rapid succession and only Nikita Pan's men remained behind to guard their transport.

Yermak and his hundred were now on firm soil, and Yakob Michailov was ashore, too. Matvei Meshcherak was snorting like a bear ready to bite, grumbling that the others were not moving fast enough. Ivan Koltso and his company brought up the rear.

In the village nothing stirred. The tents seemed deserted; yet newly built canoes lay by the water's edge. As the last of Ivan Koltso's men set foot on shore, the air was suddenly filled with the twang and singing of arrows. Next moment the Cossacks had dived to the ground and the advance party were scurrying back to the cover of the bushes. The hail of arrows was followed by the roar of battle-cries as the enemy broke out of the trampled undergrowth.

The Cossacks realized that they had fallen into an ambush. The heathen had let them march past the village and now another attack was hurled at them from the tents. One loud call drowned the screaming and shouting on all sides: 'Allah is great, and mighty is his Prophet Mohammed. He will lead us to victory or death!'

By this time the Cossacks' bewilderment had turned to fury. Yermak, who was in the van, threw fear of death to the winds. He planted his harquebus on Mitya's back as a stand, loaded it and fired. A searing flame shot out, followed by deafening thunder.

Boris's father, Igor, loaded, too. His breath rattled as he rested the gun on his own son. Again there was a flare of yellow and blue, with the angry crack of thunder behind it.

Another four or five shots were fired almost simultaneously and then the villagers had had enough. They started running away in all directions.

Yermak ordered the firing to stop and waited for a fresh attack. He had to go carefully with his ammunition and every shot must find its target. Still the Cossacks waited, but no target offered itself. Nothing happened. They could not credit it, but all was still. There was no one to be seen, not even in the village. Where had the people gone? If not for the arrows and a few men wounded, the assailants might have been ghosts.

Yermak jumped to his feet. 'Into the village,' he shouted. 'Come on, brothers, we must catch them there. They must be hiding.'

The whole army rushed for the village, roaring and yelling. They were almost there when they saw a group of men trying to escape from one of the *yurtas*. They wore the short coloured jerkins and the conical caps of the Tartars.

'Don't let them get away!' called Yermak. 'We must capture them.' He leapt towards the Tartars with such huge bounds that the others could hardly follow him. He reached the fugitives as they were about to swing themselves on to their horses.

'Surrender!' his voice boomed, so that their ears must have buzzed. 'Or else our thunder and lightning will be turned upon you and it will tear you to pieces.'

The Tartars reached for their swords and the eldest of them threw himself on Yermak. Yermak countered with his own sword, and took on the others who had come to the help of their leader.

By this time the Cossacks had arrived and the Tartars were overpowered. Yermak called for the interpreter.

'Who are you?' he asked the elderly man who had attacked him.

'I am a Tartar General.'

'Do all the Tartar Generals command such cowardly heathen?'

'You will find out for yourself if you come any farther in Kuchum Khan's dominions.'

'I doubt it, if all his commanders are as incompetent as those who fought me today,' retorted Yermak.

'Do not insult Tausan, Kuchum Khan's comrade in arms!'

'Oho!' said Yermak and he looked at his adversary from top to toe. 'So you are Tausan, are you?' His menacing tone altered at once and he stretched out both his hands.

'Had I known who stood before me, I should have been more courteous. I am Yermak Timofeyev, a General of the Czar of all the Russias. I have been sent to chase the usurper Kuchum Khan from the throne of Siberia, since he is not willing to keep the promises made by the rightful ruler Sultan Etiger, his predecessor.'

'I will not argue with you, for the victor is always right. Today you have conquered. Enjoy your triumph. Soon it will be Kuchum Khan's turn.'

'You are very sure of yourself. I would say a little too confident for a man in your situation.'

'I am not afraid of death.'

'Ready to die for the Prophet, I suppose. That is noble of you, Tausan. At least one person is prepared to perish for his faith. Not long ago your call rang out like the howl of the lone wolf of the steppes. But your army did not pay you much heed, it seems.'

'That was no army which I commanded. They were infidel rabble, just as you and your men are heathen, too, as far as we are concerned.'

'I like to hear a brave man speak, so I shall invite you to dine with me. Let us withdraw to one of the tents until the meal is ready.'

Yermak drew back the curtain which hung in front of the tent and ushered Tausan inside. It was better if the Tartars did not see too closely what was going on in the village, for Yermak knew what it would be like once his men were out for plunder, and there would be no one available to cook them a good meal for a while.

'Was this attack on us at Kuchum Khan's command or was it on your own initiative?' asked Yermak when they were all seated on the ground in the tent with Tausan opposite him. The Tartar's face was puzzled and wary. He guessed that Yermak wanted something from him, and if so silence was the wisest policy. But he was not quite sure of himself. Whenever Yermak looked at him imperiously, his hand travelled to his belt without thinking. But it was empty now.

'It was at Kuchum Khan's orders,' replied Tausan eventually, and as he spoke he was overcome with shame. That he, Tausan, should be a prisoner delivered into the hands of the infidels and all because Kuchum Kahn kept the Tartars for himself and expected him to fight with this cowardly mob! How could Kuchum have insulted him so!

Yermak seemed able to read his thoughts. 'Kuchum Khan cannot have much confidence in you,' he went on.

'That is not true, stranger. The opposite is correct.'

'Then his army must be a poor one.'

'Wait until the Tartars take the field against you! Then you will feel the power of the Khan.'

'I fear the Tartars as little as the Voguls and Votyaks who ran away just now.'

'But Kuchum is a descendant of Genghis Khan. When he gives the word an army will arise which will crush your warriors beneath them.'

'You do not frighten me,' said Yermak, playing with his sword which lay across his knees. 'These soldiers here are only the advance guard. A Russian army will follow us, thirty times as strong. What are the Tartars of your Khan to compare with them? Did you really think that we intended to conquer Siberia with this handful of men?'

Yermak could see that Tausan was impressed. 'Will you try to attack Isker and lay it waste?' he asked slowly .

'Kuchum Khan will force me to do so if he does not yield.' Yermak paused. 'Much blood will be spared if the Khan will surrender without a battle.'

'He will fight and all his Tartars with him. He will fight as befits a monarch of his race.'

'We shall not prove inferior, Tausan. I see that you defend your master although he has trampled your honour underfoot and made you fight with the scum of the earth. In that case, I shall release you. Go back to Kuchum Khan and bring him news of me. Perhaps you will be able to prevent bloodshed.'

Tausan sat there, his hands folded across his chest.

'Thank you for giving me my freedom.'

And that was all he said.

Between the two men stood the empty hearth with its charcoaled remains of a wood fire. Here was all the poverty of a typical Vogul hovel, dirty and ill lit, with a few skins lying on the ground. And here it was that they faced each other, two men who belonged to different peoples, each believing that he had right on his side. Each of them fought for a master who had disgraced and insulted him. They were enemies, yet they felt drawn to each other.

'You fight with good weapons,' said Tausan, staring hard at Yermak's sword. His words sounded grudging, as if he would have liked to swallow them again, but Yermak could hear the intense curiosity in his voice, his desire to find out something about those mysterious weapons which scattered the heathen like a flight of wild duck.

'Do you mean my thunder and lightning, Tausan? Shall I show

you what this fire-stick can do?' Yermak stood up, raised the curtain and called to a few of his men. He spoke to them for a moment and then told Tausan to follow him. They stepped out of the tent, and walked to an open space in the middle of the village where a few goats had been driven.

'As you have seen,' said Yermak, 'we do not need horses as you do. We can conquer with only our rafts and these.' He lifted a hand and gave a prearranged signal. There was a terrific crack so that Tausan recoiled involuntarily. The goats lay dead on the ground. 'Do you believe my words now, Tausan?'

Tausan did not answer. His jaws were working and his long narrow beard twitched at the corners of his mouth.

When he and Yermak had eaten a meal with the other Captains his horse was led in.

'Ride back to Isker and think about our conversation, Tausan.'

'I shall discuss it with Kuchum Khan.' He jerked the reins and galloped away.

When he was out of hearing Matvei let fly. 'I cannot agree to this any longer, Yermak. How could you release a General! Why, Kuchum Khan would have disgorged a high ransom for him. And you let him go as if he had come here on a pleasure visit. Do you know that five of the brothers have paid with their lives on his account?'

'Don't forget that we are waging a war, Matvei. Different considerations must apply.'

'That's all very well,' said Yakob Michailov, 'but Matvei is right. What booty have we taken so far? A few paltry skins, a handful of sheep and goats. Is that all there is to be?'

Yermak remained calm. 'We have not reached Isker yet and we still have to defeat Kuchum Khan. That victory will bring us loot in plenty, I have told you all along. Do you really think that Kuchum would have paid a ransom for Tausan? You can see how he values him by the rabble he gave him to fight us. The Khan has other surprises awaiting us, you can be sure.'

'You may be right,' said Nikita Pan. 'But all the same we should not have let Tausan go so cheaply.'

'Brothers, Kuchum Khan's army is ten times ours in number and any means is justified if he is misled about our numbers. Tausan was very much impressed by us and I let him go back to Isker so that he could pass on his information. Now stop hampering me with your childish greed and your petty little grumbles about plunder. Immensely more is at stake.'

'For whom?'

'For Russia, Matvei.'

'You can spare me that cant, thank you,' snorted Matvei and he moved away in disgust.

'You had better get us to Isker pretty quickly,' said Ivan, and Nikita and Yakob nodded agreement. 'The men are getting restive.'

'You say that as if we were out for a stroll. You must be prepared for hard fighting.'

Mitya was sitting with Boris by the fire which was slowly burning low. When they fed more wood into the glowing embers, the flames flared up brightly and their faces were lit up in the blaze and for a moment they looked frightened.

'Why don't you go and lie down, Mitya? I'm sure you have done all the bandaging that's necessary.'

'I can't sleep.'

'Why ever not? Haven't you worked hard enough?'

'That is what's keeping me awake.'

'You're a funny chap, Mitya. I fight as long as there's fighting to be done, three days and three nights if need be, but when we can rest I stretch out my legs wherever we may be and I'm off. You fight with the rest of us, then you see to the injured and still you don't want to go to sleep.'

'I'd like to, but I can't.'

'Why not?'

'There's so much to think about.'

'Thinking! You're always thinking. If you do your job properly, carry out your orders like a good soldier, there's no need to think.'

'That's just the point Boris. I don't know if I do carry out my orders like a good soldier. When I see the wounded, in pain, I keep thinking: Why don't I know more about ways and means to help them? And because I know so little I fly into a towering rage with the enemy who make our men suffer such agony.'

'There weren't so many wounded today,' said Boris, by way of excuse.

'No, but what about next time?'

'Yes, there's that, of course. But pain doesn't last for ever, you know, and after all, the injured are better off than the ones who were killed.'

'I keep thinking about them, too,' said Mitya. 'Tomorrow you and I will screw up our eyes in the bright sunshine and feel good. We'll talk about Kuchum Khan and how we're going to hack him to pieces. We'll argue about how much loot we shall take, and not one of us thinks that perhaps he won't be there to enjoy it. "I'll be there all right," we think. "I shan't be killed. The others, maybe, but not I." We dream and laugh and joke and share our rations and all the time at the back of our minds it's always the other fellow. And when the battle is over we are so pleased that it was someone else who paid with his life. I don't know how to describe it, but deep down inside there's a feeling of—well, triumph, I suppose. Hurrah, I'm still alive!'

'I disagree, Mitya. I'm very sorry for the comrades we have to bury.'

'I know, I know. I am, too. But our sorrow is always tempered with gladness that it's they who died, not we. Or am I wrong?'

'I don't know . . .'

'Whenever you want to get out of an argument you say: "I don't know". That's running away, Boris. You must be honest with yourself, even if you're ashamed of the conclusions you come to.'

'Well, this is the way I look at it. When all's said and done, it's the heathen who are responsible for the killing and I blame them. We who survive must avenge our dead and we must make their leaders pay for their crimes. I think Yermak is taking a big risk in introducing so many new customs. And now I'm going to sleep and you ought to do the same.' And with that, Boris stretched out full length and drew the fur cover right over his face.

Mitya poked about the glowing ashes with a twig. 'Boris is a decent fellow, I know, but . . . But what? He may be right. I'd better go to sleep as well.'

17 CRUMBLING WALLS AND SUMPTUOUS TENTS

Kuchum Khan lay on a broad divan. His eyes were covered with a veil, beneath which was a compress soaked in a concoction of herbs. He lay there, but he was ready to rise at any moment. The golden belt round his hips had not been loosened.

'Call the women, Mametkul; I want them to take this rubbish off my eyes,' he ordered impatiently as his hands groped blindly over his couch.

'It is not yet time, Father,' said Mametkul cautiously.

'Is it not?' Kuchum turned his head. 'Oh, if only it would help at least. But nothing does any good.'

'But, Father . . .'

'Be silent,' said Kuchum Khan sternly. 'It is the will of Allah that I should live in darkness. I must bow my head. But it is so hard. I know it is a sin to rebel in my heart, but I am not yet so weary of life that I can resign myself to a fate of perpetual night. And my people need me still. They need me in this hour more than ever.'

'I am here with you and my brother Alei as well. We shall defend your kingdom.'

'I know that you have the will and the courage, too. But you and Alei are not yet men. You were still little boys when we came to Siberia, and you have had no experience of warfare. Nor have you good counsellors to stand by your side. Tausan is a doddering greybeard now, and the thunder of the invaders, the cunning magic of the Russian General, has frightened him as much as the natives.'

'Are you angry with Tausan, Father?'

'Yes, I am, very angry. But you, my son, you will be strong and brave; you will be as bold as the stag who pierces his rivals with his antlers.'

Mametkul's face glowed with pride. He took his father's hand and pressed it.

'Thank you, Father. Let me set out now, at once. The Tartars trust me. They will fight as warriors have never fought before. And if they have to bite the invader's throat with their bare teeth, they will do it.'

‘Your hands are hot,’ said the Khan, ‘as hot as your head A man going into battle needs a cool head.’

‘I am young, Father. Cool heads are for men like Tausan.’

A smile appeared on that stern dynamic face. ‘You are my son,’ said Kuchum Khan with pride in his voice. ‘I cannot see you any longer, but I can hear you and my heart glows. But the battle must wait until we have conferred with the princes from the steppes.’

‘They ought to be here by now if they . . .’

‘They will come, my son. They all know what it means if Kuchum Khan sends them an arrow with a golden tip.’

Mametkul got to his feet. He paced up and down the great hall impatiently. ‘If only they were here,’ he said and his slim supple body in its sleeveless red-gold tunic rippled with the longing for action. The yellow skin of his face was overcast by a dark flush and his nerves were taut.

‘The friends who come the longest way will be the first to arrive,’ said the Khan.

‘You mean Gulai, the Nogai Prince?’

‘Yes, he and Prince Bardak and Prince Nemcha and also the tribes from the Baraba steppes and Prince Yanbysh. They will all come.’

‘Yes, yes, they will come,’ said Mametkul angrily, and he stretched his arms and shook his fists. ‘But when? There will never be a more favourable opportunity to strike the Russian invader than now, when they have landed on the banks of the Tobol. They have taken shelter there of necessity and the food supplies they brought with them are coming to an end. I must attack now. What is that?’ Mametkul turned and started as he heard the sound of a curtain being lifted.

One of the men from the town watch presented himself and bowed low.

‘I have to report that when we were on guard at the keep we saw a numerous army approaching from the south. They were riding swift horses and veiled in a cloud of dust.’

‘Our friends are coming. Our brothers in arms have not abandoned us in our hour of need!’ Kuchum Khan sat up. Bandage and veil slipped from his eyes. He turned his head in the direction where he guessed his son to be. ‘Help me to my chair, my son,’ and the Crown Prince hastily gave him his arm. ‘What do the soothsayers say about the future?’

‘Do not ask now, Father—not now, when we have become so powerful and strong.’

Babassan was a former Tartar settlement, now abandoned and derelict. A few crumbling walls were all that remained, just enough to identify them as the remnants of a village. Here Yermak called a brief halt. This was so that the men could go fishing to eke out their supplies. Their own stores were down to a few sacks of oatmeal, rye flour and barley for making broth. And Isker lay ahead of them still, unconquered.

True, the capital was not so far away, but with every mile they covered, they had to be more cautious. The countryside was more thickly populated here and it was not safe to linger. Next day they must cover another stretch, so that they had hardly time to build a palisade. The rocks, a wide ditch and the ruins of a former citadel would have to suffice for their protection if they were attacked.

The night was impenetrably black. Continuous rain seeped from the low clouds as the Cossacks lay down to rest, saturating the greatcoats which covered them. They had kept their swords and daggers in their belts and they slept on their guns, their bodies shielding them from the wet. The few tents which had been erected were to shelter the gunpowder from the rain. The sentries were posted and all was quiet.

Yermak awoke from a restless sleep with a start. A nightmare which he could not remember troubled him as he rubbed his eyes. He listened into the darkness, but all he could hear was the soft, monotonous drip of the rain, the everlasting rustle of the leaves in the nearby forest, the call of the owl and the beat of its wings as it searched the ruins for its prey. All the same, the dream had roused Yermak so thoroughly that sleep was out of the question. He decided to inspect the guard.

At the first post he stumbled over the slumped body of one of his men who had fallen asleep on duty. Yermak shook him so roughly that the Cossack awoke immediately .

'Forgive me, Yermak,' he croaked in terror when he recognized the Chieftain. 'I had just finished a patrol and I don't think I dozed for more than a few seconds . . .'

'Do you think I'm a fool, man? Tell that to the Tartars when they come!'

He went on his way. The next sentinel was awake and so was the third, but the fourth had dropped off like the first one.

Yermak stayed with the guard. They talked of home, of the Volga, as they always did when night hid reality and the darkness allowed their dreams and yearnings to come into their own.

The night was turning grey and less forbidding when Yermak

broke off in the middle of a sentence. He listened and the men with him pricked their ears, too.

'Horses!' said Yermak. He threw himself down and put his ear to the ground. 'There are hundreds of them. It must be a whole army.' He jumped to his feet. 'Kuchum Khan is coming! The Tartars are here.' He raced back to the village with the men.

'Alarm! Sound the alarm!' he shouted. 'Kuchum Khan's army is coming.'

The sleepy Cossacks threw off their coats, jumped to their feet and seized their guns. Powder and shot were doled out hurriedly.

The hundreds assembled, taking what cover they could behind the palisade, the rocks and the crumbling walls.

It was not a moment too soon, for they were barely in position when a mighty army came hurtling towards them. There were Tartars everywhere, as far as the eye could see. As soon as the first ranks came within firing range, the shot whipped in and out among them; the guns went off with the crack of thunder, and those who were hit slid from the saddle. The first wave of the attack came to a standstill as the horses shied and collided with each other.

A fresh charge followed and as the enemy approached, the Cossacks took aim once more. The stricken fell on top of their comrades and a cry of fury arose from the Tartars. They had expected to overrun the invader with their massive superiority of numbers, but the mysterious weapons with which these strangers fought struck terror in their hearts. Mametkul tried to collect his troops like a man possessed, but no sooner had they reached the palisade than his front line was broken once again. More and more of his followers fell, hit by the shots the Russians fired. The effect of the Tartar arrows was insignificant and there was no chance of closing in on the ruined village.

When Yermak observed that the enemy were unsure of themselves he gave the order for a counter-attack. Ivan Koltso's hundred covered the forward surge of the others with their gunfire and the Cossack battle-cries together with the sound of the shooting rose to a deafening inferno. Firing their guns and roaring their war-cries, they fell on the enemy who closed their ranks to repel the charge. If there was a chance of crossing swords, the Tartars stood their ground, but whenever the shot swept through their ranks, they turned and ran away.

Yermak commanded the right flank with Ivan Koltso in charge on the left. For years they had followed this pattern and each knew that he could rely on the other's professional skill.

For hours the battle raged and Yermak realized that in spite of the enemy's enormous losses in dead and wounded they would not give in. Fresh reserves were always to hand to throw in against the Cossacks. Yermak knew that the time had come when his own men were growing weary and that he must force a decision. They, too, had suffered, with many injured and not a few killed. He had to take to the rafts to escape the Tartar hordes. He sent a soldier to Ivan Koltso with the following message.

'When I dip my banner, we must fight a retreat through Babassan and take to the rafts. Make sure that we carry all the wounded with us. Every man counts. Your hundred and mine will cover the others and be the last to embark.'

Mametkul soon saw through Yermak's plan. He incited his men to fight harder. He did not intend to let the enemy get away; he wanted to kill every man of them. But his intentions foundered on the flaming guns of the Cossacks, who drew nearer and nearer to the rafts minute by minute. And by the time the sun was past its zenith the whole Cossack army was safely in midstream floating down the Tobol.

Mametkul was fuming with anger. 'Why have we no river craft to pursue them? Why did we not build rafts like these infidels?'

Prince Gulai who had led the Nogai Tartars in support of Kuchum Khan, looked at Mametkul with a superior air. He did not care to take orders from the Crown Prince who was no more than a youth.

'Why do you hesitate, Mametkul? The Tobol flows into the Irtish, and Isker lies on its banks. Can't you see how the forces of the infidels have been reduced? Many of their rafts are empty as they tow them. If they anchor before the town of Isker, the timbers of their rafts will rot, or you can set them alight—just as you please.' He smiled and pointed to the Cossacks. 'But for the moment, how would it be if we harried them on their voyage? Many of our soldiers still have arrows left.'

'Yes, come on,' said Mametkul swiftly. 'We shall shoot at them until every quiver is empty.'

That was a voyage none of the Cossacks would easily forget. Evening would not come. The sky grew dull and rainy again, but still the afternoon stretched out into eternity. The current was strong and every raft which was forced too near the right bank was harassed by the Tartars, who rode along the bank, accompanying the rafts yard by yard. From behind every rock the arrows rained down upon the Russians.

When darkness fell at last all was quiet. The Cossacks could breathe again and after the long arduous battle, complete exhaustion set in. The baked oatmeal was shared out and each man took it in the hollow of his hand. Squatting on the rafts they leaned forward with open mouths, retching as they forced the cereal, dry as sawdust, down their reluctant throats. The fish they had caught had been left behind in Babassan and they could not cook broth, for they did not dare to land in the darkness. They moored off shore among the reeds. Then sitting back to back, they settled down to sleep.

Yermak was with his Captains. They had been silent for a long time until at last Yermak spoke. 'There are seven hundred and twenty of us left now,' he said quietly, 'and we still have the hardest task ahead. We have plenty of ammunition, but things will not be easy.'

'What we need is decent food,' said Nikita Pan.

'Don't say you would like to be back in Oryol!' laughed Ivan.

'We can't live on memories!' retorted Nikita. 'Broth, oatmeal and fish—I'm fed up with the sight of them.'

'So am I,' agreed Matvei. 'And my throat is so parched I shall lose my voice if it isn't lubricated with a sip of beer or spirits.'

'You think of nothing but stuffing yourselves,' Yermak rebuked them.

'Yermak,' said Yakob Michailov quietly. 'The others are quite right. We all need proper food and a few days' rest, too, so that the wounded can recover. Then you can lead us wherever you want.'

'We shall watch out when we sail again tomorrow,' Yermak promised them. 'According to the map which Maxim Stroganov gave me, it is not far now to the land of Prince Karacha. There we shall take whatever we need.'

Mitya put an arm under Boris's head and cradled him in his lap.

'Is that comfortable?'

'Yes.'

'Then try to sleep now.'

'Have you finished dressing the wounded?'

'It's too dark to see any more.'

'Are there many of them?'

'More than eighty.'

'Have you seen my father?'

'Yes. He's on guard on the provision raft behind.'

'Thank God. I saw someone on the ground as they were carrying me to the raft. It looked like my father and he did not move. I was frightened for him.'

'Does it still hurt?'

'Yes, the pain is terrible. Shall I be able to walk again?'

'I think so, and in any case, we shall soon have horses again. We can't live on these rafts for ever.'

'I'm sick of them. I say, Mitya, how many Tartars do you think there were?'

'Do you mean the size of their army or how many we killed?'

'Both.'

'Oh, there must have been a few thousand of them all told, I imagine, and I am sure they suffered ten times our casualties.'

'I'm glad about that. It makes the pain easier to bear.'

Mitya put a hand on Boris's shoulder.

'Go to sleep now and don't talk. The fever might come if you do.'

'I'm glad about that.' Mitya could hear his friend's voice still. 'Yes he is right. They were our enemies and their dead will never raise their swords against us again.'

'All the same,' Mitya's thoughts went on. 'I can't rejoice. When they charge, I don't think, I just hit out as hard as I can. But when I see them lying there afterwards, you can only tell by their clothes which were the enemy and which were our brothers.'

The first they saw of Prince Karacha's territory were the green meadows with horses dotted here and there, grazing peacefully. They could not take their eyes off them, so much did the scene remind them of home.

In the distance, beyond the paddocks, were small fields where the yellow-green crops stood high. Sheep searched for fodder between the low native huts. Presently they caught sight of the big roomy tents, the *yurtas,* with their vividly coloured curtains to screen the entrance. This was the town of Prince Karacha.

The Cossacks did not wait for night to fall. They anchored their rafts in a broad front along the river bank and while Yakob Michailov's hundred mounted guard, the others leapt ashore. The Prince came galloping towards them with a horde of his devoted followers, but it needed only a few shots to disperse them. Once 'thunder and lightning' broke loose among them, they turned their horses and fled.

The victors found everything they needed. Sheep were quickly slaughtered for meat, and to wash it down there were great casks of *koumis,* fermented mare's milk which was a staple drink of the Tartars. Not many of them went to bed sober that night. But the most wonderful sensation was sitting on horseback once more. After those long months on the rafts, nothing pleased them more than riding.

The wounded, too, got proper care. They lay in the big tents on thick padded cushions and Mitya tended them all. By now he was used to gaping, festering wounds, to disfigured faces and shattered limbs. He knew that most injuries looked worse than they were in fact. A time came when the patient could laugh again as his hands learned afresh how to hold a sword, even if the effort made him grit his teeth. When Mitya saw the wounded lift an arm which might otherwise have been for ever useless, when he saw men limping about who might never have walked again, he felt pleased. 'I played my part too,' he thought. 'At least they were not left to bleed to death on the battlefield, alone with their pain.'

But Boris still tossed back and forth in high fever and in the evening Mitya lay by his side. All through the night he would keep getting up to place a cool wet cloth round the hot sweaty forehead, or to pour a few drops of medicine into a beaker and put it to his friend's lips.

Karacha's tents contained many precious things: rings and bracelets, and furs heaped high; beaver, sable and squirrel. The Cossacks found lances, swords and daggers. There was room on the rafts for the precious booty and for the fresh food.

'How long will you stay here, Yermak?' asked Ivan Koltso one day.

'Until the whole army is ready to fight again. But we must not be idle meanwhile. I shall ride off tomorrow and find out where Kuchum Khan is waiting for us.'

'I expect it will be in Isker.'

Yermak spread out the map on his knees. 'Isker lies here to the east, on the banks of the Irtish. Kuchum will never let us get so close. Can you see this point where the Tobol flows into the Irtish? I think that this is the spot where he will assemble his army, but I want to make sure.'

'Let me come with you,' said Ivan.

'No, I want you to stay here and take charge. I shall take only the Votyak from Oryol as an interpreter. If we are not back in four days' time, you had better send someone to look for us.'

Next morning, while the camp still slept, Yermak and the Votyak mounted their horses and rode off at a sharp trot. They avoided the villages and made wide detours around them. They found it difficult to cover much ground, however, for there were often marshes blocking their path or dense forests. The land was flat, but in spite of it, one could not get a clear view of how it lay except in a few places. Their course was roughly parallel with that of the Tobol, whose rushing waters sometimes sounded near and sometimes far away. They used every inch of height they could find to survey the landscape.

In the late afternoon the pale dazzling sun melted into golden beams. As they slanted through the thick roof of ash and oak leaves the forest grew lighter for once, and they spurred on their horses. 'At last we can see where we are going,' thought Yermak. Through a gap in the trees they caught a glimpse of bright green meadows, when suddenly the Votyak reined in his horse alongside Yermak's.

'Stop, Master,' he called softly in an excited voice.

Yermak pulled up and looked at the native.

'I can hear Tartars, Master.' And he slipped like a shadow from his horse.

There was the rustle of branches being pushed aside and the Votyak vanished. Yermak listened. He could hear horses snuffling and the muffled tread of hoofs on soft soil. He tugged the horses away from the path, tied their reins together, jumped down and crept after the Votyak. He heard the cracking of twigs ahead and soon he had caught him up. The man was lying prone, parting the thick undergrowth to get a better view.

'Can you see them, Master?'

A Tartar camp lay before them. Their two-wheeled carts were arranged in a circle to fence in the horses and a few hastily-pitched tents. Camp-fires smoked; meat turned on the spit. In the centre stood a tent with a flag flying from a tall mast. It must belong to the Commander-in-chief.

Yermak made a sign to the Votyak, and they crawled back to the horses as silently as wolves. They made a wide detour round the Tartar camp, and swerved due east and then north again. When ever they came to a clearing they galloped swiftly, but soon the forest swallowed them up again.

Evening came and the summer night was warm and clear. The way grew more difficult and wherever they stopped they could hear the Tartars in the neighbourhood and the stamp of their horses' hoofs. Yermak let the native lead him. Towards midnight the forest thinned out again and the land was covered with thick brushwood. They stopped and listened. All was still. They rode on, guiding their horses cautiously over the marshy ground. The starlight was deceptive, however, and the brushwood came to an end sooner than they expected. Then the Votyak reined in once more and pointed ahead.

'Small fires,' he said softly. 'Many Tartars, Master, many . . .'

Suddenly a horse appeared before them with a figure crouching low in the saddle. Yermak was about to turn his horse away when the stranger sat up abruptly. What happened next was a matter of seconds. Yermak kicked his horse hard in the soft parts so that it bounded forward in alarm; then he swung himself up to stand on the saddle and struck. His dagger found its mark. There was a gurgle and the Tartar dropped to the ground. Yermak fell with him, but he picked himself up, leapt on his horse and trotted away as quietly as he could with the Votyak following close behind.

When they thought they were out of hearing they worked up to a gallop once more. They skirted the camp, tied the horses to a tree and crept across to the far side. At the edge of the camping site a fire was burning. Two Tartar sentries were on guard and they patrolled a short beat to left and right. After a while they returned and sat down together to have a chat.

Yermak and his companion listened to the shreds of conversation which drifted across in gusts of wind.

'What are they saying?' whispered Yermak.

'There are many thousands of Tartars waiting for you, Master. The Crown Prince Mametkul will lead them all to victory, they say . . . They are waiting for you by the banks of the Irtish. Kuchum himself will remain in Isker . . . He is building strong defences . . . He is praying to Allah for victory . . . They are sending all the women to Isker before the battle. But you will never get to Isker, Master. That is what Prince Yanbysh has said, and he is leading this contingent here. They say that they are frightened of your thunder.'

'What else?'

The Votyak put a finger across Yermak's lips. 'Siberian soothsayers have prophesied that evil will overtake Kuchum Khan . . . But the Crown Prince is clever, they say. He will save the kingdom for his blind father, and for himself too.'

For several hours Yermak lay in hiding with the Votyak, listening. When the sentries went on their patrols once more they slipped away. They found their horses and rode back to the Cossacks.

Yermak had discovered all he wanted to know and one of the first things he did on his return was to send for Mitya.

'How long do the wounded need to make them fit to fight again?'

'You must wait until the moon has changed again, Yermak, if you want them to have their old strength back.'

'A whole month?'

'Most of them were seriously injured, Yermak. Some of them have suffered great pain. And I don't know much about these things even now. Doctor Ivan from Oryol would have known better, but . . .'

'You have no need to reproach yourself, Mitya. You have done splendidly.' Mitya turned to go. As he raised the curtain of the tent Yermak called him back. 'Don't go. Sit down a moment.'

Mitya looked at Yermak in surprise. He sat down near him on a log of wood over which a rug had been draped.

'I wanted to tell you that I have never regretted taking you with me that day. But do you feel the same, I wonder?'

Mitya hesitated. Then he looked at Yermak frankly.

'Many things are different from the way I imagined them, Yermak—but I do not regret it either.'

'Do you often think of home?'

'How shall I put it? Sometimes it doesn't occur to me at all for weeks on end. Then suddenly the thought of home overwhelms me so fiercely that I hardly know where I am.'

'I wonder if they think of us, too, Mitya?'

A hot wave of emotion flooded Mitya's body. 'Us!' Yermak had said 'us'! And during these last few months, Mitya had often wondered if Yermak remembered his very existence!

'Oh yes, Yermak. They think about us very often. I know. I'm sure they talk about us, too.'

'When you go home again, Mitya, you must tell them everything. Even Granny, do you hear?'

'Why I? When you have slain Kuchum you will go back to Russia yourself. You will be welcome everywhere, in Moscow and the village, too.'

Yermak stared into space. His mouth twitched, half smiling, half in pain. 'Maybe,' he said, but it did not sound as if he meant it.

Suddenly Mitya felt afraid. It came over him so suddenly that it took him unawares. Suppose something happened to Yermak? Suppose he was one of those who remained on the battlefield one day? He always led the advance; he was always in the thick of the action.

Mitya had to speak. 'I cannot protect you, Yermak, I know,' he blurted out, 'but let me fight by your side, always.'

'But the brothers need you, Mitya.'

'That comes later. You come first, Yermak.'

'Very well,' he said.

As Mitya left the tent his fear for Yermak was still with him. It had never occurred to him before that Yermak might be killed. What would happen to them then? We would all perish, we would die here in Siberia and no one would ever return. I would never see my father again nor Irina, nor Vassili Metyanov . . .

Then Mitya realized that he was thinking only of himself. The possibility of Yermak's death had frightened him because it might affect his own future. He hadn't been thinking of Yermak at all. He felt ashamed of his selfishness.

18 JEWELS, BROCADE AND GOLD

The days still seemed long and flooded with sunshine when a cold wind blew a sudden blast across the land of Siberia, announcing the arrival of autumn and warning everyone that winter would follow soon.

Yermak knew that he must be in Isker before the cold weather started or else his whole conquest of Siberia would be in jeopardy. He needed stout winter quarters and they could be found nowhere else. His mind was made up. Booty and foodstuffs were piled on to the rafts and the voyage down the Tobol continued. When they reached the Irtish they would follow it, too, even if the enemy tried to bar their way. Yermak was well aware that his army was too weak to defend itself against Mametkul. He must take the initiative and attack.

For some distance the Cossack army travelled as a body. Then, one day, instead of the usual ten Cossacks on each raft there were only five, and Ivan Koltso and Nikita Pan had apparently disappeared. As far as the Tartar scouts were concerned, and Yermak did not doubt that they were being closely watched, all the rafts were still manned.

The Tobol grew broader and no doubt they would soon reach its mouth. Every Cossack knew that Mametkul's attack could come at any hour. More and more Tartars showed themselves wherever they looked.

Then the moment came and the first hail of arrows descended on the rafts. Yermak did not alter course.

'Let them shoot,' he said calmly. 'The river is so broad that it is still our ally.'

As suddenly as the shooting started it was over. A furious shout of rage went up from the bank. Yermak gave the order to land, for he knew that Ivan Koltso and Nikita Pan with their men had attacked the Tartars in a broad flanking action.

Yermak led a frontal attack with the rest of the men who were carrying the weapons the Tartars feared more than anything else. The Cossacks fired and the guns gave all they had to give.

The surprise was successful. The Tartars had been expecting their enemies from the river and had not suspected that they might charge from the land as well. With gunfire from both sides at once, a terrible confusion arose. 'God be with us!' shouted Yermak and stormed on at the head of his men. The Tartars fled from the terrible onslaught. The tiny Cossack army threw themselves on the superior enemy with a grand contempt for death.

It was not long before some of the Cossacks had captured Tartar horses and were threshing wildly with swords and axes. Matvei Meshcherak, thick-set as a bulldog but as agile as a cat for all that, was standing on the saddle of the nag he had won. He had dropped the reins and his tall fur cap had slipped to the back of his head. With his knife between his teeth, he charged a horde of Tartars who had encircled a smaller group of Cossacks. He hit out first right, then left, and the next moment he had swung round and dealt a blow behind him. Still he kept his footing, dancing with the rhythm of the horse's trot. Then he gave a marrow-shattering yell and made straight for the Tartars once more.

Yakob Michailov had the job of looking out for particularly stubborn resistance and of keeping up a steady fire when necessary to support the other attacks.

According to Yermak's plan, Koltso was to harry the enemy's flank and to try to drive them into the River Irtish. Yermak knew how Koltso would revel in such a task and he would do it magnificently. The long chain of his men did not yield an inch once. Ever and again Ivan would vanish from sight, but wherever the fighting was hottest he would reappear. He had seized a horse right at the beginning and he came to the aid of hard-pressed comrades like a man possessed.

Mitya was fighting close by Yermak's side, beating off Tartars whenever they tried to attack him personally. It was the first time Mitya had fought without inner revulsion, for he regarded it as his private duty to deep danger away from Yermak. When he saw that Yermak had managed to unhorse one Tartar, he did all he could to get a horse for himself, so that he could stay at Yermak's side.

One of the enemy had turned his horse to bar Yermak's way. Mitya reached for the stirrups; then, running close behind the horse, with one bound he sprang up behind the Tartar. His sword swung down on the yellow-brown neck, one strong push in the man's side and the horse was Mitya's.

A wild joy overtook him. It lent him strength such as he had never known before and gave him courage and resolution to trounce the enemy, so that he could ride over the fallen in cold blood. He knew why he was doing it. That was what had been wrong until now. He hit and stabbed because he had to guard Yermak. His head felt hot. His face glowed, his dark gold hair flew out like a pony's mane, his eyes sparkled. He stood on horseback like the others with his dagger between his teeth, and he was one of the most daring of them all. When he and Yermak stormed side by side, their enemies fled in terror. Mitya took no heed of their obstinacy. His sword was like a flail and with every blow he felt his arm growing in strength.

The onset of evening saw the end of the battle. The Crown Prince fled with the remnants of his vast army.

The Cossacks gathered together down by the river. Hastily they pitched their tents and lit camp fires. They collected their wounded and helped Mitya with his work, as the broth simmered in the cauldrons and the meat roasted on the spit.

'What price have we had to pay for our victory?' asked Yermak, who was sitting with his Captains near the fire.

'We don't know yet how many of the wounded will live,' said Koltso evasively.

'The Tartars fought bravely,' said Yakob Michailov.

'The Crown Prince led them well,' added Nikita Pan generously.

'And we hit them pretty hard, too,' growled Matvei.

'How many men did we lose?' persisted Yermak.

Then they told him.

Yermak got up and paced back and forth. One hundred and three killed and many wounded, too. And still they had not conquered Isker.

'We must not allow Mametkul much time. He will rally his army again in Isker and the next battle will be no easier than the one today. I should like us to move on tonight.'

'That is too dangerous,' said Ivan Koltso thoughtfully. 'I do not think that Mametkul mustered his full strength here today. Kuchum Khan must have a similar army waiting for us in Isker. You cannot challenge them with an army which has fought itself to the point of exhaustion.'

'I know that. But winter forces us. Farther into the countryside beyond Isker there are Tartar settlements which provide Kuchum Khan with food for the town. We shall have to make them supply us with bread and meat. Otherwise our Siberian campaign will be over, and next spring when the Tobol is in flood, it will carry our frozen corpses into the Irtish with it.'

It seemed as if Yermak had not only the fortune of war on his side but the weather favoured him, too. The autumn that year was uncommonly long and mild and at the beginning of October the Cossacks sailed their rafts up the Irtish. They moored them not far from Isker and landed boldly. There they found a village whose inhabitants had fled to the capital and they took up their quarters there.

Meanwhile, Isker was being fortified in a great hurry. A thick earthwork was thrown up round the wooden walls which enclosed the city and the Tartars manned it in great numbers.

But still Yermak waited. A handful of his men who had been wounded in the last battle were on the road to recovery. They were all men he had known for years, men he could rely on, who were equal to twenty of the others, whose daring inspired their comrades. It was worth waiting for them, for Yermak knew that this was the decisive batle, one in which all would be won—or lost.

The twenty-fourth of October 1582 was a cold damp day. Large wet snowflakes mingled with a fine drizzle and a biting north-easter blew across the land.

Yermak had taken his decision. Tomorrow morning he would lead his army into battle. The wind tugged at his tent as he sat there with his Captains and explained his plan of attack.

'As soon as it gets dark we will light our camp-fires and cook our supper as usual. Then the whole army will disperse gradually in ones and twos, so that the enemy will notice nothing. The fires will be kept alight as if nothing were happening, but one man will do to tend them all.

'Every man must know his position in advance. Ivan, you and your men will take the far left and Yakob the extreme right. You two will have the longest way to go and so you will start off first. But watch my camp-fire all the time. I shall keep it down to a glow, but presently you will see it flare up high, and that is the sign to move in close to the city's ramparts. Keep reminding the men that they must make no noise. It will be pitch dark tonight, and if we can take the enemy by surprise, we shall conquer.

'The signal for the assault is a shot, but that will not be until daybreak. Then no one must falter, no one must hang back. The Tartars must find themselves attacked from every side simultaneously. There you are, brothers, that is all. And let us hope that tomorrow evening we shall all be sitting safely in Isker.'

Yermak was alone again. He sat by the fire and stared into the embers, lost in thought. He put on very little wood and the fire burnt steadily. Sometimes a gust of wind made the flames spurt up; then they sank down again. The smoke worried Yermak's throat, but he suppressed a desire to cough.

'If we win,' he mused to himself, 'if we gain the day, we can leave behind for ever the shame of a brigand's life, the stigma of being an outlaw.' He laughed bitterly. 'I, who intended to remain an outlaw all my life, am now engaged in conquering an empire for the Czar whom I hate with all my soul. Conquest! A fine word! Yes, when robbery is committed at the order of the highest authority and on a large enough scale we call it conquest! Kuchum Khan conquered Siberia, although he had no right to it. And I shall do the same, although I have no right here either.

'Or have I? After all, Sultan Etiger was the lawful ruler and once he swore an oath of allegiance to the Czar. But what are these oaths worth? Tartars, pagans, Russians, they keep them or they break them, just as it suits their convenience. And each of us calls on his God and prays for victory because he believes he is better than his enemies and more fitted to rule. I wonder if the Almighty is ever embarassed by all these conflicting prayers! If he answers those of one side, it can only be at the expense of the other!

'And what is all the fighting for? For the sake of power, for better trading routes, for more markets where the sweet chink of money can be heard. It has always been like that and so it will go on. Four hundred years ago the hordes of Genghis Khan burst over the borders of Asia into Russia. And Mother Russia, good, patient Mother Russia, received them into the vast, unending steppes of the south. The Tartar flood flowed away and dried up. Some powerful tribes settled and patient Mother Russia, whom they had so ill-treated, tamed them gradually into subjection. And now it is Russia's turn to stretch out her hands, only the direction is reversed. It is we who are marching east.

'What did Maxim Stroganov tell me? That the Czar was looking for routes to India and China. Why not? These roads will be oiled with blood, for there's nothing like blood to make the money roll along smoothly. What else did Maxim say? That it was like that everywhere. Many new lands were being discovered and whoever got there first claimed them for his country. He told me about a brave sailor from Spain who had discovered a whole new continent less than a hundred years ago. He, too, was looking for a route to India and he found—what was its name now? Yes—America. He discovered America. But everything depends on the initiative of the few and their tenacity in carrying it through.

Maxim Stroganov paid me a compliment when he placed his confidence in me to carry out his plans. I am merely the Stroganov tool, as it were. Very well then. I shall show them that I am not such a poor instrument for their purpose. I gave Maxim Stroganov a promise. I shall stand by my word.'

The crack of a shot at daybreak had the Cossacks on their toes and ready. From every side they stormed the earthwork which they had surrounded during the night. But only the first impact took the Tartars by surprise. After all, they had been expecting an attack and preparing for it.

The rain of arrows was thicker than anything the Cossacks had experienced so far throughout the campaign. There seemed no end to them. The men sought cover in every hole and behind every stunted bush. If a head showed itself above the wall they fired their guns, but these targets were too elusive for them to hit many of them. There would be a moment's pause: then the arrows whizzed past once more. A mighty army must have been lying concealed behind the ramparts.

Here and there the Cossacks succeeded in breaching the wall and this spurred on the others, too. Defying death, they hurled themselves against the Tartars. The screams of rage behind the earthwork grew louder and louder as the gaps in it spread.

Nikita Pan's hundred was fighting hard at one side when a forest of lances sprang up out of a trench and a company of frenzied Tartars hurled their spears in a wild advance. At their head was a slim figure in a red tunic edged with white fur and his broad golden belt shone in the grey light of dawn.

'It must be Mametkul,' thought Yermak in a flash. Mametkul was leading his army in a counter-attack! There was little doubt about what it would mean if he succeeded. Inspired by their leader's example, spears appeared along the whole length of the walls. The Tartars were going over from defence to attack.

Here and there the Cossacks were beaten back, but not everywhere. There was hand-to-hand fighting all along the line. Yermak urged on one half of his hundred to storm the rampart. He had to stop the Tartars from breaking out at all costs. With the others, he attacked the bodyguard round the Crown Prince and the heaps of dead mounted on both sides. Yermak's mind was working fast. He had to find a way out of the dilemma. He knew that if he lost this battle, that would be the end. The tiny Cossack force could never overpower these mighty hordes in hand-to-hand fighting.

His last hopes were pinned on Ivan Koltso and Yakob Michailov. If they stormed the wall on both outlying flanks, Mametkul would have to divert his men to go to their aid. He would have to retreat. Yermak looked round. Near him he saw Boris and Mitya both striking hard and both had their backs free.

'Mitya,' shouted Yermak. 'Get through to Ivan Koltso and tell him he must stay by the wall. He must not try to come to our assistance here whatever may happen. And Boris, you find Michailov and tell him the same.'

The fighting was more bitter than ever. Yermak, whose great height towered above the others, struck out like a madman. He hewed the Tartars down as they came at him, no matter how many of them there were. The Cossacks' resistance built up round him all the time. Ever and again he managed to collect the scattered brethren into one group and to lead them. In blind rage they pressed nearer and nearer to the Prince. When they were quite close one Cossack appeared unexpectedly in the midst of the Tartar bodyguard. Like a spring he uncoiled against Mametkul himself and stabbed him with his sword: once, twice. As he raised his arm for the final blow, he was mown down. The Tartars had avenged their Prince.

The next few moments were utter confusion. A cry went up over the battlefield: 'The Crown Prince is wounded!'

Yermak tried to reach the Tartars who were bearing Mametkul away, but he could not penetrate their close formation. So he turned aside, gathered his Cossacks together for the last time and once more attacked the wall. And now he found virtually no resistance. The whole of that enormous army was in flight. The Tartars tried to hide behind the wooden city wall, but the Cossacks charged after them. This was no battle, but the hectic pursuit of a leaderless mob, with each man trying to save his skin.

With his clothes torn and head bleeding one rider dashed through the streets of Isker ahead of the fleeing troops. He spurred on his horse towards the palace of Kuchum Khan and there he alighted quickly. The guard stood aside to let him pass as he dashed breathlessly into the royal house.

'The battle is lost, Kuchum Khan; your army is fleeing. The soothsayers prophesied the truth,' he gasped when he reached the inner apartment which was hung with carpets.

'Where is Mametkul?' asked Kuchum Khan, his mouth trembling.

'Wounded or dead, I do not know which. You must flee,

Kuchum Khan. The infidels are coming.'

'You are the messenger of evil tidings, Tausan,' shrieked Kuchum Khan, losing all self-control. 'Collect the womenfolk; the wagons are ready. Our destination is the southern steppes.'

'You who know everything, great Khan, why has Allah punished you with such misfortune?'

'Be silent, Tausan. Do as I order. We have no time to lose.' He groped his way into the ante-room. 'Bring the horses,' he called aloud and waited tensely for the sound of trotting hoofs.

As the Cossacks came rushing through the town they found it deserted. With drawn swords they forced a way into the first houses. They were all empty. These were the simple dwellings of the slaves: bare mud floors, narrow pallet beds against the walls and a curtain dividing the women's quarters from the living-room.

Back they went into the street and discovered the bigger houses of the merchants and traders. They found warehouses from which they dragged out heaps of goods, bolts of cloth, rugs, golden bracelets, necklaces, weapons of fine workmanship and furs. Furs! They loaded themselves up with armfuls of what appeared to be most valuable, and ran out into the street. And so to the next house where they found golden plates, thicker carpets, more costly brocades. They dropped what they were carrying and clutched the latest plunder to them. And so it went on until they came to the palace of the Khan himself.

While the others were rummaging in the houses, Yermak had made straight for the palace. The thick carpets deadened his footsteps. He flung open the door to the living-quarters. There were carpets and divans, but nothing else. Behind him came a horde of Cossacks who slashed the walls with their swords. To their astonishment the walls yielded. Another room was hidden behind this one. It was small and dark but when their eyes got used to the dimness, they could make out long wooden chests.

They rushed for the coffers, but when they thrust back the lids there was nothing there. The first one was empty, and so were the next ones. The looters started cursing and swearing, but suddenly they stopped. Kuchum Khan could not take away all his treasure in such haste, and as Yermak came up behind them they discovered in the darkness a hoard of jewels as big as a man's fist. Some were as red as sunrise, others deep blue like a lake beneath a cloudless sky, or golden brown like honey, or green as the new leaves on the trees in spring. They saw golden chains, rings, clasps, belts and diadems. But their admiration soon gave way to their greed. Eager hands reached out to grasp the treasure.

'Leave everything where it is!' thundered Yermak. 'These jewels do not belong to us simply because we arrived here first. They belong to all the brothers. In any case, there is much more to be found if we take our time.'

But the Cossacks would not leave the treasure alone.

'I shall strike you as I struck the Tartars if you don't take your hands away!' And Yermak slammed down the lid.

Then they searched further and they found valuable clothing made of soft supple velvets, women's robes with rustling billowing folds, delicate gauze as fine as a spider's web. There were painted leather harnesses for the horses, blankets, lances and spears, and they found great vats in the store-rooms with salted meat and fish and barrels of *koumis*.

Yermak assembled his army in the open square in the centre of the town. There he stepped before them and he spoke.

'Brothers,' he began, 'we have entered Isker after a hard fight. Kuchum Khan has fled; his son was severely wounded and has been carried off by a few of his devoted servants. All that was left of his mighty army has been blown to the four winds. We have conquered Siberia and our banners are flying from the citadels. We must thank God for being with us, for not forsaking us at any time on the long way to this spot.'

Yermak knelt down on the trampled earth and all his Cossacks with him. He uttered aloud a simple prayer of thanks and his voice rang out over the square in the midst of the deserted town.

Then they rose to their feet and Yermak continued, 'Let us bury our brothers who did not live to see our victory. Every hundred must help with tending its own wounded. Mitya Nikolayev will tell you what to do.'

He allocated various houses to each hundred and arranged who was to keep guard along the wall. All at once a whisper flew along the Cossack ranks. It grew stronger and louder until one voice rose high above the murmuring.

'Long live Yermak, Yermak Timofeyev who has led us to victory! Huzzah for our Chieftain, the father of his men!'

More voices joined in, shouting the same words over and over again until the town rang with the cheering.

'Long live the new ruler of Siberia, Yermak Timofeyev!'

'Yermak Timofeyev!' they thundered. 'Prince of Siberia!'

And before Yermak knew what was happening, they had pushed towards him and carried him shoulder high into Kuchum Khan's palace.

'You must be out of your senses,' he protested. 'I am no prince. I am your Chieftain, but that's all.'

They would not listen to him. They bore him into the great hall and placed him on the Khan's chair. And then there was no holding or restraining them. The *koumis* barrels were prised open and they drank Yermak's health from anything they could find, goblets, dishes, even their own caps. Hunks of meat were stewing in the cauldrons and they stabbed at the biggest ones and ate them with the fat dripping down their beards. The heady *koumis* foamed and frothed and soon they began to dance and to sing. The foremost dancers sprang into the centre of the clapping, swaying circle. They flung off their greatcoats and stamped their feet. They whirled and spun and took flying leaps, clicking their heels in mid-air before they landed on the ground again. Their arms flew everywhere, behind their necks, across chest or hips, and as they danced they shouted aloud their fierce joy in living and twirled back into the circle again. Others leapt up to take their place, urged on by the singing which grew louder and livelier from moment to moment.

Mitya was standing at the entrance to a house watching the dancing from afar. He did not want to join in. For one thing he had never learnt these dances. For another, his hands were red with the blood of their comrades whom he had been tending. Many of those now lying in Tartar houses would never dance again, he knew. By now he had seen too often what happens when a man's face grows pale and grey. He could tell more or less at a glance who would live and who would die. And there were the others dancing and singing, and for many of them it was the merest luck that they could still do so.

Lord God, thought Mitya. What souls you have given us! At one moment we kill our fellow men and a few hours later we dance. We are like ravening wolves for plunder and yet during the battle we have only the simplest aim, to stay alive. We fight each other for the biggest piece of meat and a little while before we were satisfied with a handful of grain.

Mitya lowered his head. What kind of men are we? he asked himself as he drew a basin of hot water from a cauldron to wash a man's spintered leg. Perhaps I would be dancing, too, perhaps I would feel as gay as the others if only I did not have to see to all these ghastly wounds. I should never have undertaken this nursing. I ran away to see life, not death. If Irina knew she would say, 'There, what did I tell you? Everything is different from the way we imagine it.'

How did she know? Oh well, she was always the cleverer of the two of us. But she was right. And it occurred to him suddenly that he might see her again quite soon, now that Siberia had been conquered.

A great joy overwhelmed him. He would go home before long, perhaps when the new corn was sprouting in the fields, or when the honeysuckle was in blossom or when the ears of the yellow oats rustled in the breeze. He would go home and Irina would not recognize him because he had a beard and his long greatcoat and the tall fur hat which so altered his appearance. He would not disclose his identity at once, he would tease her a little first, the darling! And she would gape when he asked her: Did you look after Grivka for me, and what about old Nikolai, my father?

The voice of a wounded man brought Mitya back to earth. 'What would we do without you, Mitya? Your hands are as gentle as my mother's. God bless you, Mitya.'

Mitya did not know what to answer. He merely nodded and took the cauldron back to the fire. 'What would we do without you, Mitya?' That's what the man had said.

It was only as he repeated the words to himself that he realized what happiness they brought him. They rely on me, they believe in me, they need me. So it was a good thing I ran away. There was some point in it, after all.

His hands began to quiver, and the sadness which had troubled him as he entered the house was all forgotten.

19 SLEIGH-DOGS

The next morning dawned cold and dry. From the dark wooded plains which stretched behind Isker came the first breath of approaching winter. A rough wind came tearing among the timbers of the city walls, pushing its way through the weak places.

But it did not worry the Cossacks. They sat in warm houses with wooden bowls on their knees, waiting for the steaming broth to cool.

'I wonder what will happen next,' said Boris to his father.

'You'll see by and by,' said old Igor calmly.

'I suppose we'll go home?'

'When?'

'Now, of course,' said Boris.

'You must be mad. What do you think would happen if we left tomorrow?'

'Why? What would happen?'

'Kuchum Khan would come back immediately. No, it won't be such a quick business getting home. We will have to see the winter through here, you can be sure of that, my boy. How can we use our rafts when the rivers are icebound? No,' he repeated. 'We must be patient. And in any case, where is "home"?'

'By the Volga, where we came from.'

'Oh, Boris, Boris. Do you think we can just go back and resume our old lives? Even you must see that some things are over and done with, once you've turned your back on them. Do you really think that Yermak will become a highwayman again now that he has been a general?'

Yermak paced restlessly up and down Kuchum Khan's palace. He had just come in and he felt cramped in the dim, gloomy hall with the swaying tapestry walls. But even out of doors his main worry had not vanished: the problem of how to feed his army.

His army? Could one still call it an army? There were hardly five hundred of them left, including the wounded. A ridiculous handful when it came to conquering an empire, but a vast crowd when they had to be provided with food. He could give them no respite, although they had earned a rest. They must go fishing and he had sent them down to the river. But that was not enough. Any night now the hard cruel frost could set in and even fishing would become impossible. The stores left behind by the Tartars would be gobbled up in a few days.

Yermak had been up to the top of the watch-tower not long before and he had been able to see for miles over the countryside. Forests, nothing but forests. In one place he had caught sight of a green strip of land, but that was probably marsh. Hunting might help, and possibly they might recapture a horse or two which had dashed away during the fighting and could find its way into a cooking-pot, but that was not going to satisfy five hundred men a whole winter long.

'We must find some Tartar settlement to raid. Perhaps they did not all flee with Kuchum. But that means fresh fighting,' thought Yermak, still pacing up and down.

The next day was spent in organizing. The gunpowder was stored away carefully and the damaged rafts were pulled ashore for repair. There was widespread grumbling at the torn fishing-nets. 'There must be something in the water which gnaws them away,' they said and hunted everywhere for suitable materials to mend the holes. 'Tapestries, velvets, brocade in plenty,' they cursed, 'but not a bit of common yarn anywhere to mend a fishing-net.'

On the fourth day a heavy downpour set in at daybreak. The rain was cold and mixed with hail and it beat down hard on the town of Isker. The guard on duty at the eastern gate saw a group of men emerging from the forest, one man in the lead and three behind him. They hesitated before they dared to leave the cover of the trees. Then the leader took a few paces forward and when the others saw that nothing happened to him they followed. They carried no weapons except the knives in their belts and they wore long leather tunics below which one could see high boots. Their hair was black and shaggy. Only the leader wore a hood which was edged with fluffy white fur.

The three men had tightly-packed bundles on their shoulders. The nearer they came to the city gate the slower grew their steps.

'What do you want?' asked one of the sentries, barring their way.

'*Barin*,' said the native and lifted his hands. A string of incomprehensible noises followed, from which the Cossack could catch only the same word *Barin* over and over again. One of the men from Oryol who was there intervened. 'I think *Barin* means "Master". They want to see Yermak. We had better fetch the interpreter and take them along.'

'Come on,' said the Cossack and pushed the new-comers ahead.

As the little band entered the palace Yermak shook off his worries and gave the new-comers his full attention. The natives lowered their small darting eyes and fell on their knees in front of Yermak. Then one of them began to speak. The Votyak from Oryol could not understand all they said, but he managed to get the gist of the words.

'He is the Prince Bohar,' he said to Yermak. 'He is the chief of a tribe of Ostyaks not far from the Isker. They do not like war and he brings you offerings of peace.'

Yermak grasped the Ostyak's hands, raised him to his feet, and made a sign for him to sit down.

'I am glad that you have come to make peace. Sit down by my side. Who are these men with you?'

'They are my best hunters, my lord,' replied the Ostyak. 'What they have brought with them is all for you.' At a sign from their prince the men took the bundles from their shoulders and untied them.

Yermak threw them a swift glance.

'I, too, want peace, Prince Bohar, but I can only believe that you will keep your word if you will take an oath of allegiance. As long as you keep faith, nothing will happen to you or your tribe.'

Bohar looked at Yermak fearlessly. 'I want to be your friend, great lord. Trum the Almighty, to whom we pray, has given you strength as to no one else I have ever met. Trum lives within you, otherwise you would never have conquered Kuchum Khan, for he was mighty, too. He had a big army, but you, great lord, were more powerful still, for Trum has given thunder and lightning into your keeping and he has made you invincible. I shall swear an oath of fealty to you.'

'Kiss my sword and swear it.'

Prince Bohar bent over the naked sword reverently.

'I swear to you my allegiance.'

Then he laid at Yermak's feet the bundles his men had brought. There were white fox furs, so thick and silky that Yermak had never seen their like before. There was black fox, too, and sable and squirrel. The last bundle of all contained dried fish.

Yermak looked up.

'Have you more fish at home in your huts, Prince Bohar?'

'Yes, my lord, we have plenty. I can bring it all to you, if you wish.'

'I do not want your people to go hungry.'

'Oh no, they will not do that. The forests are full of game. We shall have enough to eat.'

'Then bring me supplies. I need them for my troops.'

'Yes, my lord. I shall bring you what I have.'

'Let us dine together first, Prince Bohar. You must be my guest.'

A joyful smile lit up the Ostyak's face.

'Oh, my lord, you are strong and kind, too. I thank you.'

In the afternoon the Ostyaks left the town. The food and beer had put them in a good mood and they were no longer afraid. They had made friends with the man in whom the great god Trum resided.

Prince Bohar was not the only one who brought food to Yermak during the next few weeks. The news of the friendly reception which had greeted the Ostyaks flew like the wind from hut to hut. It reached even the Tartars who had fled to the forests with their tents and whom the approaching winter drove out once more. Nervously they ventured back to Isker. Yermak did not treat them as enemies, but as friends, provided they swore an oath of allegiance to him. Their friendship brought particular benefit to the Cossacks, for in summer-time they had grown crops in small fields round their tents, and these fields had yielded maize, rye and oats. So the Cossacks could bake fresh bread and cook broth. Life would not be luxurious, but at least no one would starve in the coming months.

Soon winter unfolded its whole strength. The frost set in with a grip more savage than anything the Cossacks had endured the previous year. The Irtish and the Tobol are both broad, swift-flowing rivers, but they were frozen several feet thick. The Cossacks had to dig fresh holes in the ice every morning when they went down to fetch fresh water.

The snow fell in monotonous symmetry. Nothing interrupted the even descent of the big white flakes. Then came the raging hurricane which roared day and night, and piled the snow into thick white walls as it drove everything before it. It blanketed everything in the open plains, and only the thick impenetrable forests stood up to the power of its onslaught.

The days were short in Isker and darkness fell early. There was time for endless talking; time for the men to sing and to play their instruments, the *gusli* and the *balalaika*. Mitya was always present when someone started strumming a tune. He would quite forget where he was and how he came to be there. In the dusk of the room, where only the fire glowed, everything was blurred and reality disappeared from sight.

Mitya leaned against the wall and yielded to the clear rhythm of the notes. 'It's good to be alive,' he thought. 'I love listening to these songs and they make me so happy.' The music carried him far away from Siberia. He was sitting in the *troika* next to Irina and they were both well wrapped in thick furs. They flew over the ice and the wind sang with its clear loud voice and the harness rattled dryly, keeping time with the wind. And Irina would laugh aloud, for she could never drive fast enough, and even the swaying of the coachman in front of them on the seat had a soft melody of its own and the deep voice of Vassili Metyanov as he towered over them was like music too. . . .

'Have you gone to sleep?' asked Boris and prodded Mitya in the ribs.

Mitya was so startled that his daydream vanished with a stab of pain.

'No.'

'You looked as if you were miles away.'

'So I was.'

'Fast asleep, I know.'

'Only dreaming.'

'That's the same thing.'

The heavy storms were followed by days that were clear and bitingly cold. The sun looked down through a veil of mist on the dazzling whiteness. Myriads of snow crystals glistened and blinded the eyes until they watered. The loose blanket of snow became rock firm.

It was on a day like this that strangers from the north came sweeping down towards Isker. Even from a long way off one could make out the narrow sledges drawn by a team of dogs. The nearer they came the more clearly could be heard the cries of the driver urging them on.

The Cossacks watched them coming inquisitively. They went to the gate and opened it, and the speed at which the sledge entered showed how well the dogs could pull. Most of them were white, but there were a few grey ones among them. They had thick, long coats, broad heads with pointed muzzles and small ears. They held their tails high, curled into a ring.

A deafening barking set up as the Cossacks approached the team. The dogs bared their teeth and snapped.

A man stepped out of the leading sledge. As far as the Cossacks could tell from his clothes, he must be an Ostyak. The barking was so loud that everyone came running out of the houses and Yermak, too, stepped into the street. The Ostyak turned to the dogs and gave them a loud command. Reluctantly they obeyed, and lay down quietly in the snow.

'Are you the mighty lord who has conquered Kuchum Khan?' asked the Ostyak, bowing the knee before Yermak.

'Stand up,' said Yermak, grasping him by the arm. 'I am Yermak Timofeyev. And who are you?'

'I am Ishberdei, the Prince of a great Ostyak tribe. I have come here to swear an oath of allegiance to you. Accept my gifts and let us live in peace side by side.'

'I am glad that you desire peace. Where have you come from, Prince Ishberdei? Where does your tribe live?'

'Beyond a great marsh by a river called the Konda. The river is good, my lord. It gives us fish in abundance, and many ducks and swans nest in the reeds. The forests there are thick and dark, but they give us food, too: elk and reindeer—not the small ones which live in the tundra, but big strong beasts. And there are deer and foxes, sables and martens, everything you could want. Hunting is very easy.'

'Who are these men who have come with you? Tell them to alight from the sledges.'

'They are the village elders. And this, mighty lord, is my son Voksar who will be Prince of the Konda one day in my place, if Trum deems it good.'

Yermak stretched out a hand to the young man.

'Come into my house,' said Yermak. 'Take the oath of allegiance and be my guests.'

The Ostyaks devoured with gusto the roast meat set before them, and the dogs lay outside in the square before the palace to guard their masters' sledges. If a Cossack ventured anywhere near them they sprang at him in fury as if they wanted to tear him to pieces.

The leader of the pack was a snow-white dog and the others seemed to wait for it to tell them what to do. Its team-mate was a grey and white bitch and she appeared to be even more vigilant and aggressive than the leader. Mitya kept watching her. She seemed to obey the leader with the greatest reluctance and remained standing at the alert when all the others were lying quietly.

Mitya liked the look of her. She reminded him of Grivka, and, taking no notice of the hostile growling, he went close up to her. Gently he started coaxing her. 'Good dog, there's a good dog.

Stop growling, lassie.'

Boris, who was standing near, warned him to be careful.

'Keep your distance or she'll have her teeth in your throat.'

Mitya ignored his friend. He went on coaxing and the bitch put her head on one side and stared at him. The others began their hullabaloo again, but the bitch did not join in. She let Mitya come closer still and after a while she allowed him to touch her. Mitya had the feeling that she did not care much for the caress, but she did not protest. It was just then that Voksar, the son of the Ostyak Prince, came out of the palace to fetch the gifts which the party had brought with them. He had pushed back his hood and Mitya could see him properly for the first time. We must be about the same age, he thought.

Voksar remained rooted to the spot as his eyes went from Mitya to the bitch and back again. Then he stepped towards the sledge saying something Mitya could not understand. He unfastened the harness. The bitch was free. Mitya still could not grasp what the youth meant, even when he pushed the animal towards Mitya's feet.

The interpreter came to his aid when they returned to the palace. It seemed that Kushla, as the bitch was called, belonged to Voksar. She had never let a stranger touch her before. Not even his father Ishberdei could handle her with impunity. If she let Mitya stroke her, it was a sign that she had given him her heart and she would leave it behind in Isker if Voksar took her home again.

When Mitya learned all this, he was very pleased. But he was troubled too, for he could not fail to see the sadness in Voksar's eyes.

'I thank you for your present, Voksar, but I do not see how we can look after her here. We are soldiers and this is only a short rest for us while the winter lasts. When summer comes again we shall have to go into battle once more, and what would happen to her then?'

Voksar was in a dilemma. He had not thought of that. He passed his hand over the splendid creature which lay between them.

'And what is more,' went on Mitya, 'I can see she is your hunting dog. What would you do without her?'

Voksar's eyes lit up at once. 'There's not a dog to touch Kushla when it comes to hunting,' he said enthusiastically. 'She finds the best sables. When she pounces she kills with a single bite. Her teeth are stronger and sharper than a wolf's. She is never frightened. She even worries Ashninika from his bed in winter and attacks him, although I have forbidden it. She is the finest hunting dog you ever saw.'

'And who is Ashninika?' asked Mitya curiously.

'He is a god, lord Mitya, not so powerful as Trum, oh no, but still one of the gods. Many of the gods live in our forests and one of them is Ashninika.'

'What does Ashninika look like?'

'He is tall, very tall, and fat, very fat. His fur is either brown or black. He can go on all fours or on two legs. He tears elks and stags to pieces, he eats fish and sweet berries, and when he is angry he growls.'

And Voksar imitated the growl of a bear so cleverly that Yermak, Ishberdei and the village elders all turned to look. Mitya laughed aloud.

'Oh, Voksar, your god Ashninika is only a bear. You should be glad if Kushla rouses him, for then you can kill him.'

Voksar raised his hands in horror.

'Do not speak like that, my lord. He will attack you and tear you limb from limb.'

Mitya turned away for a moment, unclasped his belt and lifted his shirt. 'See Voksar, Ashninika did attack me once, but I am still alive.'

Voksar gazed with horror at the terrible scar on Mitya's back.

'Yes, it was truly Ashninika,' he stammered wildly. 'I can tell that. Oh, my lord, then Trum dwells inside you, too, for you are invincible and never will an arrow strike you. If only I could be your friend!'

'So you shall, Voksar, but do me one favour. Take Kushla with you and keep her for me until I go back to Russia. My father is a hunter, you know, and perhaps I shall become one, too. When I go home I shall take her with me, but until then let her remain with you.'

Voksar looked into space. He was wrestling with himself. He wanted to take Kushla back, but was it right when she had given her heart to the young foreigner? Would she hunt so well if she missed her real master? But how could she live without hunting, for hunting was in her blood?

'I shall grant your request, my lord,' he said at last .

'Don't call me "my lord", Voksar. Call me Mitya, for we are friends.'

Meanwhile Yermak was talking to Ishberdei.

'How did you get the news of our victory?'

'The word came floating along the river; it sailed in the swift canoes of our people and it flew through the forests. The wind carried it from village to village.'

'Have other Ostyak tribes heard the news, those who live in the same region as you?'

'Yes, my lord.'

'Why do they not come as you have come, and swear their loyalty to me?'

'Many of them are afraid. They are terrified of the thunder and lightning which you command.'

'Is it only fear, or are they opposed to me? Will they attack me if I come near?'

'It may make you angry, but there is something in what you say, too.'

'Do you know where to find these tribes and their princes?'

'Yes, my lord. I do.'

'Prince Ishberdei, will you come with me when spring arrives?'

The Ostyak hesitated. Then he spoke. 'You can count on me. I have sworn an oath of loyalty to you.'

The Ostyaks remained in Isker until the following day. As they got ready to leave, Yermak sent for Mitya.

'The Prince has asked me if you will return with them to the village. He says that you have made friends with his son. Would you like to see his home?'

'Would you allow me to go, Yermak?'

'Yes, if you wish. It will not be for long, since Prince Ishberdei has promised to come back and pay me tribute before the winter is over, and then you can return.'

'Very well, Yermak. I'll go.'

Mitya fetched his furs and his gun and climbed into the sledge behind Voksar.

'It is narrow, I know, but it keeps you warm!' laughed Voksar with beaming face.

The Ostyaks bowed several times to Yermak and his men and then Ishberdei whistled through his teeth. With one bound the first team started off and the hectic journey along the ice of the River Irtish began. At first Mitya could neither hear nor see. The snow blinded him so that his eyes hurt and the wind blew so hard in his face that he thought it would be flayed. His head began to ache. He tried to keep wriggling his toes inside his boots, for he felt they were getting numb.

And still they raced on at the same pace. Sometimes Voksar

turned round to him. Although his mouth was covered and only his eyes and nose peeped out of the fur of the hood, Mitya was sure the lad was smiling at him.

When it began to grow dark they left the river and guided the dogs ashore. When he leaned over the side a little Mitya could tell that they were following a definite path, for they hardly sank in the snow. He was listening tensely. He thought he could hear barking in the far distance. Now he saw that the dogs were going faster than ever. They took their bearings from a tall wood which bordered the route like a wall. A hundred yards farther on he could make out the outline of some huts, and a little later he heard voices coming from the village.

A wild barking greeted them and Mitya felt he was driving straight for the mouth of Hell. The darkness which surrounded them, the black menacing forest and the sound of so many dogs combined with nightmare effect. Without thinking, his frozen hands tried to grasp his gun and when he found he could not hold it, his uneasiness mounted.

Then the sledges stopped and Mitya was surrounded by so many faces he could hardly believe his eyes. Voksar had scrambled out of the sledge and, placing his hand under Mitya's arm, he pulled him out, too. It was only then that Mitya realized how stiff his body was. He could not walk and his legs gave way beneath him.

Voksar carried him into one of the huts. He had to stoop as he passed through the doorway. He groped his way down two steps and laid Mitya on the floor, which was spread with reindeer skins. He spoke to a woman who was sitting by the fire. She brought hot water in a wooden cup and Voksar gave Mitya some to drink.

The other men crowded in. They crouched round the fire and Mitya saw how respectful they were to Ishberdei. They kept a pace away from him, and when the cup with hot water was sent the rounds, they passed it first to the Prince. Then each man was handed a lump of meat. From the distance it looked black and tough. Voksar gave Mitya a piece, too. He took it in his hand and looked at Voksar uncertainly. The meat was cold and raw.

'What shall I do with it?' he asked. Voksar must have understood him, for he took a huge bite from his own piece. Mitya tried to follow his example. There was the taste of meat in his mouth, but although his teeth were strong, he could do no more than tear off a few shreds and even that effort seemed to paralyse his jaws. The welcoming warmth after the penetrating cold of the journey was too relaxing for such exertion. He let his hand drop and watched the dark outline of the men against the flames. He could hear them smacking their lips and chewing heartily with open mouths, but he could not understand a word of what they were saying.

Voksar squatted devotedly close by his side and the blissful relief of being able to stretch his limbs, and of being warm from head to foot—indeed the whole atmosphere, gave Mitya the sensation of floating on air. And as so often when he warmed himself by a fire and knew the protection of a hut, the image of his father came back to him and he remembered those nights they had spent together by the big stove at home. Everything began to swim before the boy's eyes and reality was blurred with reminiscence.

When Voksar leaned over him Mitya had fallen fast asleep. The Prince's son took the meat from Mitya's hand and ate it himself. He did not want the others to know that the stranger could not eat their food. It was better if they thought he was like the rest of them.

Next day, before they went on again, a man from the village came over to Mitya and presented him with a tunic such as Voksar and the others wore. It was like a shift of thin supple reddish-brown leather, and over it went a long robe of white fur with a hood attached. A wide band of soft dog-fur edged the brim. A pair of boots made of a coarse brown leather completed Mitya's new outfit.

'Thank you, friend,' said Mitya.

As he was about to put on his new garments, it grew deathly still in the hut. What were they waiting for, he wondered. He took off his shirt and Voksar turned him away gently, so that he was not facing the men. This baffled Mitya even more, for the others had all undressed without embarassment. Then a murmur went up behind him. Of course! Voksar was showing them his scar. Before he could stop them, the whole assembly was bowing low before him.

As soon as he was dressed they went on northwards. The dogs knew the way and needed little guidance. The men started them off with a loud 'Hey, hey!' and away they shot. They had to spend one more night in a village hut, but the next day they reached their destination.

Mitya was led inside the *yurta* which Ishberdei shared with Voksar. It was roomy and warm. Over the dark felt foundation there was an outer layer of brown deerskin and an inner one of grey reindeer skins. Fishing-nets hung from the walls as well as knives, spears, harness for the dogs, cooking-pots, and vessels of various sizes. Voksar's mother was seen only when she prepared meals for the men, but Mitya found it difficult to tell which were the women, for they were dressed exactly like the men.

When they had rested thoroughly, Voksar took his guest out of doors. They whistled to Kushla and the three of them made for the forest. Voksar inspected some small traps he had set and not one of them was empty. There were three martens, five sables, a fox and two squirrels. Then they went eastwards and examined the big traps for stags, which were dug like pits, but here he had no luck. He replaced the icy twigs with great care and they went on farther.

Voksar took Mitya to a small lake and showed him the holes in the ice which the beavers make when they seek the land. At the first one he shook his head and pointed to the smooth surface. There was not a grain of sand nor a scratch in the snow. No animal had been there recently.

It was the same at the next hole, but Voksar did not give up easily and if he felt any disappointment he did not show it. A pit had been dug in front of the next hole and there something was stirring. The bitch sprang down and before Voksar and Mitya could reach it the beaver's death cries rang from the quiet woods. Kushla had bitten through its throat and she dragged the big brown animal out of the pit and laid it at her master's feet. Mitya scratched her head in recognition.

On the way home Kushla went snuffling along ahead of them. She kept her nose close to the snow and Mitya found it hard to follow her through the undergrowth. Suddenly Voksar gripped Mitya's arm and they both stopped. The dog's paws were scraping away furiously at the arching roots of a cembra pine tree, hurtling the snow away in lumps as she dug. There was a quick leap, a yelp, a wild shake of the head, and back she came. Between her jaws dangled the lifeless body of a black sable. Voksar put it with the rest of the game.

Mitya enjoyed his stay with Voksar and his father immensely. Before long he could talk to them a little, although he had to use a good deal of sign language, naturally. Voksar made an effort to learn a little Russian from Mitya and the two of them managed to understand each other tolerably well.

Every day there was something new for Mitya. The trapping lost its novelty, but one day the men prepared to go stag-hunting, as meat was running short. They used the dogs to chase the deer over the frozen snow until they collapsed. The snow was stained with red as the Ostyaks knifed the exhausted animals to death, but the men rejoiced at the abundant supply of venison they had to take home with them.

Mitya learnt, too, how to use the broad snowshoes which were curved at both ends, and that made hunting in the forest and over the fields still more exciting. Often they took a whole pack of dogs with them and they could hardly follow them when they hunted hares who tried to save themselves in the thick undergrowth. But there were always plenty of victims, for the forest housed more game than Mitya had ever seen before. And the men of the Taiga certainly knew how to hunt.

The days went by much too quickly for Mitya. He saw how the men drew fibres from the roots of the pine trees and knotted them into fishing-nets. He saw them sew their clothes using sharpened fishbones as needles and the fine reindeer sinews as thread. He watched how they tanned deerskins and then cut belts from them.

The evenings were never dreary either. He liked to sit with the men round the fire and the better he could communicate with them the more it pleased him.

Voksar introduced him to every hut in the village. 'Trum!' they whispered revently, and 'Ashninika!' they murmured, and everywhere they bowed low before him.

20 THE TRAITOR

Yermak received Prince Skulem in as friendly a fashion as he had welcomed Ishberdei. Skulem, too, swore an oath of loyalty and said that he wanted to live in peace with the Russians. His sledges brought with them the tribute he had formerly paid to Kuchum Khan, which he now offered to Yermak. The warehouses in Isker were heaped high with furs.

After the Ostyak princes came the Tartar chieftains, ready to make friends in their turn with the new ruler. Yermak received them as courteously as ever, but he had his private reservations. The Khan he had defeated was one of their own people, after all, while to the Ostyaks he was a usurper, an invader who had forced them into subjection. Yermak did not allow the Tartars to forget that in spite of all the protestations of friendship, it was he who was master.

Among the first of the Tartar princes to make their peace with him was Abish. He was small and sinewy with a coal-black beard and particularly slanting eyes. As he spoke he put his head on one side. His mouth smiled obsequiously, but his eyes observed Yermak closely. He ignored Ivan Koltso, who was also present at the audience.

'Be on your guard, my lord,' said Abish with his soft caressing voice. 'Kuchum Khan is still alive. You will not have peace until he is safe in the arms of Allah.' The smile grew wider.

Yermak smiled back. 'I am not frightened of him, Abish. If he returns, things will go no better for him than at our first meeting.'

'That I do not doubt for a moment. Only your soldiers grow fewer—' Abish broke off abruptly. 'If only Mametkul had not escaped.'

'His father needs him,' said Yermak innocently.

'Of course. But you do not know the Prince. He is young and very proud. He will never swallow defeat. He is already thinking of revenge, my lord.'

'Have you definite information, Abish?' asked Yermak bluntly.

'What is definite in these uncertain times?' smiled Abish and lowered his eyes. 'Only that he lives and dreams of vengeance and that he turns up in all kinds of places, now here, now there, with a few faithful followers.'

'Where?'

'How can I tell you, Prince, when he has no fixed abode?'

'A pity,' said Yermak with a bored shrug of the shoulders. But his eyes were still fixed on the crafty expression of his visitor. 'The Czar of all the Russias at whose behest I am here would be very grateful to anyone who helped his Commander-in-chief. What a pity you don't know more.'

The Tartar licked his lips slowly.

'I shall be helpful, when the time comes.'

'Thank you.'

When the Prince had gone Ivan Koltso called for a mug of ale at the top of his voice.

'I must swill away my vomit. Pah! He made my gorge rise. The treacherous vulture! Devil's spawn! What a hypocrite! I wanted to knock him down.'

'It would be a waste of energy. No, it's hanging or nothing for him.'

'Why don't you string him up then?'

'Because a man like that can be useful. The promise of a reward will draw him to us as the whirlpool sucks at a drowning man.'

'Will he let himself be used, though?'

'He might. Or he may try to play a double game with us and go straight to Mametkul. We must always be careful when dealing with the Tartars, and with a man like that, especially so.'

'Oh, Yermak, how long must we stay here in this land with its uncanny forests and lonely swamps, with these people who swore eternal loyalty to Kuchum yesterday and do the same to us today? Let us go home.'

'But you know for yourself how things stand! Mametkul is mustering an army and his father still has a large kingdom left. So much remains for us to do. We must stay here.'

'And what will happen when our magic weapons will not fire any more, when powder and shot come to an end? Do you know how our stocks stand?'

'Of course. Do you really think I would overlook something so important?'

'What will you do?'

'I am thinking of sending an envoy to Moscow.'

Ivan Koltso jumped up from the couch on which he had been sitting opposite Yermak.

'A messenger to the Czar?'

'Yes. We need soldiers and arms, and if the Czar thinks it right and proper to send them under the command of one of his Generals, then I for one will raise no objection.'

'You speak as if you had kissed hands before we set out, as if the Czar had sent you here with his grace and favour. Have you forgotten everything, Yermak? Has our victory befogged your wits?'

'Oh Ivan, will no one else ever think of the future? Why do the rest of you see only the present? We cannot take up a task and then leave it half accomplished, even if it would be easier and pleasanter to rest content with what we have. And admit it, Ivan, was it not much more of a gamble to fight with eight hundred men against ten thousand Tartars than to report a Cossack victory to his Majesty the Czar?'

Ivan Koltso turned away.

'If you put it like that, I suppose you are right. It would be a welcome change to fight Kuchum Khan side by side with Russian soldiers, to have ample stocks of ammunition and not to think with every shot that's fired: now wouldn't the sword have done instead? But there is the death sentence . . .'

'A condemned man can be reprieved,' said Yermak quietly, 'and high favour can turn overnight into sentence of death. It depends quite simply on which his most gracious Majesty considers most useful at any given moment and how many friends or detractors the man in question possesses at court. Don't let that worry you, Ivan.'

'Does that mean . . . Do you want me to go to Moscow?'

'Yes, that is what I mean. I would go myself if our situation here were a little more settled, but I am convinced that Hell would break loose if the Tartars knew that I had left Isker.'

'Of course, Yermak. That is quite true. I did not expect you to go, of course, but one of the other Captains might be a better spokesman than I.'

'Ivan, if anyone is going to Moscow, it is you. In all these years you have been my right-hand man. You were the first to know all my plans and only you can report our victory as it should be done.'

'When did you want me to set off? Now, while it is still winter?'

'Yes, Ivan, as soon as possible.'

'I'd like to sleep on it, Yermak.'

'Very well. But do not keep me waiting too long for an answer.'

Two days after this conversation Prince Abish visited Isker once more, this time in a great hurry.

'To Prince Yermak!' he shouted to the sentry and he drove his horse so furiously up the street that the sleigh jiggled to left and right.

'You come in haste, Abish,' said Yermak and led him into the palace. 'Your beard is frosted. Look how it is steaming in the warmth! You must have ridden hard, but that is not wise. The path for the sleigh is very narrow and it would be a pity if your horse slipped and broke a leg.'

'Your concern is very flattering, Prince Yermak, but the news I bring would not wait.'

'Mametkul?' asked Yermak swiftly.

'Yes, with about forty soldiers. Not more.'

'Where are they?'

'Come outside and I will draw it for you in the snow.'

'Good,' said Yermak when he had seen the rough sketch. 'Thank you for telling me. I think it would be best if you remained here in Isker until my Cossacks return.'

'Oh Prince, I thank you for your protection,' said Abish, obviously relieved, and he tried to grasp Yermak's hand so that he could kiss it humbly. Yermak draw back in revulsion. 'I was afraid you would want me to lead your men,' Abish went on unabashed at the rebuff. 'I should have been glad to do so, but . . . once we encountered Mametkul and his men . . . those loyal followers of his . . .'

'Loyal!' thought Yermak. 'I wonder he can still pronounce the word!'

'You know, Prince, it might be better if . . .'

'I understand, Abish. Tell my cooks to serve you. I must leave you now, otherwise all your haste will have been in vain.'

The Cossack Captains were informed within the hour and Ivan Koltso begged to be allowed to lead the raiding party. He pressed so insistently that Yermak was puzzled. When the others had left, he challenged him: 'Why must it be you? You know that I have earmarked you for other duties.'

'I do know, but I feel as if I must put my luck to the test. If I manage to capture Mametkul, I shall set out next day for Moscow. You can have everything prepared and I shall make no excuses. But if I don't, you must find someone else.'

'Very well, Ivan. But remember I need Mametkul alive. He is no use to me otherwise. Kuchum Khan will have no consideration for a dead Crown Prince.'

From the top of the tower Yermak watched his most faithful comrade depart. He did not leave until Koltso and his men had dwindled to a faint blur in the distance. How long would they take? Yermak felt impatient. Would they achieve their aim without blundering? Would everything go smoothly? He knew that Ivan was most capable, yet he would have felt easier in his mind if he had gone himself. He turned away and set about making the arrangements for Koltso's visit to Moscow.

The candle had burnt down to a stump before Yermak put down his quill. The letter to the Czar was finished. As he wrote, many thoughts had flashed through his head and his memory conjured up a portrait of his Majesty, Ivan the Terrible.

It was a faded image from the days of Yermak's childhood which often haunted him; but that evening it came to life more vividly than ever before. If only the Czar knew who Yermak really was! He looked down at the pattern of the carpet at his feet, but he did not really see it. In the weak flickering light the elaborate curves and whorls grew into the domes and windows of the Kremlin, where he had spent his childhood. He saw his own childish clumsy fingers playing with the strands of his mother's red-gold hair and at the same time he could hear his own voice begging, 'Granny, tell me what my mother looked like.'

'I cannot bow the knee before the Czar,' thought Yermak, rising to his feet. 'I shall never see Moscow again.'

It was about noon on the fourth day after Ivan Koltso had left Isker when a wild shout went up from the soldiers at the eastern gate. Soon the noise reached Yermak.

'They are coming back! They've captured him.'

'The Crown Prince is a prisoner.'

Yermak immediately summoned his own hundred to the gate so that the Cossacks were drawn up on either side lining the street as the triumphant procession rode in. Yermak was waiting with the symbols of office in his hands, the staff and the pike with a horse's tail waving from it. Thus he went to meet the Prince.

'Welcome to Isker, Prince Mametkul. Pray accept the respectful greetings I offer to a valiant enemy.'

The Prince stood there with a stony look on his face. He glanced at Yermak contemptuously. No one could tell if he was surprised or not at receiving such an honourable reception.

'With bound hands it is difficult to believe in protestations of respect,' he said cuttingly.

'Even with hands free, the defeated must always feel resentful before the face of the conqueror.' Yermak gave the Cossacks a sign to remove Mametkul's fetters. 'But while we both remain here in

Isker, you will have time to convince yourself that I am a man of honour. I cannot spare you all the unpleasantness of imprisonment, of course, but I shall do what I can to relieve it. This is the house I have set aside for you. Please enter.'

These were formerly the women's quarters and they lay next door to the palace in which Yermak now lived and which Mametkul knew so well.

'Tell me everything,' demanded Yermak when he was alone with his friend once more.

'If everything went as easily as that, then waging war would be child's play,' laughed Ivan Koltso. 'We discovered his tent and we waited until it was dark. Then we surrounded it. They were all fast asleep and no one made a sound. They had not reckoned with treachery. Only the Prince and his bodyguard defended themselves. If we had known for sure which one was the Prince, we should have killed the others. But there were three men close together so we brought them all.'

'All the better. We can use them all.'

'Have you prepared everything for my visit to Moscow?' Ivan went on after he had answered a few more of Yermak's questions.

'Yes, Ivan. Two sleighs have been packed and there are six reindeer ready to draw them. The interpreter from Oryol will go with you. On the way you will have to exchange the reindeer for dogs and there the native will help you. Once you are over the Urals, you will be in Russia again. Go by way of Oryol and call on Maxim Stroganov as soon as you arrive. Once you are there, you need not worry about the rest of the journey.'

'So I imagine. The worst will be over then.'

'Here is a letter to Stroganov and one to the Czar. I think Maxim will want to send Masupov to Moscow with you. Tell him that I should like that.'

They discussed at length the details of the journey and next morning when the reindeer were put to the sleighs all the Cossacks stood round and pressed Koltso's hands. They kissed him on the shoulder and the beard and told him, 'Greet Mother Russia from us all. Tell her we'll be back soon.'

'Tell her that we long for her. Greet her kindly and don't stay too long.'

'And bring back plenty of ammunition so that we can get home sooner.'

'Good-bye, Ivan, God speed you.'

And the Cossacks of his own hundred ran alongside the sledges till they were well beyond the town.

'Give our love to Russia and come back soon!'

Then they stood and watched the sleigh tearing away across the snow. He was going home to Russia, they kept thinking, and they could hear the Volga's running waters and see the sun shining over the endless steppes . . .

Shortly after Ivan Koltso had left, one of the Tartars captured with Mametkul left the town of Isker. He bore a message for the Khan and this was it:

'Do not fear for the life of your son, Kuchum Khan. He is an unfortunate prisoner, but he has reconciled himself to the will of God who placed him in the hands of the victors. He is not short of food or drink and he is not wounded or in pain. But should your followers attack my victorious soldiers who are seeking fresh supplies of food, things might be different. His fate depends on the way your people behave to the members of the conquering army.'

21 THE GOLDEN GOD IS SILENT

During those winter days they often spoke of Ivan Koltso, but once spring came their minds turned to what lay ahead, the conquest of the Ostyaks in the land of Yugor. A hundred men were to stay behind to guard Isker, but the rest were to travel northwards, farther, ever farther from Russia. And last autumn they had talked about going home again!

As the campaign started Yermak gave his orders to Yakob Michailov, who would be in charge of the garrison. 'Take care of the Prince,' he reminded him once more as they walked down to the river. 'And see to it that the Tartars and the Ostyaks pay their tribute regularly. Be friendly towards them but firm. Do not accept any excuses.'

As the little flotilla of rafts reached the mouth of the Konda, Ishberdei was waiting on the banks with his son, a soothsayer and one of the village elders. Mitya and Voksar were delighted to see each other again. They embraced warmly and Kushla ran to Mitya and put her front paws on his shoulders.

'I would like to come with you so that we could be together,' whispered Voksar, pressing Mitya's hand, 'but I must remain at home. Father insists. How I envy you the excitement of it all!'

Mitya smiled.

'Do not envy me, Voskar. You will be spared many things that I must see. But I should like to greet your father. Come on.'

As they approached the others they saw how respectfully the soothsayer bowed to Yermak, and Mitya heard him ask to read Yermak's hand.

'You are a man who has more courage than anyone here in our country, great Prince. Show me your hand so that I can tell you what fate Trum has in store for you,' he said.

Mitya translated the words for him. Yermak hesitated. Then he stretched out his hand. A silence fell on the men all round. The native's dirty brown fingers travelled over the lines on Yermak's palm.

'There is much written in your hand. Here are victory and fame. No enemy will slay you; all will bow their heads before you, great Prince. Your name will echo through Siberia long after you are dead; long, long after, lord Yermak.' The soothsayer dropped his hand abruptly and gazed into space with a peculiar expression. Then he bowed low.

'Thank you for a good horoscope,' said Yermak, 'but we must not tarry any longer. Come, Prince Ishberdei, let us row back to the rafts.'

'Good hunting until we meet again.'

'Farewell, Voksar,' said Mitya, and pressed his friend's hand.

'I shall wait for you, Mitya. I shall be looking for you when the sun turns its face away from the earth once more, for you and for my father.'

Voksar stood on the river bank and waved to Mitya until he could no longer make him out from the others. But still he remained standing there until the rafts themselves were out of sight. He was so preoccupied that he started when the soothsayer placed a hand on his shoulder.

'Let us go home, Voksar.'

'Yes.' Then Voksar remembered something. 'Before, when you released the great lord's hand, you looked away with such a strange expression. Did you see something frightening there?' he asked.

'Yes. I saw the Prince sinking suddenly, like a stone. I don't know where, though.'

'But you prophesied such fame and honour for him!'

'Fame, yes. Great fame. But he has not long to live.'

'Oh,' said Voksar and his eyes were troubled as he turned them once more in the direction the rafts had taken.

Ishberdei sat on the raft near Yermak.

'Your heart is heavy, Prince,' said Yermak.

'Yes, my lord. You must understand that it hurts me to fight my own kin.'

'You do not need to fight, Ishberdei. You need only show me the way.'

'It is the same thing. Only the words are different.'

'Would you prefer to turn back?'

'No, my lord, I stand by my oath. We shall soon reach a Tartar fortress and then my heart will laugh. These Tartars have always looked on us natives as dogs. They beat us to death. I will show you the easiest way to take this stronghold. I know a gap in their defences.'

Ishberdei was a good guide. The Cossacks landed in the dark and they entered the fortress so quickly that the battle was half won before the Tartars could recover from their surprise. Their firearms did the rest. There was a short sharp conflict and the defenders surrendered.

But just as the fighting was over, a fresh horde of Tartars arrived and fell on the Cossacks with all the ferocity of bitter hatred. The other Tartars regained heart and the battle flared up once more.

Again it ended in defeat for the Tartars, but Yermak felt that he must assert his supremacy more emphatically. He had the leaders brought before him and he ordered his men to shoot them before the eyes of their followers.

'Now are you ready to swear allegiance?' he thundered as the shot re-echoed. And there was not a man among them who refused to kiss his sword.

A damp mist rolled in over the plains. It spread in thick clouds, covering the vast marshland, which was overgrown with reeds. Here and there the clouds parted and swirled back and forth. Then they closed in again in a sinister ghoulish dance which made one shudder.

Along the narrow path which swayed under their feet filed a column of men. This had been going on since the first light of dawn and still not all of them had reached Trumchar. There must have been well over a thousand of them, nearer two thousand perhaps. They were Vogul and Ostyak subjects of Prince Demian, whose capital, Trumchar, stood by the banks of the Irtish. The Prince knew that he must expect an attack from the invading army, who where rumoured to be invincible. The reputation of these foreign soldiers had been growing ever louder day by day and the people hunched their shoulders and bowed their heads whenever they were mentioned. So Demian had summoned his fighting men to Trumchar, and Racha, the idol of gleaming gold in which resided the invisible god Trum, would give them all courage and would make them as strong as the bulls of a herd of reindeer, who will do battle even with Ashninika the bear.

When the two thousand heathen were assembled in Trumchar and had sacrificed fawns and fish to the golden god, the priest went into the temple. He bowed low before Racha and begged for strength and courage for all his faithful host. He implored the god to pardon him for disturbing its rest, lifted the idol bodily from the floor of the temple and dipped it into a vessel of water. Then he replaced the image and chanted a prayer.

'Save us from these warriors who threaten us,' he conjured the idol, but Racha remained silent. Then the priest took the vessel of water and carried it out to the gathering.

Prince Demian was the first to bend down and drink the water which Racha had filled with magic strength. And after him every one of his subjects bowed down and drank, too.

The moor seethed and heaved beneath the feet of the returning men and they sank deep into the treacherous soil. But now they believed that they were strong.

When Yermak caught sight of the fortress in the distance and gave his orders for the plan of attack Ishberdei asked him a favour. 'Let me row ashore and speak to them before they see your army.'

'Is that not rash? Why do you want them to recognize you? Remain here.'

'If you will grant my wish, I hope to spare much bloodshed. They may reject my advice and resist you, but I should like to try. There are many of my kinsfolk there.'

'All right then, go.'

The Cossacks rowed Ishberdei ashore. When they offered to give him an armed escort, he refused. He disappeared into the forest and the Cossacks had a long wait until he returned. When they saw the defeated look on his face they knew that his journey had been in vain. They rejoined the others and continued on their way.

'You look very depressed, Ishberdei. Why is that? You have done what you could,' said Yermak.

'It is not that Demian insists on fighting which makes my heart heavy, but the fact that he refused to see me, that he would not give me an audience. He sent a message that he did not wish to set eyes on a traitor, and he was right.'

Yermak wanted to reply, but Ishberdei refused to listen to him and remained crouched in a huddle. Yermak felt much sympathy with this honest man. But was he really betraying his people? How different he was from the ruthless, contemptible Prince Abish who had betrayed Mametkul! Nevertheless the Ostyaks were bound to see Ishberdei's services to the Russians as treachery, services he had to carry out under the oath of allegiance which he had sworn.

'Prince Ishberdei,' said Yermak, 'I hate the soul of a traitor. For you I have nothing but respect.'

Ishberdei nodded, but Yermak did not know if the native fully understood the words which Mitya translated for him.

In the fortress Ostyaks and Voguls were preparing for the battle.

'We have drunk the waters of courage,' they whispered, 'but Racha did not speak. The god was silent . . .' And they hunched their shoulders high.

As the rafts drew nearer to the fortress a few of the defenders looked out over the walls. Yermak told his men to open fire. The pagans vanished. The fortress fell to Yermak without a fight.

Their plunder was a wealth of furs such as they had never seen before. Prince Demian swore an oath of allegiance and promised to pay tribute. Yermak found plenty of meat from the enormous herds of reindeer. The inhabitants who had fled returned before long, bringing him gifts and kissing his sword.

'The invincible stranger is sent by Trum. Who can defy him?' they told each other.

The day after the victory, Yermak was sitting in Demian's *yurta* and Ishberdei was in attendance.

'What is the next place we come to?' he asked.

'It is a large settlement called Narymsk, and then you will reach the land of the most powerful of the Ostyak princes whose name is Samar. You will have hard fighting there, for Samar is as respected among our people as Kuchum Khan among the Tartars.'

'What next?'

'Then you will come to the River Ob, my lord. Do you want to go any farther than that?'

'Who live by this River Ob?'

'More Ostyak tribes.'

Yermak glanced at Ishberdei, who was staring into the fire and he hoped that he would look up. But Ishberdei sat there without stirring.

'My friend,' said Yermak coming a little closer.

Still Ishberdei did not move.

'My friend,' repeated Yermak and touched the man's arm. 'Go home to your tribe.'

'Do you not need my help any more, my lord?'

'I did not mean that. But I cannot see you breaking your heart over this conflict of loyalties.'

Isrberdei refused. 'It is all the same if I go with you or back home. I have told you what you want to know.'

'Oh no, my friend. That is not why I asked you. If I go on, I shall soon discover where my enemies live. What I wanted to know was if they were Ostyaks, men of your race, against whom I must wage war. As it is, I beg you, go home. Go back to your own people. If you need a raft or a boat, I will give you one. Take what food you need. But remain my friend.'

In the darkness the boat with Ishberdei in it pushed off from land. Mitya could hear the even strokes of the oars.

'Give Voksar my love,' he called aloud over the water.

When the Cossacks reached Narymsk a few shots were enough to send flying the band of defenders who had collected on the banks of the river. Ever faster went the news of the invincible General, and the way was cleared for the Cossacks wherever they went. The Ostyak leaders were powerless in the face of the terror which paralysed their subjects and they themselves were gripped by this same fear when they heard the crack of the firearms thundering over the river.

The men had fled and the women and children crouched in their tents, raising their trembling hands in subjection to the mighty foe, but expecting death. Mitya, who could speak the language a little, kept close to Yermak and had to interpret for him.

'Why are you afraid of us? We do not come here to harm you. Come out of your tents and cook some food for us. Kuchum Khan is defeated. Your new overlord is the Czar of Russia, who sent Yermak here. Look, this is Yermak. He does not wish you to be frightened of him.'

The women listened. Nervously they crept out of the tents. They stared dumbly at the foreigners and went to fetch reindeer milk and meat. Before sundown the men returned. They brought with them all the furs they possessed and spread them out before Yermak. They kissed his sword and slowly their faces lost the distorted look of mortal fear.

'If the conqueror wants no more than tribute, why should we not pay him? Kuchum Khan used to demand it, too,' they told each other.

There were no dead and no wounded, and Yermak could go on. The summer-time must be used to the full.

'Samar will not have to wait long,' said Yermak to his Captains. 'He wants to save the land of Yugor, or so the natives say.'

'If he can!' laughed Matvei, confident of their victory.

'I have been told that he has a large army assembled, and many tribal princes,' said Yermak.

'So have others before him,' retorted Matvei's booming voice. 'If they all run away, it hardly matters if he has hundreds or thousands.'

Nikita Pan joined in Matvei's laughter.

'Would you prefer a pitched battle, or do you think we can take them by surprise?' he asked.

'I want as little bloodshed as possible, on our side especially.'

'Then let us attack them at night. A surprise attack is always best. Remember our first battle with Yepancha.'

'It will be a good thing if we can bring it off,' nodded Yermak.

'What are we waiting for, then?' asked Matvei. 'We shall sing them such a sweet lullaby that they will go to their gods smiling.'

They decided to land well before they got to the Prince's camp, while it was dark, and to attack the enemy at night as they slept. The weather favoured them. It was raining in torrents as they left Narymsk. The clouds were very low and veiled the land in a grey haze. It also concealed the army as they came ashore.

Evening came and still it rained. The forest offered the Cossacks excellent cover and they advanced in darkness as far as the outer patrols. The drumming of the rain muffled the cries of the startled sentries as they set out on their journey to meet their great god Trum.

The Cossacks went on, working their way right round the camp. Then they closed in gradually. In spite of the darkness they could make out the tents quite clearly. At first they had to grope cautiously, but when they reached the shelter of the low, black fir trees they could walk upright. All was still.

'The general with a large army can sleep in peace, that's what I always say,' guffawed Matvei, amused at his own joke.

'Don't laugh. You'll wake the high command!'

Making sure of every inch of the way, they pushed on. The rain turned to a cloudburst. Matvei reached the edge of the trees. Again he listened and peered into darkness. Then with a handful of Cossacks, he leapt across the clearing to the first tent.

Nothing moved, no one heard them. Out they came again, pricking their ears as they made for the next tent. The same happened on all sides: the cautious inspection, then the attack, one leap forward into the skin-covered tents. Then suddenly there was a cry which roused the sleepers. The guns fired, aiming at the centre of the encampment. They were only isolated shots, for the rain made it difficult to ignite the powder, but the Cossacks knew how much depended on the accuracy of their shooting.

Samar, who had darted out of his tent, sank to the ground, hit.

'Flee!' he cried and made a great effort to raise his head. 'Flee as long as darkness lasts.' And to the man who tried to lift him he said, 'Leave me, save your own life.' His body sank to the wet ground. 'The foreigner is invincible; save yourselves.'

Prince Alach turned him onto his back, so that his face did not lie in the water. 'You did not want to believe me, Samar. Now you have paid dearly for it.' And Alach crouched by the dead man's side until the Cossacks arrived.

Next morning Yermak was sitting with him in the tent. 'Why must we always fight, Alach?' asked Yermak. 'Have you not heard of all my victories?'

'Yes, my lord. But we love freedom.'

'I will not take yours away. Pay me tribute, bring it to Isker and no one will hurt you. Can we not be friends?'

'Friends?' Alach looked up dubiously. 'My reason tells me that friendship is only good and lasting if the friends are of equal strength. Will not your friendship remain a condescending favour shown to a people who were not strong enough to resist when they were threatened?'

'Do not say that, Alach. I know how bitter you must feel, but believe me, that is not my way of thinking at all. I want peace with all your tribes.'

Alach's face was full of grief, but he did not lose his dignity.

'I know what makes you so strong, so unconquerable. It is not only your skill in war which makes you successful. You are also a man of understanding. Perhaps you dislike sitting here with me, the luckless leader of a poor tribe. But you do it because your head tells you that it is the right way to act. You think not only of today, but of tomorrow, too. You really do want friendship; I am sure you mean it sincerely. There is something about you . . .' And again Alach looked searchingly in Yermak's face. 'There is something about you that is hard to define. You are alone, are you not? A lonely man, I would say. For you there is only the task before you, and because you recognize nothing but our duty, you always do the right thing instinctively. You do not need long to make up your mind. You are like the lone bear who can smell every danger in the air and guard against it. That is what makes you so strong.'

And so Yermak achieved his object, which was Alach's friendship. Alach was Samar's successor and prince of all the tribes in this territory. He undertook to keep order, to collect tribute and to send it to Isker.

Yermak had conquered the land of Yugor. Now he could return with his army.

22 THE ENDLESS CHAIN

It was a laborious journey back to Isker, rowing the clumsy rafts against the current. The days were long and hot. When the Cossacks passed through the marshes they felt they could cut the air with their knives, it was so heavy and oppressive. The sweat streamed down their backs and thighs. They tore off their shirts and trousers and breathed with relief. But it was not long before they had to put them back again as swarms of mosquitoes and stinging gnats descended on their sticky bodies.

They had to beg for a rest more and more frequently and it was only when it rained that they made good progress. Yermak realized that it was better to rest during the day and to travel at night, so they pitched their tents at noon. Hot as it was inside them, it was easier to bear than the terrible plague of gnats and flies.

Since Mitya had become Yermak's interpreter he often shared a tent with him. One day as they were lying side by side Mitya asked, 'Do you think Ivan Koltso is in Moscow yet?'

'I hope he is on his way back to Isker,' replied Yermak.

'I wonder what kind of a reply he will bring you.'

There was no answer.

'Suppose he met Vassili Metyanov at court,' Mitya went on. 'If Vassili has to do his service occasionally, it is possible.'

'But Ivan does not know him.'

'Of course not. I had forgotten.'

'And in any case, the Kremlin and all the royal apartments are so big, they would never meet except by design.'

'Do you still remember what it looks like?'

'Yes, I often recall it all—the pillars, the lofty state apartments, the many servants.'

'What does the Czar look like?'

'He was still young when I saw him last. He was of medium height, not quite as tall as my father. He had glossy black hair and a keen face. But my mother was often frightened of his eyes. She often used to say he could kill people with a look if he wanted to.'

'Vassili said that he spends whole days on his knees, praying.'

'That is perfectly true, but when he gets up again he spends whole weeks murdering.'

Mitya did not answer. Then as if he was thinking aloud he said,

'You hate him yet you fight for him. You could have gone back to Oryol instead of conquering Yugor. I cannot understand you.'

'By the Volga I was a bandit and there were few to equal me, I assure you. Now that I am in the service of the Stroganovs, I am just as thorough. When they sent me out to conquer this land, I became a conqueror. That this meant winning Siberia for the Czar was only incidental. I had a task to perform and I did it.'

'But when you speak to the natives here, you always say that the Czar has sent you.'

'Do you think I should say the Stroganovs ordered it? What would the name mean to the foreigner? No, Mitya. This lie is part of my mission if I am to carry it out. The means is bad, I admit, but what it will achieve is good, though good for whom is not important. You see, Mitya, one day this Czar will be followed by another, and I hope, a better man who will not have to kill to keep his throne. But whoever it may be, Siberia will belong to him, and all because we set out to conquer it.'

'When I first came with you to the Volga,' said Mitya with strange emotion, 'Boris said that you always think a step ahead of the other Captains. And all the time I have been a Cossack, I have noticed that he was right. But it is only now that I realize just how far ahead you look. I don't know how to say it, but my heart is so full of admiration and respect that I don't know how to show you what I feel. I would like to do something . . .'

'I'll tell you what to do, Mitya. Go to sleep now so that you will be able to pull a good oar tomorrow.' Then a moment later he added, 'I know what you mean, child.'

When they approached the Konda once more Mitya felt pleasantly excited. He kept looking out for Voksar long before he could possibly have come into sight. 'Perhaps he will come a little way to meet us now that his father is back,' thought Mitya hopefully. But there was no boat to be seen on the broad surface of the river. They rowed on and Mitya became impatient. Soon they would reach the spot where Ishberdei had joined them on their outward journey. Mitya grew more and more tense as he watched the right bank. Then from the distance he could see several figures. He could not make them out yet, but they must be Ishberdei and his men.

'Look, Yermak, our friends are expecting us. They will bring us fish and fresh meat.' And Mitya's eyes kept searching for Voksar. He could make out the prince and the soothsayer; only Voksar with his dog were not there. Where were they hiding? Why had they not come, too?

Yermak steered the raft towards the banks and Mitya, who had been rowing for all he was worth in eager anticipation, was seized with a curious premonition. Where could Voksar be? His arms grew heavy; he did not want to land. He could not think why Voksar was not waiting for him. What was there here for him if . . .

Yermak waved to Ishberdei, who bowed and waved back. But his greeting had no warmth in it.

The Ostyaks waded out into the river and towed the raft ashore. Yermak leapt on to the dry land. He approached the Prince and kissed him on the shoulder as was the custom between friends.

'I rejoice to see you again, Ishberdei.'

'I am glad, too, my lord.'

'You say that you are glad, but you do not look it.'

'Was the campaign successful?' asked Ishberdei evasively.

'Yes, we were very lucky. Fortune favoured us throughout. But tell me, where is your son?'

Isberdei stared in front of him with a frozen face. 'Oh, my lord, Trum did not wish him to greet you. He has made the journey to Trum. He has been laid in his boat with all his weapons.' Ishberdei's voice was hoarse. His face looked grey and his features slack.

Mitya stared at him helplessly.

'Voksar is dead?' he asked and forgot to translate the words for Yermak. But he did not wait for an answer. 'No!' he shouted. 'I don't believe it, Ishberdei. It isn't true!'

Ishberdei stood there and looked at him.

'Was it hunting . . .?' asked Mitya.

Ishberdei shook his head. 'He was dead when I returned. They were followers of Prince Demian who murdered him. They wanted to avenge my deeds.'

'But you did nothing wrong . . .' Mitya broke off when he saw how Ishberdei stared at the ground.

'It cannot be altered now,' he said.

But Mitya did not know if he meant the death of his son, or that his services to Yermak would always look like treason to the Ostyaks.

'I want to thank you for your friendship to Voksar, Mitya. He valued it greatly.'

As in a nightmare, Mitya told Yermak what had occurred. And all that happened afterwards seemed like a dream, too: the gathering round the fire and the loading of the supplies which Ishberdei had brought. Mitya did not want to talk to anyone. He wanted only one thing, to be alone. Voksar was dead. The Ostyaks had taken their vengeance on him.

No, no. It couldn't be true. Why had they done it? If they wanted revenge, why did they not kill Ishberdei himself? Why Voksar, who was in no way to blame? And where was the blame, in any event? What crime had Ishberdei committed and what was Voksar's?

'Where is Kushla?' asked Mitya as he clasped Ishberdei's hand in parting.

'She died with him. She was lying by his side in the tent when the men came in the night.'

Skeins of geese flew over the river as the Cossacks rowed on. They flew in such numbers that the sky seemed to be overcast with grey cloud. The air was noisy with the beat of their wings. The sun turned to red as it set and from the sedge came the call of the ducks, orr . . . orr . . . orr . . . The oars cut the water in steady time. Everything was just as it had been before, but Voksar was dead.

'Can you tell me how these things happen, how innocence becomes guilt, Yermak?'

'Who can say, Mitya? Perhaps it all began when we launched our rafts into the Tura. Perhaps it was when Kuchum Khan killed Sultan Etiger. Perhaps it was long before that. Maybe no one is really to blame in that sense. Perhaps things happen according to some universal law which we do not understand.'

'According to a law? That does not help Voksar. He is dead and he will never go hunting again. His heart will never again leap with joy when he catches sight of the elk and hears the baying of the stag. This law of yours must be a law of hatred, Yermak.'

'Yes, that is so. There is hatred everywhere, and if you pursue even the most righteous cause long enough it turns to injustice.'

'I suppose that is how Ishberdei's conduct looked from the Ostyaks' point of view. But then injustice breeds new hatred and lust for revenge. Are we not men with understanding in our hearts as well as hatred?'

'To understand is to forgive, Mitya, and that is much harder than taking revenge. A man must renounce something of himself to forgive the man who has wronged him.'

'And is that more difficult?'

'Then pardon those who killed Voksar. Can you do it?'

'That's different,' retorted Mitya.

'No, it is just the same. You see, you are aggrieved that the men who killed your friend should not have pardoned Ishberdei, but you in turn will not forgive them.'

'But if anyone was to blame it was Ishberdei and not Voksar. Why did they kill him?'

'That was how they could hurt him most deeply. And if he has the opportunity, Ishberdei will avenge his son's death. It is like a chain, Mitya, a chain forged link by link. Don't you see?'

'Yes, yes. I can see. And all because we hate where we should forgive.'

They said no more, and as they sailed along the river Mitya remembered Ilya that night after the battle on the Chussovaya, and how he had left him dying there because he wanted his revenge. There was a terrible turmoil within him. 'I am no better than the men who killed Voksar,' he told himself. 'But then Ilya would have died even if I had carried him to the camp with the other wounded. No! You can't talk yourself out of it like that. You must take the blame. You would not forgive him.'

Four days after they had left Ishberdei the Cossacks made out on the left bank the watch-tower and the roofs of Isker. They rowed with all their strength, oblivious of the sun and the sweat.

'We're nearly home! There is Isker. We shall soon be home!'

And when Yermak heard them speak he thought: Now they look on Siberia as their home. This land is Russia now. Yes, Russia stretches farther to the east than ever before.

The river bank was crowded with what looked like scurrying ants. The Cossacks who had remained behind in Isker flew their banners and waved their hands in wild delight.

A few of them jumped into the water and swam towards the rafts, pulling them in towards the land. Everything must be well here, thought Yermak, and he went straight up to Yakob Michailov. Yermak embraced him and he did not need to ask any questions. Michailov reported everything of his own accord:

'The tribes brought in their tribute regularly. Now and then we had to keep order, but there were no attacks on our men when they went out foraging for supplies. Kuchum Khan is abiding by your conditions.'

'And how is Mametkul?' asked Yermak.

'He is well, too.'

Yermak was greatly relieved as they entered the town together. And as he told Yakob about their experiences in the north, the Cossacks' words kept running through his head, 'Now we are back in Isker. Now we have come home.'

Siberia was truly conquered.

23 THE CZAR'S EAGLE IN THE FIRELIGHT

When was Ivan Koltso coming back? In spite of the satisfaction he felt at what had been achieved, that was the question which tormented Yermak soon after his return. What news would Koltso bring? The garrison's gunpowder was running low. If the Cossacks were to hold what they had won, if they were to retain the awe and respect of the natives, then they must have effective fire-arms.

The men needed a thorough rest after the strain of the recent campaign, and this enforced inactivity made Yermak more impatient than ever. It aggravated his mounting uncertainty. He could not bear such idleness. Sometimes he went fishing and hunting to kill the time, but more often he visited the Tartar villages which had been detailed to supply food for his army. Usually the chieftains received and entertained him with obsequious protestations of loyalty, but he could not help thinking of his ammunition supplies and how swiftly this humility would turn to revenge if the Cossacks could no longer load their guns at will. Then the yellow skins and slanting eyes became unbearably repugnant and Yermak would end the meal and the conversation the moment politeness allowed and gallop home to Isker. Perhaps Ivan Koltso had returned during Yermak's absence and he spurred on his horse until its mouth dripped with foam.

There were other Tartar chiefs with more pride and self-assurance, and their mask-like faces were less distasteful to him. At least he knew where he was with them. They did not show open hostility, but they would dare to fight again if they had the opportunity. Kuchum Khan might be a fugitive wandering over the steppes, but they still considered him their lawful ruler, a descendant of Genghis Khan's.

Among these was Prince Karacha. He had been conquered at the outset of the campaign, but who had not been forced to yield to the invader since then? Yermak had defeated them all, even the Crown Prince with his ten thousand men, but Karacha was still humiliated by the recollection of his defeat. It tortured him so much that when he was alone he had fits of rage which left him almost unconscious. Even when Karacha came to Isker to pay tribute, Yermak knew that he at least remained an implacable enemy.

The remaining Tartars seemed merely indifferent. They did not care who ruled in Isker as long as they were left alone. Yermak could not count them either for him or against him. All they wanted were peace and settled conditions so that trade could be resumed. So far the merchants from Bukhara and China had not found their way back to Isker, for the River Irtish, their main trade route, was too unsafe. Kuchum Khan's followers now lived as free-booters on the steppes and they lay in wait on the river banks to attack merchant shipping. No, the traders were still waiting, and who could blame them when the risk of losing everything to these pirates was so great? They were bad times and business was at a standstill.

Yermak knew that the only chance of restoring commerce to its previous prosperity was to consolidate his position. This in turn depended on Ivan Koltso's success or failure, and Yermak chafed more than ever at the inevitable waiting.

'I'd like to know what's wrong with you, Mitya,' said Boris one evening. 'You sit around brooding all the time. You hardly do anything with yourself. Why don't you learn some of our Cossack dances? You always said you would like to when there was time, but now you just sit there gaping at us. What is the matter?'

'Nothing,' said Mitya, reluctant to be drawn into an argument. 'The dances are all the same really. There's nothing to choose between them.'

'You're thinking again, that's what it is. I'm right, aren't I?'

'Why shouldn't I?' retorted Mitya sharply. 'You prefer to dance and I would rather think, that's all. Just leave me alone, there's a good chap!'

'What good is all this thinking of yours in the end? It will never alter facts, you know. No one can prevent things happening if they have to be. Why, next summer, I may find I don't like *koumis* any more, but that does not stop me from enjoying it today! No, Mitya. I don't think, I live. And that's the best way. Enjoy life as it comes.'

Mitya did not answer. You are alive and that's fine, he wanted to protest, but what about Voksar? He, too, would have loved to live, and Ilya and all our friends whom we have buried. No, I can't accept things as simply as Boris does.

The summer came to an end and the first storms of the autumn began to pluck the golden-brown leaves from the oak and aspen trees. The belling of elk and stag boomed through the forest and every day the triple-spanned carts arrived in Isker delivering the freshly gathered harvest.

A raft was speeding down the Tobol towards its junction with the Irtish, towing a boat behind it. The man steering had to use all his strength to keep it under control.

'This will make them stare all right,' he muttered to himself. 'Oho, they'll open their eyes, and their ears into the bargain.'

From the citadel of Isker, the Cossack sentinels watched the river. They saw the raft floating along and there were two men on it.

'Isn't that . . .?' said one of them.

'Can that be . . .?' called the other.

They waited a little until it was nearer.

'Yes, it is he!' cried the first one. He ran down the steps shouting at the top of his voice: 'Captain Ivan is here. Ivan Koltso is coming!'

Like wildfire the word spread through the streets: 'Ivan Koltso is back!' 'Down to the river! Ivan Koltso is coming!'

Everyone was gripped by the excitement. What would he have to tell them? At least the Czar had not arrested him in Moscow. That surely must be a good sign.

'Long live the Czar! Long live the Father of his people!'

The Cossacks from Ivan Koltso's hundred jumped on to their rafts to be the first to meet their Captain.

'Ivan!' they called, waving with both arms. 'Good old Ivan. We've been waiting for you so long. Now you are back with us.'

Ivan Koltso laughed across to them. 'My brothers, my comrades!' And when the rafts were side by side, they jumped across to him. They insisted on bringing him in to shore and they bombarded him with questions.

'Presently, lads,' said Ivan, refusing to be rushed. 'I'll tell you when we're all together. Otherwise I'll have to repeat it for the rest of them, and it's a long story. I'd rather hear how you've been getting on. A few more scars, eh? No one missing, I hope?'

Then he saw Yermak waiting on the bank and he could hardly wait to get ashore.

'You always rebuked the Tartars and Ostyaks when they adressed you as Prince,' he said, when he and Yermak had embraced. 'But now I bring you the title from Moscow—Yermak Timofeyev, Prince of Siberia.'

Yermak stopped and looked at him inquiringly.

'Don't you believe me?' chortled Ivan Koltso. 'I have it in writing, too. I know I cannot read, but he told me so himself.'

'Do you mean the Czar?'

'Yes, the Czar, may Heaven protect him.'

The words sounded strange in Ivan Koltso's mouth and the men looked at each other.

'Come home with me, Ivan. And the rest of you, prepare some food and light a fire in the square. We shall all meet there and then Ivan will tell us about Moscow.'

'Haul the boat up into the town,' said Ivan Koltso. 'No, don't unpack it. Take it just as it is.'

'So he has pardoned us?' asked Yermak, and closed the door behind them.

'Yes, not only you and me, but all the Cossacks on the Volga. And you are Prince of Siberia as long as you live.'

'Don't you mean as long as we stay here?'

'But why should we leave, now that Moscow is behind us?'

'How many soldiers are coming? How much powder and shot, Ivan?'

'Oh, you're always worrying. Now that you are Prince of Siberia . . .'

'Ivan,' Yermak interrupted him firmly. 'We both know just how little this precious title is worth. It has nothing more solid behind it than our guns, and their barrels will soon turn to rust unless we . . .'

'You'll get everything, but damn it all, have you forgotten how to feel pleased?'

'Of course I am glad, Ivan. I did not mean to be ungrateful, but I have many cares on my shoulders, you know.' Yermak stood before Kuchum Khan's chair and kicked the toe of his boot against its legs.

Ivan watched him and suddenly he had to admit that Yermak was right. What did it mean if the Czar created him a prince? He has been a prince for a long time, at least as long as I have known him. Probably he was born a prince. We were just Captains, but he was always so much more. He was always a prince among us men. And this sudden insight helped him to bear his disappointment at Yermak's indifference.

'The Czar is sending out a Commander-in-chief. He is called Bolshovski and he is a prince, too. He is coming here with three hundred sharpshooters and with adequate supplies of ammunition. He was due to leave soon after my own departure.'

'Then we can expect them before the winter sets in. I hope they are hurrying. They must arrive before the rivers freeze over.'

'They are not coming by river. They are mounted.'

'What? Riding here on horseback?' Yermak was almost screaming. 'And you did not talk him out of it?'

'Do you think a General, and a Russian prince at that, will listen to a poor Cossack Captain? I did try to stop him, you can believe me, but his Highness knew better.'

'Then I don't know what . . .' Yermak controlled himself. He dropped into the Khan's chair. 'Very well then,' he said at last. 'We shall have to wait for him to arrive.'

Ivan Koltso sat down on the couch and looked at Yermak for a moment.

'I have some more news from Moscow which will not please you, either,' he said presently.

'Information do you mean? Or is it an order?'

Ivan kept his eyes on Yermak. 'You are to send the Crown Prince to the Kremlin immediately.'

'Mametkul?' Yermak jumped to his feet. 'I might have known. He wants to celebrate his triumph. The Czar of all the Russias, may Heaven . . . And as for us, we can let ourselves be picked off by Kuchum Khan's arrows.'

'That is the Czar's command.'

'Command, command!' Yermak paced up and down with deep emotion. 'A fig for such commands! I have conducted a victorious campaign without any of his instructions. I had a handful of outlaws, but no commands from the Czar. He must leave it to me to decide when to send him Mametkul.'

'Yermak,' said Ivan Koltso quietly, 'I told you before I went that I was not the right ambassador to send to Moscow. You might have been able to argue with the Czar, but I did not dare.'

'No, no, Ivan, it isn't that. No one could have done more.' And as he spoke Ivan Koltso could see that Yermak's thoughts were far away. 'But the winter can set in any day now. Bolshovski is not yet here and no one in Moscow knows how long you have taken to travel. I must get through this winter without any incidents. I shall not send Mametkul before the spring.'

Ivan looked at his friend.

'That's a good way out, Yermak,' he said with genuine relief.

The men lit a big fire in the square outside Yermak's house and everyone sat round and ate. When they finished and the flagons were passed from mouth to mouth, Ivan Koltso told them all about Moscow. And the picture which his simple words painted was like a fairy tale. They listened in breathless silence.

'Feodor Masupov came with me. You all know him—Maxim Stroganov's right-hand man. We had a terrible journey to Moscow. The thaw had set in and we could hardly move. Damn it all, it was a miserable business. But the horses battled through the mud until the sweat ran down their necks. They were fine horses.' Ivan Koltso paused and took a deep draught of beer. Then he wiped his beard with the back of his hand, cleared his throat and went on.

'As we got nearer to Moscow, I kept thinking, "I wonder if you'll ever come back along this road?" I can tell you frankly, you know I'm not a coward when it comes to facing the enemy, brothers, but to put your head in the bear's den . . . I don't mind telling you, my knees felt pretty weak . . .' He pulled a face so that they could hardly see his eyes. 'Mind you, I did not say so to Masupov. I wasn't going to let a wretched shopkeeper like that, a fellow who only knows how to swindle his customers, know how I felt. There was I, then, conquering Siberia one day, and the next, with my bowels turning to water . . .' He did not say any more, but the men understood him, and they kept their eyes glued to his face, which was red from the firelight and the beer.

'From a long way away we could see the domes of the great town where the Czar lives. It's a beautiful city with so many towers, big and small, pointed and round, like the churches in Byzantium. That's what Masupov told me. I don't know if it's true, because I've never been there. Neither has he for that matter, but he knows! He says that foreigners built these churches with their spires and domes: Germans, Swedes, Greeks—I don't know if it's true, but Masupov told me it was. Some of them gleamed like gold and some were bright blue like the sky in early summer over the steppes. Oh, they were splendid!—Well let me go on. We did not go straight to the Kremlin. "There's a storm brewing there," said Masupov, and we went to the house of Boris Godunov, who is a friend of the Stroganovs. The war with the Swedes and the Poles was not going too well, so Masupov did not dare to present me to the Czar right away. I did not mind, of course. I was quite happy where I was. I had a good bed and as much to eat and drink as I wanted and everyone pricked their ears when I told them of our expedition and how we had chased Kuchum Khan from his capital.'

Then Ivan Koltso had another drink and he thought for a while before he went on with his tale.

'In those days before I was allowed to see the Czar I learnt a lot. "Do not strut before him as a conqueror, but approach humbly as a petitioner, as a penitent who has come to beg for mercy from the Czar." That was what Masupov told me!' Ivan Koltso cleared his throat again. 'A petitioner, a penitent? I did not know how you go about such things, you understand me, brothers, don't you? But Masupov said I had only to learn to hang my head. So I said to myself, "Well, Ivan, that's better than hanging by the neck." So I practised bowing and scraping a bit and I found it doesn't do a fellow much harm.'

The Cossacks looked at their Captain with shining eyes.

'And then the day came. We drove to the Kremlin. It's a huge place, I tell you, a fine building and as strong as a fortress. The walls are thick, with massive towers. There are sentries everywhere and I walked in front of Masupov through the great gates as he had told me. I wasn't swaggering exactly, but neither was I cringing. We went into a courtyard and through a wide gateway, then across a big hall with doors to the right and doors to the left, and through all kinds of doors which opened for us as we approached and then closed behind us. You couldn't hear a single footstep, so thick were the carpets. In one hall we were made to wait. Then a pair of doors in front of us flew open and Masupov nodded to me. So in I went, alone, moving slowly step by step. This was where I had to walk as a penitent, so I could only squint with my head down to make sure I was keeping in the right direction, for I had given a quick glance inside as the door was flung open.

'It was hard going, brothers. There was a red carpet under my feet and it ended in two steps. Right and left all I could see were the tips of various pairs of boots, and it was so still in the audience chamber that you could have heard a mouse squeak. That is if there had been a mouse there, squeaking, I mean. Two steps to go, then one, and there I was at the foot of the dais, and I fell on one knee. "Exalted Czar," I said, "you who by the grace of God are Czar of all the Russias, allow one of your despised subjects to come before your eyes. Be pleased to listen to him while he announces that Siberia has been conquered for you, and in your great goodness read this letter which Yermak Timofeyev has written. Here he tells you how he has won Siberia with five hundred Cossacks and three hundred soldiers from the Stroganovs' militia. Kuchum Khan has fled and his son and heir, Mametkul, is a prisoner in Isker. All the vassals and subjects of the Khan have sworn an oath of allegiance to you, your Majesty, and they send you their first tribute, two thousand four hundred sables, fifty beavers, and twenty black foxes. Now accept us in your service. Rule over us, most exalted Majesty."

'That was what I said, brothers, and all was still again in the chamber. Then I heard him speak. "You bring us good news, Captain Ivan Koltso, and to someone who has struck so honourable a blow for us, we shall not refuse our mercy." I felt as if the heavens had opened. Mercy, I thought, he said "Mercy". That must mean a pardon for us. His voice was soft and suddenly I saw a hand before my face. "Kiss our hand, Captain, and with this kiss you and your brothers are pardoned." I did as I was told and the Czar told me to stand up and take my place with his nobles. So I looked up, and I discovered Boris Godunov in whose house I was staying standing there with Masupov. He moved aside a little and I stood near him. The Czar looked at me and I at him, for I was no penitent in sackcloth and ashes now, was I? Then he had Yermak's letter read aloud and when Boris Godunov had finished the Czar took off his cloak of sable and ermine and said: 'Take this to Yermak Timofeyevich, who now, according to our will, is Prince of Siberia. He shall receive also the goblet out of which we have drunk until this day and we will send him a suit of armour which it is our pleasure he shall wear. You and your brothers shall each receive a dagger from our armoury as a sign that we have forgotten all our previous displeasure."

'By this time I was beginning to feel positively uncomfortable at so much grace and favour and I thought to myself, "We must have done something extraordinary to be given such rewards." Then the Czar inspected the presents and I was dismissed.

'I left that chamber with its red carpets and tall windows a good deal lighter in heart than when I entered it, you can believe me. I thought of you all and I think I felt happier than ever before in my life. I went back to Boris Godunov's house with Masupov and you can't imagine how delighted everyone was. I spoke to Bolshovski as well, the general who is on his way to us, and Maxim Stroganov appeared unexpectedly one day with Semyon, too. And everyone was in the kind of mood I cannot begin to describe.'

'Did you hear what happened to Murashkin when we left the Volga to march to Perm?' asked Yermak after a while.

'Oh yes, I had almost forgotten. Yes, Murashkin did set out with an army for the Don and the Volga, just as Yermak told us he would, and they were evil days for our brothers who remained. Many of them were killed in battle or hanged afterwards and only those who could flee escaped death. The steppes, thank God, are wide and kind and some were able to hide. And when I heard about it, I thought what a good thing that we followed Yermak.

And now, brothers, I shall finish my story. I visited the streets in Moscow where the various traders live, and I sat in inns, and I went into the churches, too. Then came the day when I had to leave. At last, I thought, at last I can get back to my brothers. I rode back to Oryol in Maxim Stroganov's *troika*. He greets you all and thanks each one of you individually. Well, that's what happened, lads, and now I am back again.'

At first it was very still and then a voice came from the circle:

'Long live Ivan Koltso!'

And this was repeated first by one and then another and the cry went up from every throat:

'Huzzah for Ivan! He was a fine spokesman for us in Moscow. He was the right man to send.'

Everyone came crowding round the boat which had been lying by Koltso's side all the time. He unpacked the daggers and the mantle of sable and ermine which the Czar had taken from his own shoulders. Then he showed them the heavy armour which the Czar had sent and they fingered it reverently.

'Now nothing more can happen to you, Yermak,' they said. 'And we shall be safe, too. As long as you live, all will be well.' And they clamoured for him to try on the magnificent suit of armour.

Yermak put it on and stood there before the Cossacks. The fire-light poured a red glory over the polished steel and the imperial eagle glowed across the breast-plate.

A heavy silence descended on the gathering.

'Well, why don't you say something,' teased Yermak. 'Don't you like me in it?'

There was a pause before he received an answer .

'Oh yes, we like it,' they answered, but there was no warmth in the reply.

Then Boris's father, Igor, spoke up for them all. 'It's only that you look so different, Yermak, as if you don't belong to us any more. It's so stiff, so hard. . . . It takes you away from us, sets you apart. . . .'

24 A RICH BUT CRUEL LAND

Winter came as suddenly and violently as it almost always does in Siberia. One morning the Cossacks awoke to find that the land was muffled in a thick blanket of snow, criss-crossed with the spoor of the wild creatures. The heavy snow bore down on the tall, ancient trees and the branches drooped under its weight. The Cossacks set about building traps and every day they went to fetch the game they had caught.

The days grew short and the time of darkness inevitably longer. The men got out their instruments and from behind closed doors could be heard the plucked strings and the voices as the songs echoed down the streets. Mitya joined in, and as he sang he remembered how he had dreamed of songs like these back at home. He thought, too, of Voksar, to whom he had sung them last winter as they sat round the fire in Ishberdei's tent.

Often Mitya sought Yermak's company. He badly wanted to talk to him about Voksar, but whenever they were alone together something prevented him from speaking. Gradually he became aware that it was because Yermak could not forgive either, that his hatred went with him, accompanying him through life.

Yermak was waiting for General Bolshovski. But day after winter day passed by and nothing was heard of the Russian reinforcements.

'Just as I thought,' said Yermak to his Captains. 'Who knows if we shall ever see him? Perhaps he has turned back long ago with those horses of his. Or perhaps he has perished in the ice and snow.'

'But he has three hundred gunners with him,' protested Ivan Koltso. 'They can't all have . . .' His failure to convince Bolshovski not to go on horseback worried him more and more as he thought of their dwindling supplies and saw Yermak's worried face.

'We must wait,' said Yermak in reply. He never reproached Koltso.

'I wouldn't waste any tears on that nincompoop from Moscow,' thundered Matvei. 'We don't need him, if only we had the gunpowder he's bringing. That's all we really want.'

'We could use the soldiers, too,' said Nikita Pan frankly.

'I don't know if Bolshovski is a nincompoop or not,' said Yakob Michailov thoughtfully, 'but he does not seem to take his mission very seriously or he would have been here long ago.'

Bolshovski came with the spring floods when the Tobol rolled in yellow torrents past the walls of Isker. He came by river as the Cossacks had done in their time. Fifteen hastily-built rafts contained all that was left of his reinforcements and supplies.

When he stepped ashore, he was already a dying man.

'Welcome to the capital of Siberia,' said Yermak, and embraced him. Bolshovski's eyes were sunk deep into their sockets and his face had fallen in. The fur mantle hung loose and wide from his shoulders as if it had been made for a much bigger man. It seemed to weigh him down to the ground. The tall fur cap was perched on his head like that of a scarecrow.

'You have had to wait a long time for me, Yermak Timofeyevich,' he said, holding himself erect. Yermak saw what a strain it was for him to stand and led him to the divan.

'Sit down, Prince Bolshovski,' he said. 'You have a weary journey behind you.'

'Yes, Yermak Timofeyevich. And what I bring you is only a small part of what I set out with.' He was too ill to spare himself. He collapsed on to the couch. 'This is a terrible land,' he said and his head was bowed. 'We have had to bury many of our soldiers on the way; we haven't a single horse left, and our food is finished. Most of it went bad and the rest we have eaten. Many of the men are as ill as I am.' He stopped. 'Why, oh why did I not listen to Ivan Koltso? Why did I not take his advice?'

Yermak did not add to his self-reproaches.

'What about ammunition? It would be most useful if we . . .'

'Whatever is still usable is on the rafts.'

'Good.'

The general sat up.

'How did you conquer this enormous country with all its snow and mud, Yermak? However did you do it?' He sank back again and buried his head in his hands. 'It is a terrible land, a cruel land,' he groaned.

'But it is also a rich land, Prince Igor, so rich that it will take many years even to calculate the full extent of its wealth. When you see it in summer, you will soon forget the winter.'

'I shall never see the summer, Prince Yermak.'

Nine days later they buried the general in Isker and during the next few weeks they had to dig many more graves by his side.

'So much for soldiers from Moscow!' said one Cossack to his friend as he paused in his grave-digging and leaned on his spade. 'And they didn't even have to fight their way as we did!'

'They have meant nothing but extra work for us,' grumbled the other. 'They would have done better to remain where they were.'

In the previous spring the Cossacks had often talked about going home, but this year they hardly mentioned it. Perhaps they were getting used to Siberia. It was no longer a foreign land to them, but home. Perhaps also there was a certain pride in having conquered a country where others had succumbed so easily.

Then bit by bit the picture changed, and things began to happen too fast for them to dwell on their homesickness. With a heavy heart and the greatest secrecy, Yermak had equipped a small troop and sent it to Moscow with the Crown Prince. Nevertheless, Kuchum Khan must have got wind of it, for just as Yermak had feared, the Tartars began to make themselves a nuisance once more. Now that Kuchum had no need to take consideration for his son's life, he set about trying to dislodge the Cossacks.

The first attack was on Nikita Pan and his men, who had gone to one village to collect supplies long overdue. On the way, archers shot arrows at them and two men were wounded. Nikita immediately gave chase, but the distance was too great for them to shoot their assailants and the enemy soon reached the cover of the forest and were safe. All the Tartars escaped.

A few days later a similar thing happened to Matvei Meshcherak and from then on the Cossacks had to be continually on their guard against ambushes. Yermak at once strengthened the patrols round Isker and watch was kept day and night. The ammunition supplies worried him greatly, but he did not despair. The escort he had sent to Moscow had been instructed to ask for urgent and effective help, not a mere drop in the ocean like General Bolshovski's gunners. It was this hope of help from Russia which sustained Yermak through these trying times.

The attacks were not the only sign that Kuchum was stirring. The Tartars became careless about paying their tribute. They came with excuses: the harvest had been bad, the winter hard or the cattle were still too lean. They told the Cossacks that Kuchum Khan's men often descended on them and stole what they needed.

'Then mount a guard and resist them,' Yermak retorted. 'I am the Prince of Siberia. You have sworn me an oath of loyalty and I insist on my tribute. Don't think that I am trifling. You know my weapons. I shall use them ruthlessly if you do not pay up.'

The Tartars bowed before him, but Yermak could sense their defiance and hostility.

Prince Karacha sat with his guest in his tent. He finished chewing his meat and threw the mutton bone into the fire.

'Do you really think Yermak will come himself?' he asked.

'Why not, Karacha? If he cannot get enough meat and grain for his soldiers, the game is up. I should have thought it was vital for him.'

'Then Allah be praised if he strikes the infidel with such blindness. But suppose he does not come, Abish?'

'Then he will send one of his Captains and I should not think it will be the worst of them either. Whatever happens, it must surely weaken the might of the invaders and Allah be praised for that, too.'

'You speak as if the deed were already done.'

'Trust me, Karacha, and all will go well. You can see for yourself how Yermak has to wait for tribute. Would he have sent for you to come to Isker otherwise? He will ask you why these payments are delayed and you will answer him as we have agreed. Allah is with you, believe me. You have been chosen by him to restore Kuchum Khan to power and to avenge his son, Mametkul.' An ambiguous smile played round the lips of Prince Abish, for it was he who had betrayed Mametkul to Yermak.

'Praise be to Allah. I shall do it.' Karacha stood up. He girt on his scimitar and walked to the entrance to the tent. 'Ride away in this same hour, Abish, and rally all the tribes for Kuchum Khan whom Allah has blessed with such courage and wisdom.'

Karacha raised the curtain and went out of doors. His servants must have been watching for him, for he had hardly time to drop the hanging again before his horse was led to him. As he mounted two youths who were hardly more than boys darted across to him.

'Let us ride with you, Father. Take us with you,' they cried.

'Today I must go alone, but you shall come with me quite soon. Until then, keep your swords sharpened.'

'Father!' they cried aloud and their narrow faces flushed with excitement.

'But do not talk about it, my sons.' He whipped up his horse.

'Allah be with you, Father!'

'And with you, too.'

It did not look as if the conspiracy which Abish the traitor had plotted would succeed, after all. Yermak turned a deaf ear when Karacha explained to him that it was Kuchum's soldiers who were stopping the tribes from paying tribute to Yermak.

'They attack us as soon as we prepare to come to Isker, Prince Yermak. We do not dare to come to you any more. We have no soldiers like you. I do not need your whole army, of course. If you and a few of your Cossacks escorted us personally, that would do. Kuchum's followers are no cowards, believe me, but they are afraid of you.'

'How can you ask me to do such a thing? Was Kuchum in the habit of going out himself to collect his due? What do you take me for?' And Yermak's armour clanked indignantly with every movement.

'It is no use,' thought Karacha. 'It was not a good plan. Yermak will not come and even if he did we cannot wound him. No dagger can pierce this armour of his.'

All the same, Karacha tried again. 'I could bring you even more tribute than you have asked for. My tribes will give you everything they possess. We do not want to be enemies. We want peace. But I do not see how we can fulfil your demands without your help.'

'Very well, I shall think it over, Karacha. Be my guest and then ride back to your own people.'

A few days later Yermak gave in and Ivan Koltso got ready to leave with forty Cossacks to escort Karacha's wagons back to Isker.

'If it were anyone else but Karacha, I would not let you go, Ivan, but I trust his word. He may be an enemy, but he is a man of honour and he would not behave like a hypocrite. Farewell, Ivan, and bring it home to Kuchum's men that we mean business.'

'You know me well enough,' laughed Koltso from the saddle. 'I hope you won't be bored here in Isker while we are away.' And he waved his sword gaily. 'Come on, brothers. We have no time to lose.'

They galloped away in a whirling cloud of dust and the Cossacks went back to their usual hunting, fishing and riding.

It must have been in the third week since Ivan Koltso's departure that a solitary rider drew near to Isker. He crouched in the saddle, exhausted. His face was crusted with dirt and his horse was worn out. The sentinels in the watch-tower tried to guess who it might be. They could tell he was a Cossack by his clothes, so they ran down the steps and flung open the gate. The man collapsed into their arms, not listening to any of their questions.

'I must see Yermak!' he gasped. His mouth was parched and he could barely speak. They propped him up in the saddle again and led his horse forward.

Yermak was at home. When he heard the excited voices in the street he ran to the door. He saw the haggard figure tottering towards him.

'You are Sergei, one of Ivan Koltso's men,' he said rapidly. 'What has happened? Why are you alone?'

'Yermak!' Sergei spoke with the greatest difficulty. 'They are all dead. The Tartars stabbed them to death, every one of them—Ivan, too.' And it was as if, until that moment, he himself had not grasped exactly what had happened. He dropped to the ground and clutched Yermak's knees with his hands. A dry sob shook his body. 'Karacha had them butchered, every man. I am the only one who escaped and I don't know how I did it. They are all dead, but not in battle. They stabbed us at night, in the tents. . . .'

Yermak lifted Sergei and carried him indoors. He laid him on a couch and then sat down at the far end. The Cossacks crept closer, making no sound. They hardly dared to breathe when they saw Yermak sitting there. His expression was frozen, his shoulders bowed. His face was grey and his arms dangled as if they were too heavy for him.

Sergei managed to summon a little strength.

'Be on your guard, Yermak. Karacha will not stop there. There was not a Tartar village where anyone would give me shelter or a morsel of food.' His voice shrilled hoarsely, so that everyone wished he would be silent. It was agony to hear him.

Yermak did not move. Igor gave a sign with his head and one after the other they left the room softly.

That evening Yermak called for Mitya.

'Would you like to move in here with me?' he asked as Mitya hesitated by the door. He had heard how Yermak had taken the news, and he had been nervous about meeting him. Now it gave him pleasure to think that he could be of some use to Yermak.

'Of course, if you want me.'

'Then fetch your things.'

They sat down on the couch and neither of them spoke. The silence grew more and more oppressive. If only he would say something, prayed Mitya, not just sit there, staring into space.

At last Yermak rose. He pointed to the left wall and said, 'Lie down over there, Mitya. We had better go to sleep.'

Mitya listened to Yermak's breathing. He was so absorbed in waiting for each breath that he started when Yermak began to speak.

'I spent most of my life with him. He was my teacher, if you like.

He taught me how to ride, how to fight, how to pillage and how to live as a Cossack. I learnt everything from him. He was like an older brother. Indeed, there was no one I called "brother" more readily. And then came a day when I knew more than my teacher. But still things remained the same between us. He was delighted. There was never a spark of jealousy or resentment. We were quite different and yet we were like brothers. And all at once, I am alone. I cannot quite grasp it yet. And he had forty faithful men with him. Why was I so stupid, so gullible? I cannot forgive myself. No, don't seek excuses for me, Mitya. I know you would like to. But I shall avenge them yet, every one of them!'

25 THE SIEGE

The Cossacks had not much time to brood over the deaths of their comrades. It seemed as if the Tartars had been waiting for a signal. Revolt broke out everywhere and wherever the Cossacks went they were attacked. The tribes stopped paying tribute altogether, and if the Cossacks needed food, they had to go and get it by force. Now they realized just how precarious was their conquest of Siberia.

The Ostyaks still refrained from attacking the Russians physically, but even they did not dare to come to Isker with meat and fish and furs, because they feared the Tartars would lay waste their villages if they remained loyal.

Yermak arranged for iron rations to be shared out fairly and for food to be stocked. They filled large vats with salted fish and daily meals were cut down to a minimum. But supplies of powder and shot were even shorter than food and Yermak did not know how he could replenish them. If a strong escort were provided, the river could still be fished, but there was no means of finding fresh sources of ammunition.

The other Captains did not seem to be so concerned about their situation.

'Who cares about powder and ball as long as we have our sabres?' grunted Matvei Meshcherak. 'I for one would much rather fight with the sword, in any case. What does it matter if we can't use the guns?'

'And we have horses now,' said Nikita Pan. 'There's no need to worry, Yermak. We'll be all right. Just let them come.'

Only Yakob Michailov shared Yermak's concern. 'You are right, Yermak. We must think twice before we fire a single shot. We simply do not know what they are planning next.'

'If you ask me, the best thing would be to smoke out that viper's nest of Karacha's,' thundered Matvei. 'It would be a pleasure to do it and so avenge Ivan Koltso.'

'And meanwhile the rest of us would be stuck here in Isker. No, that's no use. We must wait,' said Yermak.

They did not need to wait too long. The patrols round Isker brought more and more reports that they had seen Tartar encampments in the forests. They were closing in on Isker from all sides. There were frequent skirmishes; and burnt-out Tartar wagons, slaughtered horses and slain Tartars, too, were often left lying on the ground.

But the Cossacks had their casualties as well. Whenever they fought without firearms the enemy defended themselves to the last drop of blood. Then came a day when the first Ostyaks were pressed into battle on the side of the Tartars, and the Cossacks' anger mounted day by day when they saw how the Tartars exploited their weakness. They began to curse this land, which concealed such untold wealth. They thought of the houses in Isker, stacked to the roof-tops with precious furs. They could see the countryside spread out so temptingly with its forests, meadows and rivers; yet it seemed mysterious and sinister, like the faces of the aborigines. This was the realm they had conquered with such supreme exertion, in which so many of their brothers lay buried. Moss and ferns were already smothering their graves.

'It will swallow us all, this accursed land. It is like a bloodthirsty monster and everything we fought for will have been in vain.'

These words came to Yermak's ears.

'No,' he said one evening when they were sitting round the fire. 'This land will never conquer us. Do not forget that Mother Russia sent us here and when a mother sends her children, there they stay no matter how desperate the struggle. Even if we are driven out, others will come back. Remember that.'

During the night which followed this conversation the town of Isker was beleaguered. The enemy used the darkness to press closer and tighter round the town, until an unbroken ring of sturdy Tartar wagons hemmed in the Russians on all sides.

The Cossacks behind their strong defences waited for the attack. They could see that the enemy were well armed and their superiority in numbers was overwhelming. They guessed it would be a hard fight, but that made them only the more eager for it. Too many of their comrades had been left behind in the recent litle skirmishes. Now they would be avenged.

But no attack came either by day or by night. The Cossacks lay captive in their fortified town, their guns in their hands, their unsheathed swords stuck in their belts, but nothing happened. One week went by and then another.

'They dare not attack, the cowardly assassins,' said the Cossacks. 'They will withdraw again without having smelt our steel. We want to go over to the attack, just as we always did.'

But Yermak gave no orders. All he did was to send out a few raiding parties at night in which the Cossacks were to take prisoners and bring them into Isker for interrogation. It took a long time, but he managed to get out of them eventually that it was Karacha who was leading the enemy and that he was trying to reconquer Kuchum Khan's kingdom. Yermak learnt, too, that Voguls and Ostyaks were fighting side by side with the Tartars. The whole country had turned against them. Would he be able to subdue it yet again?

Days and nights passed and meals grew less and less satisfying. Isker was sealed off. The Cossacks could not even get down to the river, for the enemy's boats and rafts were moored side by side lying in wait.

'Let us attack them,' demanded the Captains loudly.

'No.'

'But they are trying to starve us out and they will succeed.'

'Their soldiers must be as tired of inaction as ours. Their supplies will be running short, too.'

'But ours are practically finished. The moon has changed twice since the siege started. We are slaughtering our horses for food.'

'The moon may change again before anything happens. But this is not the first time we have waited for dawn with empty bellies and night has fallen without any improvement.'

'But something must happen.'

'So it will. You must trust me.'

They went away grumbling.

On one of the following nights Mitya was on guard duty. Boris, who shared the watch with him, had dozed off. Mitya listened to the noises in the darkness. He heard the wing-beat of the owls which flew from the forests and prowled round the walls. He heard the stamping and snorting of the Tartar's horses. Scraps of conversation in foreign tongues drifted through the quiet of the night towards him. Sleep tormented him. 'If I sit down,' he told himself, 'I shall drop off right away,' and he jerked himself awake. 'Later, I shall sleep later. It's Boris's turn now.' He paced over to one side and then came back again. Then he explored the other side. Suddenly he thought he heard a rustle near the ground. He stopped at once and strained his eyes. Nothing. Oh well, on a night like this even a ghost could be heard. There it was again, the same pattering sound, as if someone was groping his way forward a few steps at a time.

Mitya did not move. Suddenly he saw a black shadow moving. Perhaps it was an animal. But an animal would not keep stopping like that. Mitya waited, sword in hand. The shadow came nearer slowly. It was a man. In a few feet he would have reached the fortification. He raised his head a little.

'Mitya!' came a whisper through the night.

Mitya stood there paralysed. It must be one of the Cossacks, he thought. But why was he creeping like that? Was the enemy behind him?

Again the soft call, 'Mitya!'

Who could it be? Whose was the voice? Then a hot wave of emotion flooded his body. He knew now who it was.

'Ishberdei!' he answered, just as quietly.

Still crouching, the man advanced two paces and he was there. Mitya stepped forward so that he could see him. The Ostyak prince dropped to the ground at his feet. 'Ishberdei, how do you come to be here?'

'They forced me to help them, Mitya. I am speaking the truth, believe me. There weren't many of us, but they made us come. Here, I will show you where we are sleeping. Can you see that tall clump of firs which reaches almost to the sky? Count as many fingers as I have on my two hands, and take so many paces on either side. Now you know where our tents are.'

'Why are you telling me?'

'You must tell my lord, Mitya. But hurry! Karacha is preparing to attack. He knows that you are hungry in Isker. Tell my lord that we Ostyaks sleep soundly, very soundly.'

'Come to Yermak with me.'

Ishberdei shook his head. 'I must go back.'

Mitya grasped his hand. 'How did you know what I was on duty tonight?'

'I know many things, friend of my son. Suffering makes a man clear-sighted. Farewell.'

'Are you doing this for Yermak's sake?'

'I am doing it to avenge Voksar.'

'Farewell, Ishberdei, farewell.'

The Prince disappeared as cautiously as he had come. Mitya shook Boris awake and took the news back to the town himself. As so often these days, he found Yermak sitting on the divan with his head in his hands.

The next day was spent in preparation. The last of the gunpowder was shared out and the plan was drawn up for the men to leave the city in small groups and then to attack. They must hide their intentions from the enemy at all costs.

When the night was dark enough Yermak set out with the first hundred. Yakob Michailov followed and Nikita Pan with Matvei Meshcherak brought up the rear. But the hundreds no longer deserved their name. They had dwindled to less than eighty men apiece.

They reached the spot where Prince Ishberdei and his Ostyaks were encamped without meeting any opposition whatsoever. Nothing stirred. They crept on soundlessly and before long they were through the besieging ring. The Tartars had taken no precautions to defend their rear. They guarded only their front lines which faced the town. Not a single sentry kept watch beyond the encircling wagons.

Towards dawn the Cossacks launched a fierce attack on the enemy with complete disregard for their own lives. The Tartars were taken wholly by surprise, for Karacha had never envisaged such a break-through.

But Yermak had to pay dearly for his victory. He lost more than a hundred men, among them two of his three remaining Captains, Nikita Pan and Yakob Michailov.

As day declined the Cossacks returned wearily to Isker. They herded the prisoners in their midst and carried the wounded brethren. There were not many of them after this terrible battle, for the Cossacks fought to the last and when they fell they were mortally wounded indeed.

Mitya heated water and carried on his work with bandages and medicines. It was sticky indoors and he had taken off his tunic. But it wasn't the heat alone which made his pores run with sweat. He was afraid for Boris. The blood spurted from his chest whenever a spasm of pain made him arch his body. His father Igor crouched by his side on the fur rug.

'Let him live, Almighty God, let him live,' prayed Mitya. 'If you are so powerful and good, let him live. He so loves to sing and dance and he is my friend and he has an old father who has only one eye—Good heavens, I must be going mad.'

Mitya dipped the cloth in hot water and as he bound the head of one of the Cossacks, he looked back at Boris. He saw the old man stroking the corn-gold hair and his lips moving in a whisper. Suddenly Mitya was seized with longing for his own father. If I were lying there, wounded to death, who would watch over me? A feeling of utter loneliness seized him. I want to go home, thought Mitya, I want to go home. And his hands worked all the more surely and swiftly, so that they might speed up his return.

He went out to get some water from the well. 'Have you heard?' a voice called out to him. 'We've captured the sons of that Tartar hell-hound.'

'Do you mean Karacha's sons?'

'Who else? And tomorrow they'll be hanged.'

'Who said so?'

'Yermak.'

'Do you know for certain?'

'Yes.'

Mitya filled the kettle and carried it over to the fire. He built it up with a log of wood which he pushed between the twigs. Revenge, he thought, revenge for Ivan Koltso, revenge for the forty murdered men, revenge for the siege, revenge for Nikita Pan, for Yakob Michailov and all the others. The endless chain! Mitya was seized by such violent revulsion that he wanted to stand up and shout at the top of his voice, 'No, no! For God's sake, stop!'

The whole evening as he tended the wounded, he thought: 'I must go to him. I must speak to him.'

It was deep night. He was already in the street when he heard Boris's father calling him. The panic in his voice made Mitya turn.

'Mitya, come quickly. I think . . . I don't know . . .'

Mitya pushed the old man aside and went back into the house. There was cold sweat on Boris's forehead. His chest rose in spasms, gasping, struggling for breath with his mouth wide open. Cautiously, Mitya raised his friend's head and supported his back. It took a long time before the agony passed and he grew calm again. He lay with his eyes closed. 'He can't hear us speaking,' thought Mitya, 'but he must be in pain, otherwise he wouldn't keep rearing his body as he does.'

Mitya mixed some medicine in a wooden beaker. He bent low over Boris, and in the dim light he gave him drops of the mixture one by one. And all the time his mind went on, 'I must stop Yermak from carrying out this act of vengeance. If I can do that, Boris will live. I know it, I can feel it. I must make him stop.'

He passed the beaker to Igor.

'If he struggles for breath again, give him a little of this. It will help him to sleep.'

The old man nodded.

When Mitya entered Yermak's house it was empty. He sat down on the floor and leaned his back against the couch. He left the door open so that he should see Yermak the moment he came in.

It must have been a good hour later and Mitya was already

beginning to feel anxious about the wounded men he had left when Yermak came in.

'It's I—Mitya. Don't be afraid, Yermak. I have been waiting for you.'

'Why didn't you strike a light?'

'The darkness will do for thinking.'

Yermak did not reply. He felt his way to the table, struck a light and lit the wick of the candle with the thin taper. He shielded the flame with his hand so that it could burn steadily.

'Well? What is it you want?' he asked curtly with his back to Mitya.

The question was so abrupt that Mitya was taken by surprise, but he answered just as shortly, 'I came to ask you not to hang Karacha's sons tomorrow.'

Yermak went round the table, keeping his eyes firmly on the candle as if it were a thousand times more important than anything Mitya had said. Now the light fell on the jangling metal of his armour. Mitya looked at it. His gaze took in the golden eagle and then rested higher still on the steel helmet. The vizor was open, but Yermak's familiar features lay in darkness. Only the whites of the eyes gleamed and the sharp outline of the nose could be seen. The great man stood there suspended in space like a ghost and his shadow was enormous, like a giant against the tapestry behind.

'Why do you plead for them?' asked Yermak.

'This chain of vengeance must stop, this eternal clamour for blood which only leads to fresh hatred.' Mitya had jumped to his feet. 'Yermak, we spoke about this once before, that time when Voksar . . . You remember? Then you said how much harder it is to forgive than to avenge and I know that it is true. You have to wrestle hard with yourself until you can say, what do I gain by my revenge? New enmity, new bloodthirst and the knowledge that the killers are now as stiff and cold as those they murdered. But what gain is that?'

'You would have made a better priest than a Cossack, Mitya.' And the taunt struck Mitya like a blow on the face. 'You have learnt to speak the Ostyak's language, you can understand what the Tartars say, but you have never mastered the language of war. Suppose I listened to you,' Yermak went on, 'what do you think the consequences would be? Karacha would collect another army, he would advance on Isker once more, and we should have to fight and bleed all over again. No! He lured Ivan Koltso and our brothers to their death, and because I did not immediately undertake a punitive campaign he thought I was a weakling. He gathered an army and marched against us, although we demanded nothing from him but the tribute he undertook to pay when he swore his oath of allegiance. No one would have touched a hair of his head if he had behaved honourably. He wanted this battle and now he must feel the hard edge of the sword. And even if my action provokes him to a fresh outburst of wrath, his allies among the native chieftains will think twice when they see the gallows.'

'Then take Karacha prisoner. His sons are still mere children.'

'Oh, these children knew how to sit a horse and to use their scimitars. If they go out to fight, they must be prepared to die, too. If I allowed them to be ransomed, that would be tantamount to a defeat. No, the laws of warfare are not so tender-hearted. I am not going to give up Siberia, for which so many of my men forfeited their own lives, just because I am sorry for two young Tartars.'

'What you say destroys everything in me that still believes in good,' said Mitya and lowered his head. Then he threw it back and looked Yermak straight in the eyes. 'I cannot stay here with you any longer,' he said passionately. 'Let me go home. I cannot be a priest; I have robbed too many people and done too much killing for that. But I could be a hunter like my father.'

Yermak was silent. Then he stepped towards Mitya. 'Your oath obliges you to remain here with me, but I know that a man must lead his own life. Your longing for adventure drove you to us, but that was not enough to live as we do. It was Fate that made us all Cossacks.'

'Yes, Yermak, you too. I know that.'

'What do you know, Mitya? Only what Irina told you. And how much did she know? Only what her grandmother told her. But the old woman kept the worst from her and only I saw what happened. Only I saw how the Czar's henchmen from Moscow strangled my mother with their big ugly fists and my father, too. And I, I was made to watch them. That hour determined the future course of my life. Yes, Mitya, it is much harder to forgive than to avenge, I say it still. You are different. I knew it from the moment that I took you with me and all the same I took you. Now I am glad that you haven't changed. If there is goodness in a man's soul, nothing can uproot it; but it may be difficult for such a man to lead our kind of life. So I will give you back your promise and your oath as a Cossack. Go home, Mitya. And now leave me to myself.'

Without a word, Mitya went out into the darkness. He walked

slowly through the narrow streets, from house to house. Yermak's words had set his emotions in a turmoil. He walked to the end of the town, as far as the watch-towers, and then turned back again.

'I cannot understand it. I don't know if he is doing right or wrong, but what kind of a person would I have been if I were made to watch while my mother and father were strangled to death . . .?'

Beads of sweat broke out on Mitya's forehead. He wandered round and round the town until the grey of dawn appeared in the dark sky. Then he heard the sound of hammering from the highest spot in the city. They were erecting the gallows.

Mitya's legs grew as heavy as lead. He dragged himself back and went to find the house where he had left Boris. His hands were shaking as he pushed the door open gently. He felt his way through the darkness to Boris's pallet. He did not dare to touch him, for fear he would find him cold and stiff. He listened hard and tried to catch the sound of his breathing. He bent lower and lower and then he felt a faint, hardly perceptible breath on his face. Mitya leaned back. Boris was still alive.

Mitya dropped down on the floor by his side and laid his head on the ground. He could not stop the flood of tears. 'What is right and what is wrong? I cannot fathom it. Probably there is only one who knows. We must face the facts. All we can do is to search our own hearts and act in good faith.'

26 THE RAIN SINGS A LULLABY

After this victory, Yermak ruled Siberia once more. Tartars and natives swore fealty to him again and brought him the tribute he demanded.

'He is invincible,' they said. 'The might and strength which lie within him are such as we have never known.' They turned their backs on Kuchum Khan's soldiers and sent them away. They wanted to end these unsettled times; they wanted to live in peace, to hunt again and to trade.

The Princes begged Yermak to safeguard the banks of the Irtish so that foreign merchants could return. Yermak knew that he was not strong enough to do so without help from Moscow, but he did not let the tribes know this. He behaved as if his resources were undiminished, as if he were as powerful as when he arrived in Siberia.

'I, too, am concerned that trade should be resumed, but I am a soldier, not a shopkeeper. You have shown me that you are capable of great treachery and I cannot trust you,' he answered bluntly. 'I refuse to send my men to police the river until I have proof that ships are actually on their way to us.'

'Our old friends in China have managed to get messengers through to us. They have brought us news that their masters have laden ships with spices and cloth, but they dare not start on their journey for fear of piracy. And we have huge stocks of furs, such beautiful furs! Once we trade again, money will flow into your coffers.'

'People who want to trade must be prepared to take risks,' retorted Yermak. 'And the Chinese want to do business, not to shoot ducks! All the same,' he conceded eventually, 'if they come, I will help them. I give you my word.'

The Tartars withdrew, satisfied.

Towards the end of July they sought another audience with Yermak.

'There are ships from Little Bukhara on their way to us, Prince, but Kuchum's army has barred their way. The traders are having to fight them. Help us, Prince.'

'What proof can you give that you are not plotting treachery like Karacha?'

‘I have brought the Chinese messenger with me, the one who brought us the news. He is waiting outside your palace.’

‘Very well,’ said Yermak, when he saw the small figure with his slanting eyes. ‘I shall think it over.’

‘Do not take too long about it, or your help will come too late.’

Yermak had the boats prepared and he called for volunteers. Mitya was the first to respond.

Yermak selected thirty men. He had tents loaded and they took provisions: dry biscuit, and smoked meat.

‘Why are you going yourself?’ asked Matvei. ‘You should remain here. Your presence is more important in Isker than on an expedition like this.’

‘I cannot sit around waiting all the time. The days pass more quickly when one is doing something. And if help from Moscow should arrive during my absence, you can receive it just as well.’

‘And suppose it is a trap? Who can trust this Tartar rabble?’

‘I shall be on my guard, Matvei; do not worry about me.’

The Cossacks had to row hard, for they were battling upstream, and the current was so swift that it was difficult for them to get very far each day.

Yermak watched both banks of the river. The farther east they went the more often he thought, ‘This is like home.’ Right and left were plains of brownish-green stretching out of sight, like the steppes by the Volga and the Don. ‘All the same, if I am honest, I have to admit that the southern steppes were never home to me. Where is my home, I wonder? Moscow? Or the village where Vassili lives? Is it in Isker, or by the side of the Volga, after all? A few hours long ago in my childhood made me homeless for the rest of my life. But perhaps it had to be. Who knows?’

Mitya watched him and thought: ‘It is more than five years since I went away with him and there are many things he does which I do not pretend to understand. Many times I would have done things differently, but he was always right in the end. That is why I am staying with him, after all.’

For four days and three nights they rowed on, and although they kept a careful watch, there was no sign of any foreign merchant vessel.

‘Is there any point in going farther, Yermak?’ asked one old Cossack to whom Yermak always listened.

‘Don’t you think we’ll find them?’

The old man shrugged his shoulders. ‘I think we have come too late. Kuchum’s people will have plundered the Chinese ships by now. If there were any survivors they must have turned and gone back again.'

'But what about their ships?'

'The Irtish is not only wide. It is deep, too.'

'Very like you are right. We had better turn back.' He waved to the boats behind. 'Come on, we're going home.'

The Cossacks breathed a sign of relief, for they were at the end of their strength. For the first time since they had set out they need do no more than drift with the current and steer.

Evening descended more quickly than they had anticipated. Throughout the day the sky had been overcast with low clouds which now seemed to hasten the onset of darkness. They grew thick and black, and then it began to rain. At first it was only a fine drizzle, but presently it developed into a heavy downpour like a cloudburst.

'Does it matter when we arrive back in Isker, Yermak?' said the old man. 'Will half a day sooner or later make much difference?'

'Are you suggesting that we spend the night under canvas?' asked Yermak in reply.

'Yes, we need a rest. And travelling by day is easier.'

'The bank here is not very accessible, as you saw when it was light. The river is full of inlets. It may take us some time to find the right spot.'

'Do you remember that on the way out we passed a little island not far from here? If I am not mistaken, we shall come to it quite soon.'

'That would be a good idea. We'll keep a look-out for it.'

Presently a black patch loomed up out of the leaden waters, and despite the darkness it appeared to be what they were looking for. The boats steered towards it.

'This is it,' called Yermak. 'This is the island.'

The Cossacks moored the boats in the reeds, collected the tents and jumped ashore. The rain was falling heavily as they pitched camp. They shared out the smoked meat and gulped it down quickly. Their one aim was to sleep, to lie down and sleep for as long as possible.

'Who will take the first watch?' asked Mitya.

'I'm wondering if we can do without a guard,' answered Yermak. 'We all need sleep and, after all, this is an island. What with that and the weather, I think we are safe enough. No one could guess we are here, and in any case, we have seen nothing to rouse the slightest suspicion since we left Isker. I suggest we all go to sleep.'

The men were relieved that the proposal had come from Yermak himself. The effect of rowing for four days and three nights was making itself felt in every limb.

'Yes, you are right,' they all agreed. 'We need sleep. It will be better to go on first thing in the morning, but now we want to stretch our legs for a few hours.'

The rain drummed down monotonously on the canvas. It wrapped them round like a potent narcotic, lulling them to sleep. One or two of them perhaps were still a little worried. Wouldn't it have been better to mount a guard? . . .

Their sleep grew heavier and heavier. After four days and three nights of physical exertion, sleep claimed them for her own.

They had not seen the riders who had found refuge by the banks of the Irtish since they were driven out of Isker. These men had wandered as nomads so long that they knew every hill, every rise in the ground.

And the Cossacks did not hear the snuffling of their horses as the forded the river across to the island. The rain beat down in an irresistible lullaby.

Cautiously the riders came ashore. They cut the cables and let the boats drift into the current. Without making a sound they drew their scimitars and crept towards the tents. The rain muffled the cries of alarm as the Tartars entered the first tent.

Mitya felt himself being jerked violently into a sitting position. He opened his eyes so suddenly that they started watering.

'We have been attacked!' he heard Yermak's voice. 'Draw your sword. It's now or never.'

Mitya was still swaying as he wrenched his sword from the scabbard. The two other Cossacks with them in the tent, jumped up as well. Yermak hurried outside with Mitya at his heels.

'To the boats,' shouted Yermak. Figures emerged from the darkness ready to pounce. Mitya did not know how many of them there were. He plucked his knife from his belt and placed it between his teeth. His hands gripped his sword. He waited until the figures were near enough and then he smote them hard.

'For Kuchum Khan!' he heard them shriek as they parried.

That roused his fury.

'For Yermak Timofeyev!' he roared and struck out again at the Tartars who surrounded him. He did not notice that his fur cap had gone; he hardly felt the blow on his shoulder. He only wondered why he found it so difficult to raise his arm when he hit out once more with his sword. The next moment it was dashed from his hand. He grasped his dagger and ran to attack one of the Tartars.

We must get to the boats or swim ashore,' shouted Yermak. 'Go on, Mitya, run! I will fend off these dogs. They'll get short shrift from me.' Yermak was not wounded, for his armour shielded him. He mowed every man who tried to attack him.

Mitya retreated hastily, but in the darkness he could not find the place where they had moored the boats. He crept into the brushwood and crawled along the bank. Then he stopped for a moment and listened. He could still hear the cries and the clash of swords. Why did none of the others come, he wondered, and at the same time he asked himself: 'Where have the boats gone? We must have them if we are to get away.' He could not see them anywhere.

'But I must find them—I must. It's all up with us if I don't.'

Again he listened in the direction from which he expected to see Yermak and the others coming. All at once Yermak's voice boomed out: 'Save yourself, Mitya, if you're still on the island! Swim for it! They've cut the boats adrift. I'm going to jump in, too.'

Mitya hesitated no longer. He jumped into the black gurgling waters. The current there was not strong, but all the same it caught him and pulled him along. Mitya tried to make for the nearest bank but he could not do so. The stream kept dragging him back.

'What is the matter with my arm?' he puzzled. 'Why does it hurt so? I must get ashore, I must do it! If only my boots weren't such a weight. They must be full of water. They are dragging me down. I must take them off.'

He let the current carry him for a while and concentrated on a supreme effort to get rid of his boots. When he managed it at last, he was so exhausted he had hardly any strength left to swim.

'I must get to the bank—I'll never reach it—I must do it—No, I can't. But I shall drown if I don't. I don't want to drown. I have no boots now to pull me under. Swimming is easy, now—take it easy. How far away the bank is! I shall never get there. But Yermak is waiting for me.' Yermak! Suddenly a dreadful thought came over Mitya. How could Yermak reach the bank in his suit of armour? Why, even a pair of boots had nearly done for Mitya. My God, the armour, the armour!

Mitya felt a sudden access of strength. How easy it was to swim, how light he felt. And how heavy must be an iron suit of armour.

With every stroke the bushes ahead drew nearer. 'I shall be there any moment. I'm so light . . .'

His fingers caught hold of thin twigs and his hand closed round them. Mitya tried to haul himself out of the water, but the twigs were too brittle and came away in his hand. He felt for stronger ones. Would they hold firm? If only he could rest a little!

Inch by inch Mitya hauled himself into the bushes. He was safe.

He let his head drop forward into the mud and the reeds. He had just enough air to breathe. His feet were still in the water, but he did not realize it. He breathed deeply and as long as consciousness remained he thought, If only I can rest a little! As soon as I'm rested I shall go and look for Yermak.

Dawn was grey over the steppes when Mitya came to himself. It took him some little time before he could remember what had happened. He dragged himself out of the water and crawled along to firmer ground.

'I must find Yermak and the others,' he thought and groped along the bank upstream. Cautiously he peered left and right whenever he came to a part of the river bank which was not thickly wooded.

'I have no sword nor anything else to fight with, not even a dagger. I have no boots, but that's not important. I could kill a Tartar barefoot, if only I had at least my knife.'

The rain stopped as the day proceeded. Mitya walked on steadily. Sometimes he called softly: 'Yermak!' and again: 'Yermak!'

Nothing stirred. He walked until he could see the island in the distance and he watched it for a long time. Was there something moving there? Two of the tents were still standing and there were bodies lying on the earth, but nothing moved. Mitya dropped to the ground. His heart began to pound against his ribs.

'I have come back all this way and I haven't found Yermak nor even one of the Cossacks. There's no one alive on the island. Can I be the only survivor?' The realization that Yermak must be dead came as such a thunderclap that he sprang to his feet.

'No, no!' he screamed. 'No!' And he clenched his fists and gritted his teeth in wild grief. 'No, no!' he blurted out again, and pushed his hair away from his forehead. 'But what about me?' he thought. 'What can I do? I have no boat, no weapons, no boots. Damn it all, why do I have to keep worrying about my boots? I can walk barefoot.'

Mitya trudged on slowly and then he started to hurry. He did not bother to conceal himself. As often as he could, he ran. His hair caught in overhanging branches, his face and hands were torn and scratched. He began to feel hungry and thirsty, but he forced himself to ignore the torment. On to Isker, to Isker! He could endure anything as long as he was not left alone with his thoughts, not to be alone with the certainty that Yermak was dead.

He walked on until it was so dark that he could not see which way to go. Then he dropped to the ground where he stood and he slept as if he had been stunned.

The next day began where the previous one had ended. Mitya set out once more to try to reach the town. He had a feeling of such nausea that he thought he would vomit at any moment, but he told himself that it was only hunger which made him feel so ill.

'How long will it take me to get to Isker? How many days and nights? Perhaps if I drink I will not feel so famished. Perhaps you don't feel the pangs so much if you can have a good drink.'

Mitya turned back to the river, for the stinking marshy pools in the forest revolted him. He threw himself down and bent his face over the water. After a few moments he stopped and looked around. His eyes grew wide. To his left, in a tiny inlet, perhaps two hundred yards away, he saw a boat. It was one of their own, a Cossack boat.

Mitya sprang to his feet and ran as fast as he could along the awkward path. 'Yermak!' he called. 'Brothers!'

He stopped and listened. Then he ran on, keeping his eyes fastened on the boat all the time. He was nearer now. 'Yermak!' he cried and then again, at the top of his voice: 'Yermak!'

All was still. The birds were scared and fluttered up into the air, but nothing else happened. When Mitya reached the boat he saw that it must have drifted downstream. It was empty. He waded out into the water and climbed in.

Now I have a boat and do not need to walk to Isker. It won't take me long to get there now.

He grasped one of the oars and pushed off. He leaned back with trembling arms, but they were so stiff he did not know how he could get into the current. They simply would not move. For a while he closed his eyes and rested.

'This is much better,' he tried to convince himself. 'I can kill a fish with an oar and eat it. When I was with Voksar we ate fish raw. Why not now?'

This idea gave him new strength. He forced himself to take up the oars once more and this time it needed only a few strokes and the boat was caught by the current.

It was night when he reached Isker. No one had seen the boat coming. Mitya steered it in to the shore, but he remained sitting there.

For two whole days he had never expected he would survive,

that he would have to tell the others . . . And now the time had come.

Slowly he got up and crawled towards the city wall. The sentries saw him now, approaching through the darkness. 'Who are you and what do you want?' they cried.

'Open up. It's I, Mitya.'

Even from outside, Mitya could hear the thunder of the boots as the sentries came hurtling down the stairs. The door creaked and two Cossacks dashed out.

'What a sight you are! Are you really Mitya? But you have no boots and your face is black.'

'Yes, I dare say, with all the mud and dirt. But let me in, for God's sake.'

'Mitya, what has happened? Where have you come from? Where are the others? Where is Yermak?'

Everything began to spin in front of Mitya's eyes.

'Dead, every one of them, killed or drowned!' They caught him as he fell and carried him into the town. They shouted through the streets.

'Wake up, wake up! Mitya is back. Wake up!'

Matvei came rushing out of Yermak's house. His tunic flapped loosely round his body. As he met the sentries who were carrying Mitya, the lad sat up. 'They're all dead—killed or drowned.'

'Yermak?' asked Matvei dully.

'He, too,' nodded Mitya. 'His armour weighed him down. And now let me sleep.'

Mitya slept until twilight of the foowing day. When he awoke and went out of doors the whole of Isker resembled an overturned beehive. Cossacks were scurrying hither and thither with sacks crammed full. They ran through the streets and down to the river. From the distance, Mitya could hear the banging and hammering.

'What is happening?' he called out to a Cossack who was hastening by. 'What are you all doing?'

'Haven't you heard? We're going home. We're going home to Russia. We've had enough of this accursed land. Now we're going home.' And the Cossack ran on.

Mitya hurried round to the house where Boris lived. He opened the door. Boris was sitting up. His face was emaciated and his fair hair hung round his face in lank streaks. He had one hand under his armpit and he was breathing heavily.

'Mitya,' he said, and his eyes lit up. 'I'm so glad you've come back.'

'Yes, yes,' said Mitya, and sat down near him. 'Are you still in pain?'

Boris shook his head. 'Not now. Not now that we're going home.'

Mitya looked at him. 'Who said we're going home?'

'Who? Why, everybody! What can we do here in this terrible country without Yermak? If we wait any longer, the Tartars will kill us. Once they find out that Yermak is dead . . .'

'But we cannot give up everything we've fought for so bitterly.'

'How can we stay? You can see for yourself that Moscow will send us nothing. We have no ammunition left, nothing but a few rusty guns. Are we going to allow ourselves to be butchered like a flock of sheep?'

'When was it decided that we were to leave?'

'This morning, while you were still asleep. Everyone was in favour. They've been busy repairing the rafts and we're taking everything with us. And there'll be plundering as we go, here and there among the settlements on the way. We don't want to go back empty-handed, not after five years of this.'

Boris looked at Mitya. The latter's face was a blank.

'Aren't you glad, then, that we're going home?'

'For years I've been imagining what it would feel like to be going home. And now, now that the day is here, there's no joy in it. Where will you go, Boris?'

'Where? Back to the Volga, of course. Aren't joy coming with us?'

'I! No, Boris. I shall go back to my father.'

The rowan trees on the sandy river banks bowed their branches under the heavy clusters of gleaming red berries; the heather bloomed purple; the leaves of ash and willow showed the first yellow edges as the fleet of rafts sailed westwards, under the laborious strokes of the oars.

In the first few days everyone clamoured to take the oars, but now regular rotas had been arranged and they took the strenuous task in turns.

'We're going home, we're going home.' The phrase gave the oarsmen their time as they dipped the oars into the water. But it was not only yearning which drove them on ever faster. They knew, too, that Kuchum Khan's cavalry was following them. At the beginning of the journey they had stopped twice to exact tribute from two of the settlements, although it was unjust, for Yermak had already received it from them. Blood flowed once more and suddenly a posse of Kuchum's soldiers appeared on horseback with their bows and arrows. And again Cossacks were left behind, among them the last of their Captains, Matvei Meshcherak.

Now the leadership fell to Igor, Boris's father, and to one of the few Russian soldiers who had survived the journey with Prince Bolshovski in the spring.

'If only we were across the Urals,' said the Cossacks every day. They had to cross them before the winter came. And the more they increased the distance between themselves and Kuchum Khan's army, the safer they would feel.

Day and night they travelled west. Day and night they crept nearer to Russia. As biting storms announced the onset of winter, they dragged their packs, their rafts and skiffs up the Ural Mountains. It did not take as long as it had done years ago when Siberia lay ahead of them, for their rations were finished and all they carried with them was the booty they had captured. The brown leaves of the dwarf birches and linden trees rustled under their feet and swirled round their shoulders. The pines and firs which defy the seasons braced themselves against the wind, and the Cossacks had to brace themselves, too, as they toiled up the heights.

When it came to the descent there were just as many difficulties, but the men were in better heart and full of confidence. Below them a dull silver ribbon of water stretched through the valley, lying like a girdle between the rounded mountain promontories, disappearing between dark wooded hills to emerge once more in a broader band of shimmering blue.

One by one they steered as long as daylight lasted, but only the most skilful could be trusted at the helm. More than once danger threatened the rafts as the raging torrent tried to fling them against the rocks, and it needed good seamanship to keep a safe course.

When they came to the Kama the hungry Cossacks had to buckle down to the strain of rowing once more. True, the Russian settlers gave them a little food—indeed, all that they could spare—but it was only sufficient to still the direst pangs. Everyone was worried, too, about the reception they would get in Oryol. Would Maxim Stroganov at least provide food for the winter? And when winter was over, what would happen then?

In Oryol, in Doctor Ivan's house, nothing had altered. Mitya felt immediately at ease there, just as he had always done.

'Are you comfortable, lad? Are you warm enough? Come

on, stretch out your legs on the bench and make yourself at home.'

Mitya leaned against the wall and his eyes followed every movement of the doctor's. He had not heard such affection for so long that it sounded strange in his ears and he listened hungrily, repeating silently to himself each word the doctor spoke.

'Why don't you say something, my boy? You're not ill, are you?'

Mitya shook his head. He did not dare to speak for fear of destroying something that gushed like a hot spring inside him. Somebody cared! Here was someone who really cared whether he lived or died.

'Talk to me—and eat, too.' The doctor pushed over a dish full of appetizing chunks of roasted meat and another of soft, sweet-smelling bread.

'I want to go home to my father,' said Mitya, half to himself. 'And I shall be a trapper like him. Our hut is old and shabby, but that doesn't matter. Nikolai, my father, is old and a bit the worse for wear as well. I shall build a new house for us and we can go hunting together. How his eyes will stare when I tell him about hunting in Siberia.'

'Why don't you settle here like most of the Cossacks, Mitya? You would have a good job immediately. I have spoken to Maxim Stroganov already and he says you could be my apprentice. I'm getting old, too, you see, and I need someone with strong young arms and a pair of skilful hands. I should teach you to read and write and one day you would be a real doctor like me. Doesn't that mean something to you? Anyone can go trapping, Mitya, but not many can be doctors.'

'You make it sound attractive, Doctor, and perhaps you are right. But my father is getting old as well. You see, I left home without so much as "Good-bye". Is he never to see me again?'

'Of course you must go and see him, but you can come back again. Perhaps he will come, too. You said that your house is old and dilapidated and you must rebuild it. Why don't you find a fresh site for it altogether? This land can do with many more people. There is room here for both of you, for you and your father, too.'

'Yes, you are right; the land here does need people. It gulps them down like a wild beast. It crams them down its gullet and they disappear and there is nothing left of them. This land has destroyed much that was in me. It was here that someone gave me a precious jewel for a drink of water. Yes, look! Here it is still. I have carried it about in my pocket, and it means no more to me than a pebble, because it showed me how cruel is this land. It was when the Prince of Pelym attacked us here in Perm that a dying Tartar gave me this ruby in return for a drink of water. That's when it all began.'

'You don't see it in the right light, Mitya. This jewel was not payment for a drink. A dying man was trying to thank you for your kindness, for an act which made you brothers in the last hours of his life.'

'You can talk your way round anything, just as Yermak used to.'

Mitya stopped.

Yermak! The very name had conjured up everything he had been trying to forget. And now the words poured forth from him . . .

The doctor let him talk, and when Mitya had finished there was silence for some time.

'And now you think that it was all in vain, that everything is lost; that Kuchum Khan has long been back in Isker and everything is over and done with?' The doctor's round face broadened into a smile. 'No, Mitya, it is not over. Yermak conquered Siberia and that fact remains. Czar Ivan, may Heaven grant him eternal bliss, has been succeeded by his son Feodor. But the new Czar is a weakling and it is Boris Godunov who rules the land. And Godunov is not the man to make the same mistake twice. It will not be a second Bolshovski whom he sends to Siberia, you can depend on that.'

'Do you really think they will send another army over the Urals?'

'Certainly they will, and that is very important. But it is even more important that Russian settlers shall follow the soldiers. It is only then that the land will be truly conquered. The plough must follow the sword, you know.'

'Perhaps you are right, Doctor.'

'Go home, Mitya, but come back to us, my boy. Take your time about it, but come!'

27 THE NEW HOUSE

The sleigh flew over the hard frozen snow. The horses steamed in the clear air and the lash of the whip flicked over their brown backs.

'Let them be,' called Vassili Metyanov. 'They have travelled well and we are not far from home now.'

The coachman put up his whip and Vassili fell into a doze. 'A new Czar in Moscow,' he thought, 'and they say he is like a straw puppet. Ahem.' He smiled to himself. 'Why should I worry? It makes no difference to me here. What do I care who is Czar as long as I am left in peace?'

The coachman turned round. 'Look, Master. There's a man riding ahead of us. I wonder where he is going?'

'Where do you think?' rasped Vassili tartly. 'To my house, I expect. It will be someone from Moscow as usual, one of the Czar's envoys for whom I am expected to provide a bed and supply a fresh horse.'

The coachman raised his whip again, but Vassili stopped him once more. 'Why are you in such a hurry to find out? We'll learn soon enough what it is he wants.'

All the same, Vassili Metyanov let the coachman have his head in the end, and before long they were near enough to see that the horseman was not wearing the uniform of one of the Imperial couriers. Vassili was relieved and now he, too, felt curious to know what the stranger wanted and who he might be.

They drove behind him for a short distance. Then they drew level and Vassili peeped across.

The rider had drawn up the collar of his fur coat and his cap was pulled down over his eyes, so there was little of his face to be seen.

'Where are you going, my friend?' called Vassili Metyanov.

The rider jerked his head round at once. 'To the next village,' he replied, and bent forward a little.

Vassili narrowed his eyes. 'Have you some reason for going there?'

'Yes.'

'Now where have I seen that face before? Where have I heard that voice?' thought Vassili Metyanov.

'Would you like to ride with me in the sleigh?'

'No, thank you. It isn't far.'

'So you know the village, then?'
'Yes.'
Vassili could see that the rider was laughing to himself.
'And I know you, too, Vassili Metyanov,' said the familiar voice.
'You know me? Who are you, then?' Vassili gave the coachman a dig in the ribs. 'Can't you stop, man?'
The rider whipped off his cap and turned his full face to Vassili. 'Do you know me now, Vassili Metyanov?'

Irina had been watching from the window all day.
'The sleigh! Mother, Granny! Father's coming,' she cried excitedly and ran to the hall to open the door. 'Volodya, Volodya. Where are you? The Master is back. Help him out of the sleigh, Volodya.' And she dashed out into the street.
'Irina, dear. Put a shawl on. It's so cold. Your father will be angry if he sees you like that.' Her grandmother ran after her as fast as her feeble old legs could carry her, but she was too late. 'She's such a wild thing, such a tomboy,' she muttered to herself.
As she ran Irina's kerchief slipped from her head. The thick brown plaits bounced against her back.
'Father!' she cried, and waved both her arms. Then she saw the stranger by his side and they dropped with disappointment. He was bringing home a guest, and she had been looking forward so much to driving home beside him. She stopped irresolute. She could climb up beside the driver, of course, but her father would disapprove and be angry. But not for long. She knew him.
The sleigh drew up alongside and the coachman tugged at the reins.
'Father!' called Irina once more. Then all at once she had no eyes for Vassili. All she could see was the stranger's face, the face of a man by her father's side. Her eyes grew wide, her hands flew to her face and her mouth gaped. She took a step back and then another. 'Mitya?' she breathed, unable to believe her eyes.
Before he could reply, she had repeated his name and this time her voice was louder, firmer. 'Mitya! I knew it. I knew you would keep your word. You've come home!'
And she jumped up on to the driving-seat, tore the reins from the coachman's hands and made the whip sing through the air. 'Mother, Granny!' she shouted at the top of her voice. 'He's come home—Mitya is here! It's Mitya!'

Mitya went gliding over the dazzling whiteness of the snow. He had made himself a pair of snowshoes and his knapsack was heavy, for he had found a fox and three squirrels in the traps. The sun had disappeared in a veil of mist.

He wanted to be home before it was dark and he had still a good distance to cover. It would be cold and lonely when he got there. But he knew the way well enough and he could allow his thoughts to wander.

How long ago it all seemed! With an effort he tried to recall it all: the voyage on the salt transport to Moscow, buying a horse there, the ride home, the last stretch in the sleigh with Vassili Metyanov and then meeting Irina. He thought of the way she had recognized him and the expression of the others when they saw him get out, especially Granny's and Olga Metyanova's. And how they changed when he asked them about his father, how they all went dumb and did not know how to tell him, how to spare him the pain.

'Vassili Metyanov always warned us that Grivka would cause trouble. And he was right. A wolf is a wolf; that is what he always said. No creature can fight against his nature. And Yermak would have said that every man had his fate marked out for him. But none of that helps me. Nothing can stop the hut being empty whenever I come home. I wonder if it's true that Father was never angry with me or reproached me because I left him all alone? Or if Irina just said so? Why, oh why can't I ask him myself?

'Now I am quite alone, just as Yermak always was. I know I can go to the Metyanovs whenever I like, but that's not much help. They are kind to me and I have to tell them what happened over and over again. Granny always weeps when I mention Yermak, but I know she doesn't quite understand. She cannot grasp what went on during all those years. None of them can because they have never seen Siberia. They marvel at it as if it were a fairy tale. Only Irina understands. She is different. When she listens to me there is something in her face that tells me she understands.'

Mitya's thoughts wandered on.

'I wonder if Boris has reached the Volga, Boris and Igor his father? I should have persuaded them to come here with me. Then the loneliness would not be so crushing. But is it so bad? I often wished to be alone when I was away, just to be home again and to sleep by the stove with Father at my side. And now I am home, why am I not contented? Is it only because Father is dead? No, it must be something else. So much has altered while I was away, so many things are different now. But what? The houses are the same, the church is still where it was; a few people have died, children have been born. There are only one or two new faces. Perhaps it is I who have changed. Is that it? These squirrel skins are a poor quality. They were better in Siberia. There aren't many sables in these parts. In Siberia, we only bothered to skin the black ones which hardly exist here at all. And why are martens so rare? In Siberia . . . Siberia! I hate the place. It makes me restless. No, I mustn't blame Siberia. It's my own fault. Probably I'm not cut out to be a good trapper either. Perhaps I would make a better assistant for Doctor Ivan? No, I mustn't think about him. It is only this loneliness which is driving me mad.'

As Mitya drew nearer to his hut he saw smoke rising from the roof. A bluish ribbon curled into the darkening sky with a red spark soaring now and then. Mitya's heart pounded with joy. She has been there! She lit the fire so that it would be warm for me when I got home. No, no. She did not come herself. She must have sent Volodya. Her father does not like it, because there might be gossip in the village. Oh, the people in the village talk nothing but nonsense in any event. They talk about my snowshoes and the gold ingot I was given that time when I went to stay with Voksar. What a pity I couldn't bring back a reindeer or a team of dogs! Then they'd have something to talk about.'

When Mitya reached the hut he took the knapsack from his back, untied his snowshoes and pushed open the door. He threw the bag into the hall, put his snowshoes by its side and stamped the snow from his boots. He looked forward with pleasure to the warmth he would find indoors.

Then he heard a noise. Quickly he opened the inner door. 'Irina, is it you?'

'Why not, Mitya?'

'But your father doesn't like it. He doesn't want any talk . . .'

'Oh, let them talk. I don't care what they say. Did you stop to ask what the other soldiers would say if you gave a dying Tartar a drink on the battlefield?'

'That was different,' smiled Mitya. 'But I'm glad you remember what I said.'

'It wasn't so very different. You need a little help now and how can I grudge it? You mustn't be alone so much.'

'Irina,' and he wanted to add, 'sweetheart', but as he thought of it he stumbled. Things were different now. It wasn't the same as when we were children. 'How beautiful she has grown,' thought Mitya. 'Her hair gleams like those silks we found in Isker. I wonder if it feels the same.' And then he realized that, unlike the other women in the village, she refused to wear a kerchief.

'Her skin is like the velvet in those houses in Isker, too!' his thoughts went on. 'Her eyes have grown much darker. They were quite light when I went away!' But perhaps that was only because she was standing in the shadows. His eyes glanced over her neck and the embroidered close-fitting collar of her robe. It travelled down to her waist, to the flowing dark skirt and the soft white boots she wore. 'How lovely she is,' he thought and he stood there spellbound as if he wanted to gaze at her for ever.

And Irina thought, 'Why is he staring at me? Why on earth is he looking like that? You'd think he'd never seen me before! Why doesn't he speak? How tall he has grown! I hardly come up to his shoulder. His beard suits him too, and how broad his shoulders are! And the Cossack cap is so becoming it might have been made for him. There's no one like him in the whole village. But there never was, even before. But it's different now. Quite different.' And she felt herself blushing. When her eyes met Mitya's, she lowered her head.

'You must have something to eat. I'm sure you are hungry. I cooked some meat for you and I brought a loaf of bread. There's milk too. It's frozen of course, but you can chip off as much as you want.'

'Yes,' was all he said. He was still standing at the door, looking at her.

Irina was so embarrassed she did not know where to look. She felt she ought to go, but she could not bring herself to leave him, for then she would not see him any more that day.

'I must put on some more wood,' she said hastily. She knelt by the stove and fed it with a few sticks and a log. 'And now I must be going,' she said softly, hoping all the time he would say, 'Stay a little longer.'

Mitya started.

'Go? Why do you want to go? Stay and have supper with me. It tastes better in company. I miss the men so.'

'The men! Don't you ever think of anyone else?'

'Yes, I do, Irina.'

She put a dish on the table and poured out meat and gravy.

'Did you catch much?'

'Not bad. A fox and three squirrels.'

'Not bad, you say? But that's splendid. Think how many roubles you will get for them.'

'Of course,' said Mitya and he thought of the pelts in Siberia.

'Will you build a new house next summer, Mitya?'

'I don't know yet,' he answered slowly, and took a bite of meat. 'Do you think this one is so bad?'

'Yes, it is.'

'And you for one would never live here, I suppose?' Mitya was watching Irina out of the corner of his eye, and his heart pounded, wondering how she would reply.

'Oh,' she said tensely. 'I wouldn't say that, but if there was a better one . . .'

'Of course, I understand.' And Mitya's heart beat louder than ever. 'Only I'm not sure where to build, here or in Perm.'

Irina let the bread and meat slip back into the dish.

'Mitya! You don't want to go away, surely? No, no. You can't go. You promised me you would come back.'

Mitya closed his eyes for a second in sheer happiness.

'I was only joking, Irina.'

Later, as it had grown dark, he took her as far as the first houses in the village.

As they said good night Irina could not stop herself saying, 'Was it really only a joke about going to Perm?'

Mitya tried to make her look at him, but she kept her eyes on the ground. He could not resist temptation. Cautiously, he passed a hand over her glossy hair. And he thought, 'Yes, it feels like the silks in Isker, too.'

But Irina took it as a promise that he would not go away again.

All the same, Mitya did not start building a new house once the thick blanket of snow had slipped from the roof to the ground. Nor had he built one by the time the summer sun dried out the timbers so that they creaked. He did indeed make a new door and new shutters and he repaired the roof, but he found no pleasure in it. On the contrary, it made him more restless than ever.

'Why am I doing it?' he thought. 'I can't make this old hovel look like new.' And the word 'new' made him think of the new house Doctor Ivan had spoken about. He might almost have been standing behind Mitya and saying: 'The plough must follow the sword. Only then will Siberia be truly conquered.'

'Oh, that's all very fine,' said Mitya angrily to himself and he did not know with whom he was so exasperated. 'But the men must come first, men to wield the sword, and to do the ploughing, too.'

Towards the end of the summer a pedlar came to the village. He came every year just before the brief autumn started. He brought all kinds of things which the villagers would need in the long winter ahead, and he took their goods in exchange. Vassili Metyanov knew that Mitya had been waiting impatiently for this visit and he sent Volodya to fetch him.

Meanwhile, the peasant bartered honey for salt, rye for cooking-pots, and oats for a length of cloth to make a new robe. There was much haggling, for the pedlar was a good businessman and the villagers enjoyed driving a hard bargain, too. There was always much conversation as well, for the pedlar brought with him the latest news from Moscow and the other big towns.

Mitya was the last person to come and see him in Vassili Metyanov's house. He had brought a whole knapsack full of furs and he spread them out, tidily arranged according to species, size, and quality. The pedlar, naturally, tried to beat Mitya down and poured scorn on what he had to offer.

'These sables aren't worth much,' he said, pointing to four skins tied together. He undid the bundle and blew into the thick brown fur. 'They are not pure, you know. You caught them out of season. They're moulting, Mitya Nikolayev.'

'Are you trying to swindle me, or are you so stupid that you don't know how to tell quality in a sable? Look at the inner side. They're absolutely white, pure white. Well? Aren't they? If you knew the first thing about furs, you would see at once that these sables were trapped at their very best.'

Then the pedlar saw that he could not cheat Mitya and although he was so annoyed that he felt strangled, he paid out the right price in cash and placed the money by the side of the furs.

'So you came back, did you?' said the pedlar, ready to forgive and forget when the transaction was over.

'Why, did you think I was a ghost?' laughed Mitya.

'Well, you won't be off again so soon, I reckon,' nodded the man. 'A man who knows how to earn good money at home does not need to go on his travels, there's no two ways about it.'

Mitya merely grunted as he packed salt, flour, barley, and candles into his knapsack.

'Did you know that another hundred gunners have set out from Moscow?' the pedlar went on. 'I thought you'd be interested. They have been sent as reinforcements for Prince Yermak's army. A pity he died! But they are saying prayers for his eternal rest in all the churches.'

'What's that you're saying? More soldiers off to Siberia?'

'Oh yes, and they're not taking horses this time. The gentlemen in Moscow are a bit wiser now. And do you know, they have even taken a cannon with them. They say the soldiers have gone to build forts up and down the country, small ones but strong so as to protect the citizens. And they say that all the Cossacks who came back from Siberia and stayed with Maxim Stroganov—though he can well afford to keep them, a rich man like Master Maxim—anyway, they are going back to Siberia with the gunners. Yes, many a head in Moscow is being turned by the thought of those riches behind the Urals . . .'

Mitya threw the pedlar a few coppers.

'Buy yourself a mug of ale, my friend. Farewell.'

'Heaven's blessing on you, Mitya Nikolayev, may God bless you twice over.'

But Mitya was not listening as he strode away.

When he got home the hut seemed too small to hold him. He sat down on the doorstep and stared into space. Lost in thought, he traced patterns in the soil, first with the toe of his boot and then with his heel. Then he picked up a stick lying close by. He drew the mountains beyond which lies Siberia, and he made a thick line for the Irtish which flows through the Land of Yugor where the Ostyak tribes live. 'The plough must follow the sword.' He heard Doctor Ivan's voice and in his mind's eye he could see the little villages beyond the Urals and the settlements where the Russian colonists had built their houses. He saw the wooden walls and watch-towers which protected them from attack. But where would the people come from who would dare to settle in the unknown, in that mysterious and cruel land which was, despite everything, so rich and so beautiful? Everything would be new to them and strange. They would only gain experience through time. And Mitya thought: 'If a few people went with them who knew the country, how much easier it would be for them.'

He jumped to his feet and tugged at the collar of his tunic. Suddenly he felt hot, as if he were choking.

'But I shall not draw a sword again. I cannot do that. I am not a fighting man.'

And again he heard the doctor: 'The plough must follow . . .'

'But I am not a farmer either. What am I, then? I was a Cossack once, but never again. I am a trapper now, but I am not happy. When was I ever contented? What did I ever do which made me feel as if I had fulfilled myself?'

Mitya's thoughts strayed once more. They went over the whole course of those five long years. He recalled the journey to the Don, the Cossack village by the Volga, the trek to Oryol. His thoughts lingered as he remembered the first time he had entered the quiet friendly room in the doctor's house. Then there was the night of his first battle and the conversation with Yermak. 'We ought to have a doctor for the wounded,' Mitya had told him. He saw the brothers whose wounds he dressed and whose pain he had tried to alleviate. And suddenly he remembered more vividly than anything else that night when they had entered Isker. The brothers were dancing and singing in the streets and he had gone indoors to tend the wounded.

Mitya leaned against the wall of the hut and closed his eyes. He could hear the man saying so clearly, 'What should we do without you, Mitya? Your hands are as gentle as my mother's.' And the same feeling came over him again. He had never felt so happy in his life as that moment.

And now Mitya knew the way he must go.

'Did you hear what the pedlar told Mitya?' asked Granny when Irina came back to the house.

'No, I wasn't there.'

'He said that soldiers had set out for Siberia again, and he said that the Cossacks who had remained in Oryol were going to follow them. I dare say Mitya will get itching feet again and be off once more.'

'Oh!' was all Irina could say and she turned her face away so that the old woman could not see how she had flushed. She invented an excuse quickly and left the house.

'Even if you don't build yourself a new house, at least you should repair this rickety door frame,' she scolded Mitya as she saw him standing there, leaning against the wall.

He had seen her coming and his feeling of happiness grew stronger than ever.

'I am going to build a new house, Irina,' he said.

'Oh.'

Mitya grasped her by the wrist and drew her nearer. 'Many years ago when I used to talk to you about going away, you often said that if you were a boy you would come with me. Do you remember?'

'Yes,' said Irina and she looked at him.

'Would you still say the same now?'

Irina's hands grew cold and moist with excitement. 'Yes, Mitya. Does that mean you are building your new house somewhere else?'

'Yes.'

'I knew you wouldn't stay. I knew it long ago. But I thought that Cossacks did not need houses.'

'I am not going to join the Cossacks again. I am going to Doctor Ivan to learn how to be a doctor, too.'

'And when . . . when you are a doctor, Mitya, what will you do then?'

Mitya laughed and placed his arm round her shoulders. 'Then I shall help people when they are sick and try to cure them as the doctor does. But I shall need someone to help me, too. Would you like to do that?'

Irina nodded. 'And then you will go to Siberia afterwards?' she asked slowly.

'Why do you look at me so anxiously? Are you frightened?'

She shook her head emphatically. 'Not if I go with you. Will you be leaving soon, Mitya?'

'You must say: "Will we be leaving soon?" Yes, sweetheart, before the winter sets in.'

'What will the doctor say when you bring me with you?'

'When I saw him last he said I should come with my father. Do you think he will be angry if I bring my wife instead?'

And Irina looked up with a sigh of relief and her hands were hot with joy.

POSTSCRIPT

Yermak's campaign opened the way for the Russian acquisition of Siberia. Despite the fact that the remnants of his army straggled back to Oryol without a leader and Kuchum Khan re-entered Isker for a short time, the ground had been cleared. Disunity prevailed among the Tartars, and the Russians and Cossacks who followed in later years had little difficulty in establishing Russian sovereignty. From 1587, Russia's frontiers edged eastwards at the rate of something like seventy miles per year, until they encompassed the whole land-mass as far as the Bering Straits.

Many years after Yermak's death, a Mongolian who was on particularly good terms with the Russians asked the Governor of Isker—or rather Tobolsk at it was renamed—to obtain for him a certain suit of armour in which miraculous powers were said to reside. The price asked was one thousand sheep and six families of slaves. The Governor agreed to buy it, but once the Mongolian had acquired it, he refused to lift a finger to aid the Russians any more. The armour made him feel so secure that he could defy the conqueror. The mighty Yermak had been considered invincible, and when he was dragged down into the depths of the Irtish, this invulnerability was said to have passed into the armour itself. Such was the legend which was firmly believed in Siberia, where Yermak's name was kept alive in many place-names, folksongs, and stories. Even as late as 1914 there were regular prayers in Siberian churches for the repose of the soul of the great Cossack hero.

And what about today? Who knows! Siberia is still a huge, mysterious land, which knows how to guard its secrets.

CHRONOLOGICAL TABLE OF EVENTS

INTRODUCTION

The 'Free Cossack' communities date from the fifteenth century, when runaway serfs and peasants fled from their homes to escape the extortionate demands of the tax-collectors. They flocked to the steppes of Southern Russia, to the banks of the Don and the Dnieper, for these areas did not acknowledge the Czar's sovereignty. The Cossacks lived as freebooters, plundering the Russian and Persian caravans and shipping on the rivers. Surrounded and threatened as they were by Tartars, nevertheless they assimilated the Tartar way of life to some degree and they became outstanding horsemen.

By the sixteenth century the Cossacks had grown so strong that Czar Ivan IV decided to make use of them. He granted them a form of self-government in return for which they were to settle the land and protect the Russian frontiers from the Tartars.

1488

Anika Stroganov born. Grandson of Luka Stroganov. Blazed the trail for the conquest of Siberia. Enjoyed great respect at the Czar's court. Given concessions in the Province of Great Perm for his sons Grigori and Yakob. Youngest son, Semyon, excluded on account of the greed of his brothers.

1530

Ivan IV born. Became Czar at the age of three and had himself crowned in 1547. Ruthless and cruel, he consolidated his power by wiping out the other princely houses of Russia. Known as 'Ivan the Terrible'. During his reign Russia's frontiers were pushed far to the east and the south.

1556

Sultan Etiger of Siberia offered Moscow his friendship and volunteered to pay tribute to the Czar.

1558

Grigori Stroganov awarded 2.2 million hectares of land on either side of the River Kama.

1562
Sultan Etiger murdered by Kuchum Khan, a descendant of Genghis Khan. Kuchum occupied the throne of Siberia, and refused to pay tribute to Moscow.

1564
Grigori and Yakob Stroganov awarded a further 1½ million hectares of land.

1568
Further award of 1.3 million hectares on either side of the Chussovaya to Yakob Stroganov.

1570
Death of Anika Stroganov.

1574
A further concession to the Stroganov brothers, this time of land beyond the Ural Mountains covering the Land of Yugor, Mangaseya, and territory on both sides of the Tobol and its tributaries. These, however, lay within Kuchum Khan's dominions.

1575
Nikita Stroganov inherited his father's possessions in and around Kankor.

1579
Maxim Stroganov inherited his father's possessions in and around Oryol.

1580
Yermak Timofeyev and his 550 Cossacks arrived in Oryol.

1581
Spring. Prince Beguli from Pelym attacked Perm and was beaten back.

1581
Late summer. Cossacks, together with 300 of the Stroganov militia, set off to cross the Urals and attack Kuchum Khan.

1582
Cossacks captured Isker, the then capital of Siberia (later renamed Tobolsk).

1583
Submission of the Ostyak tribes on either side of the River Irtish.

1584
Yermak Timofeyev drowned in the Irtish on the night of 4th-5th August.

1584
Ivan IV died. Succeeded by Feodor I, but the real ruler of Russia became Boris Godunov, Feodor's minister and brother-in-law.

1585
A hundred Moscow Sharpshooters, unaware of Yermak's death, crossed the Urals in February as reinforcements for the Cossack army.

TITLES IN THIS SERIES

CASTORS AWAY! HESTER BURTON
THE COSSACKS B. BARTOS-HÖPPNER
DEVIL'S HILL NAN CHAUNCY
THE EAGLE OF THE NINTH ROSEMARY SUTCLIFF
EARTHQUAKE ANDREW SALKEY
THE EDGE OF THE CLOUD K. M. PEYTON
FLAMBARDS K. M. PEYTON
FLAMBARDS IN SUMMER K. M. PEYTON
FLY-BY-NIGHT K. M. PEYTON
A GRASS ROPE WILLIAM MAYNE
HURRICANE ANDREW SALKEY
I MARCHED WITH HANNIBAL HANS BAUMANN
IN SPITE OF ALL TERROR HESTOR BURTON
THE INTRUDER JOHN ROWE TOWNSEND
JUMPER NICHOLAS KALASHNIKOFF
KNIGHT CRUSADER RONALD WELCH
THE LANTERN BEARERS ROSEMARY SUTCLIFF
THE LITTLE BOOKROOM ELEANOR FARJEON
LITTLE KATIA E. M. ALMEDINGEN
MINNOW ON THE SAY A. PHILIPPA PEARCE
NORDY BANK SHEENA PORTER
ONE IS ONE BARBARA LEONIE PICARD
PASTURES OF THE BLUE CRANE H. F. BRINSMEAD
PIPPI GOES ABOARD ASTRID LINDGREN
PIPPI IN THE SOUTH SEAS ASTRID LINDGREN
PIPPI LONGSTOCKING ASTRID LINDGREN
PIRATE'S ISLAND JOHN ROWE TOWNSEND
RIDE A NORTHBOUND HORSE RICHARD WORMSER
A SAPPHIRE FOR SEPTEMBER H. F. BRINSMEAD
SIRGA RENÉ GUILLOT
TANGARA NAN CHAUNCY
THE THREE BROTHERS OF UR J. G. FYSON
TIGER IN THE BUSH NAN CHAUNCY
TOM'S MIDNIGHT GARDEN A. PHILIPPA PEARCE
WARRIOR SCARLET ROSEMARY SUTCLIFF
WHEN JAYS FLY TO BARBMO MARGARET BALDERSON